Acclaim for *Change Me into Zeus's Daughter*

"Vibrantly detailed . . . Moss's coming-of-age tale is a study in chutzpah and a fascinating exploration of a child's love-hate ties to an abusive parent."
                                                              —*Glamour* magazine

"A vivid, honest memoir about poverty, suffering, and resilience . . . traces the emergence of a little girl, with a face disfigured by malnutrition, into a women who becomes a powerful writer."
                                                    —Elizabeth Taylor, *Chicago Tribune*

"Heartbreaking . . . By the conclusion of this remarkable memoir, a marriage behind her and a new son to care for, Moss has changed, and we have been rooting for her every step of the way, sharing her rage and her joy."
                                                              —*The Times-Picayune*

"Compelling . . . incredibly dramatic . . . The Moss family knew the kind of poverty in rural Alabama found in Dorothea Lang photographs. Shocking poverty, poverty that made a sack of seed corn treated with pesticides good enough to eat."
                                                    —Jacki Lyden, National Public Radio

"A Southern autobiography fired in a crucible of poverty and abuse is nothing new in literature, but Moss makes an art of candor, which drives her both powerfully simple narrative and her burning desire to find—or make—beauty in a face scarred by a lifetime of malnutrition."
                                                    —Mike Peters, *The Dallas Morning News*

"Like Carson McCullers and Lewis Nordan before her, Barbara Robinette Moss makes immediate and intimate her own sad and funny Southern childhood. At once poetic and plainspoken, *Change Me into Zeus's Daughter* celebrates the wonders—good and bad—of discovering the world outside herself and uncovering the even deeper, more secret world of her family."

—Stewart O'Nan

"This elegant and moving memoir is nothing short of an *Angela's Ashes* for Americans, beautifully written in the female voice. Author Barbara Robinette Moss has Deep South roots, a backbone borne of deprivation overcome, and an inner beauty of the highest order. . . . The goddess of beauty, it may be said, has nothing on Barbara Robinette Moss."

—Ann Prichard, *USA Today*

Change Me into Zeus's Daughter

A MEMOIR

Barbara Robinette Moss

A TOUCHSTONE BOOK
PUBLISHED BY SIMON & SCHUSTER
New York   London   Toronto   Sydney

for my mother, *Doris Robinette Moss,*
with love and gratitude

and in memory of *Stewart Karl Moss, Jr.*
—who proved to be as powerful as sunlight.

TOUCHSTONE
Rockefeller Center
1230 Avenue of the Americas
New York, NY 10020

First TOUCHSTONE edition 2001
Originally published by Loess Hills Books

TOUCHSTONE and colophon are trademarks of Simon & Schuster, Inc.

DESIGNED BY ERICH HOBBING

Set in Adobe Caslon

Manufactured in the United States of America

13 15 17 19 20 18 16 14 12

The Library of Congress has cataloged the Scribner edition as follows:
Moss, Barbara Robinette.
Change me into Zeus's daughter: a memoir/Barbara Robinette Moss.
p. cm.
1. Moss, Barbara Robinette. 2. Adult children of alcoholics—United States—Biography.
I. Title.
HV5132.M67 2000
362.292'3'092—dc21
[B]   00-07886
ISBN-13: 978-0-7432-0218-3
ISBN-10:   0-7432-0218-X
ISBN-13: 978-0-7432-0219-0 (PBK)
ISBN-10:   0-7432-0219-8 (PBK)

This narrative is a true account of events, according to my memory. The names of some people and their identifying characteristics have been changed.

If I make the lashes dark
And the eyes more bright
And the lips more scarlet,
Or ask if all be right
From mirror after mirror,
No vanity's displayed:
I'm looking for the face I had
Before the world was made.
          —WILLIAM BUTLER YEATS

Acknowledgments

My intention in writing this book was to go back in time—to heal old wounds and reclaim my family. Too fearful to take on such an adventure alone, I took my friends and loved ones with me.

My kindred spirit and husband, Duane DeRaad, listened to my stories and encouraged me to write them. My son, Jason Freeman, from an early age listened to those same stories with interest and without judgment.

One of my graduate professors said I led a charmed life. I didn't know what that meant until I met M. T. Caen, who became my agent—and almost immediately, I was taken under the wings of Susan Moldow, Nan Graham and Sarah McGrath at Scribner. I am astounded—and forever grateful. Mary Swander taught me how to structure a story, and how to be patient. Kate Kasten and Tania Pryputniewicz read acutely, gave indispensable guidance, and made it enjoyable. Ann Wright Au, Ingrid Mazie and Melanie Parks soothed the hurt and reminded me that there is good living to be done. Karman Hotchkiss tenderly edited the first draft.

I am grateful for the support received from Jonis Agee, Michael Carey, Jack Davis, Adrienne Drapkin, Jim Harris, Susan Kratz, Charlie Langton, Shannon Miles, Robert Neymeyer, Joni Russ, Sharon-Ord Warner and Richard Webster.

My aunt, Janet Robinette Smith, rescued me as a child, told me stories about my parents I had never heard before, and encouraged me to publish this book. I am thankful for the telling and re-telling of family stories by my parents, Stewart Karl Moss, Sr., and Doris Robinette Moss, and my siblings, Alice, Stewart, David, Willie, Doris Ann, John and Janet.

The author would like to thank Diane Wakoski for the use of her poem "I Have Had to Learn to Live With My Face," from *Emerald Ice*, Black Sparrow Press.

Contents

Change Me into Zeus's Daughter

Birth Order:

Alice Jane

Stewart Karl, Jr.

David James

Barbara Allen

William Riley

Doris Ann

John Patrick

Mary Louise

Janet Lynn

Eastaboga, Alabama

1962

Near the Center of the Earth

*M*other spooned the poisoned corn and beans into her mouth, ravenously, eyes closed, hands shaking. We, her seven children, sat around the table watching her for signs of death, our eyes leaving her only long enough to glance at the clock to see how far the hands had moved. *Would she turn blue, like my oldest sister, Alice, said?* Alice sat hunched next to me in the same white kitchen chair, our identical homemade cotton dresses blending into one. She shoved my shoulder with hers as if I were disturbing her concentration and stared unblinking at Mother. Each time Mother hesitated, spoon in mid-air, Alice's face clouded and she pushed against my shoulder.

"She's dying," Alice whispered, covering her mouth so Mother could not hear her. "I told you she was gonna die."

I ignored her and watched Mother. I wanted to feel the kernels of sweet yellow corn slide against my teeth. I didn't care if they were poisoned. I was so hungry my head throbbed. The clock ticked as loudly as the clattering train that passed beside our house every day, each tick echoing against the wall and bouncing into my head, making my heart beat in my temples and my eyes want to close. I forced my eyes to stay open, to watch my mother as she ate. I stared at her; the light freckles on her face smeared into a large round blur, then snapped back into focus. No one spoke or moved. My oldest brother, Stewart, sat next to me, hands in his lap clenched into tight white balls; David, his chair pushed as close to Stewart's as possible, leaned forward with his arms spread across the table, ready to catch Mother if she fell. Willie and Doris Ann also sat together, their small legs sticking straight out, dirty bare feet dangling over the edge of the chair seat, Doris Ann's arms wrapped around the feather pillow from her bed. Mother held John cuddled in her lap, leaning over his head to spoon the beans into her mouth. He fussed and reached for the spoon, hungry and angry because she kept pushing his hand away.

Mother had waited all morning for a letter from Dad, a letter with money for food. When, once again, no letter or money arrived, she went out to the toolshed and brought in the corn and bean seeds for next year's garden. The seeds had been coated with pesticides to keep bugs from eating them during the winter. Poison. I watched Mother split the dusty sealed brown bags with a kitchen knife and empty the contents into bowls, the seeds making sweet music as they tapped the glass: "ting, ting, ting." She ran her hands through the dry seeds, lifting them to her nose. *Did they smell like poison?* She rubbed a fat white bean between her fingers and touched her fingers to her tongue, then spit into the sink, rinsed her mouth with cold water and spit into the sink again. She stood staring out the window above the sink, her hands limp in the bowl of seeds. She stood this way for ten minutes or more, staring out the window.

Then, as if released from a spell, she opened the cabinet and got out two colanders. She poured the dry seeds into them: corn in one, beans in the other, and ran water over and over them. She rubbed each tiny seed with her fingers and wiped the cool water on her forehead and the back of her neck. Her dress was already damp under the sleeves from the afternoon heat.

"Those seeds are poison, you know. Poison. If we eat them, we'll die," Alice whispered. She was eleven and knew these things. I tapped my bare feet against the kitchen chair and thought about this, deciding I would eat them anyway. I was so hungry and certain that no poison could kill me. I could just tell myself not to die and I wouldn't. I was that strong.

John slid from his chair and pulled at Mother's dress, kicking and fussing, wanting to be held, wanting to be fed.

"Alice, why don't you take the kids outside for a little while," Mother said as she churned the seeds through the water. She turned and caught Alice's disappointed face. "Just for a little while," she said.

We stumbled reluctantly out the back door. Alice peeled John from Mother's legs and carried him out; he liked to be outdoors and stopped fussing. We moved into the yard, each claiming our territory. Stewart and David ran into the garden and picked cornstalks, to joust like the knights in our storybooks. Alice took John for a walk in the shade of the oak trees, to push the leaves around and look for buckeyes. She began reciting from her favorite book—*Alice's Adventures in Wonderland*—the part where the Mad Hatter sings Alice an example of what he sang for the Queen of Hearts: " 'Twinkle, twinkle, little bat! How I wonder what you're at! Up above the world you fly, Like a tea-tray in the sky.' " I sat on the steps with Willie and Doris Ann and listened. When she couldn't remember any more, she jumped to her favorite parts of "The Walrus and the Carpenter."

"The Walrus and the Carpenter were walking close at hand. They wept like anything to see such quantities of sand. 'If this were only cleared away,' they said, 'it *would* be grand! If seven maids with seven mops swept it for half a year. Do you suppose,' the Walrus said, 'that they could get it clear?' "

Pale mountains jutted in the far distance. I could see the gas station at the bottom of the hill and farther on, barely visible, our closest neighbor's house. Directly in front of me was the garden, or what was supposed to be a garden. The fierce sun had baked it brown before any vegetables had appeared, the temperature climbing to over a hundred degrees every day. Twelve rows of shriveled corn, dwarfed and fruitless. So many tomato plants, twenty or more, the little yellow flowers dried and stiff, not bothering to form into green balls. The tomato vines weaved in with the cucumber vines like the hot-pan holders we made on our loom. Grasshoppers, thriving in the heat, had stripped the cucumber plants. Vines, like curved barbwire, ran through the dusty red clay, in and out of the tomato vines and in and out of the bean rows.

Nothing to put up and stack on the pantry shelves for winter, no steam from boiling kettles fogging the kitchen windows, the aroma seeping into every corner of the house: tomato sauce, soup stocks, creamed corn, sweet bread-and-butter pickles, succotash, green beans, white navy beans, speckled pinto beans. Not one jar to open when the coldest days arrived, when it hurt to breathe the air. There had been no summer tomato sandwiches smeared thick with mayonnaise on white bread baked in the oven, no corn on the cob dripping with butter, no crispy cucumbers to eat, straight from the garden, still warm from the sun.

That summer, in Eastaboga, Alabama, what had flourished were the daylilies: thousands of them, in the yard hovering close to the house, around the trees, alongside the road and in the ditches. Dad called them ditch lilies. "Ditch lilies! Living in the ditches, like beggars. Returning every year—more and more of 'em. We can't grow goddamned tomato but we can grow thousands of these. We couldn't weed enough to make 'em disappear, even if we wanted to. 'But Solomon in all his glory was not arrayed like one of these.' "

Dad had pulled a handful of lilies up by the roots and tossed them into the sun to dry like bones, knowing Mother loved the bright red and orange lilies, knowing she did not want them to disappear.

The daylilies had not disappeared but, somehow, my father had. Alice said she had gotten out of bed one morning and he was gone and did not show up again.

"That's disappearing," she said matter-of-factly, hands on her hips. It was, after all, more mysterious to have a father who had disappeared than one who had just gone somewhere. And this time, we were sure, he had not just been put in jail for the weekend. The black-and-white sheriff's car had not driven into the yard. The sheriff had not, this time, stepped out of the car, tipped his hat to our mother and apologized for disturbing her, telling her he would bring our father back home in a day or two. No, this time our father had been gone for weeks. We wanted to ask Mother where he was but had learned not to ask questions, or speak of it except among ourselves.

Actually, Dad had not disappeared but had gone to Scranton, Pennsylvania, where he was born and his brothers still lived, to find work. He left no money. He took the car. Said he'd write and send money soon. Mother couldn't drive anyway, so the car wasn't a great loss. The one time he had tried to teach her to drive, she had driven into a ditch. He never let her try again, claiming women weren't made to drive, they were made to take care of the home. And that's just what she did: wash clothes, iron clothes, wash dishes and cook meals for her husband and seven children.

Seven children: girl, boy, boy, girl, boy, girl, boy, like descending stairs: eleven, nine, eight, seven, six, four and two years old, some without a full year in between; four with their father's hazel eyes and dark hair and three with their mother's blue eyes, but blondes rather than redheads.

I had just turned seven years old and didn't think Dad's disappearance was such a bad thing; no more dishes shattering into the wall, no more whiskey breath and smell of urine, no more fear of being discovered, of having to peek into a room before entering to see if he was slumped in a chair waiting for you to walk within his reach.

"Now I've got ya," he would shout, like he had just caught a raccoon raiding the corn patch, pulling his leather belt from the loops as the unwary one struggled to get free. You didn't have to do anything—anything at all—to get pinched, poked, shoved or hit, just be where he could reach you when he was drunk. "You belong to me and I'll do with you what I want."

Unless, which often happened, he decided you didn't belong to him at all.

"Where did these towheads come from?" he'd chide, ruffling Doris Ann's blond hair, pulling just hard enough to make her wince. "I got dark hair, your mama's got red hair; maybe they got you mixed up at the hospital and you don't really live here."

"I live here and I got blond hair," David said defiantly.

"Maybe you don't really live here either. Maybe I'm feeding kids that don't really even live here," Dad said and thumped David on the head. "Hell, Mamie's kids look more like me than you do!"

Mamie, our closest neighbor, lived about a quarter of a mile farther down Mudd Street. We played tag and leapfrog with her children. *How could he believe Mamie's kids looked more like him than some of us? Mamie and her husband, Buck, and her kids—they're Negroes—how could he think they look more like him than us?* We ran as fast as we could to the kitchen to ask Mother.

"Did they mix up the babies at the hospital?" Alice asked, breathless and close to tears.

"Of course not," Mother frowned. She pulled plates from the cupboard and put them on the table.

"Then how come I got blond hair?!" David demanded, holding up a lock of straight blond hair.

"And me!" Doris Ann said. She held her hair out from both sides like a long-eared puppy.

"Because God gave you—"

"But how do you *know* they weren't really mixed up at the hospital?" Stewart interrupted, holding his hands out and hunching his shoulders.

"Am I eating food that's not mine?" David asked. He sucked in a sharp breath and held back tears.

"What?!" Mother asked.

"Am I eating food that's not mine? Do Mamie's kids look more like Dad than I do?" he choked, pressing his palms over his eyes.

"That's ridiculous." Mother exhaled heavily. She put her hands on her hips and glanced in the direction of Dad's crackling laughter. We turned toward the laughter but inched closer to Mother, surrounding her.

I pulled on the skirt of her dress. "Are you sure I live here?" I asked. "Are you sure I live here?"

"And me?" Doris Ann added.

"Yes, I'm positive," she said irritably. She patted my hand so I would let go of her dress. "Nobody was mixed up at the hospital. You all belong right here!"

I would not have questioned my parentage, for I had dark hair and hazel eyes like my father except: *How did I get to be left-handed if neither my mother nor my father were left-handed? Maybe I'd been swapped for another baby girl with dark hair and hazel eyes. Maybe I was the one eating food that wasn't mine; maybe I was the one that didn't really live here.*

It annoyed my father that I was left-handed. He called me "Southpaw," "Sinister" and sometimes "Middle-of-the-Road" because I was the middle child: three older, three younger. Just before I started to school he decided to remedy my left-handedness.

Dad came in the door with a six-pack of beer and a brown bag.

"Southpaw," he shouted. "Southpaw, come here! I got something for you." He dropped the bag on the couch. "Bring me a church key for my beer, there, Stu," he said, pulling a beer from the carton and sending the rest with Stewart to the refrigerator.

When I crept into the room, he was sitting on the couch drinking—small, refined, pleasurable sips, pleasure that he seemed to get from nothing else. He put the beer on the coffee table and pulled the contents from the bag: a small blackboard, a box of chalk and a length of cord. He propped the blackboard against the large family Bible on the coffee table.

"Well, get over here," he barked. "I can't reach you from there."

I walked slowly toward my father, my heart beating faster with each step. I didn't understand the meaning of the chalkboard or the rope. The fear crept higher in my chest and I could hardly breathe. I wanted to run out the door but I knew he would catch me and more than likely hit me. I looked around for Mother, but she was not there. I could hear Alice and Stewart in the next room talking. "Dad brought home a rope for Barbara." I bit my tongue and tasted salty blood in my mouth. *What had I done?*

"Now, Miss Sinister, we're gonna rid you of your problem," Dad said, pulling me toward him and shaking me gently by the shoulders. He let go of me, took another sip of his beer and opened the box of white chalk. He took out one piece and placed it firmly in my right hand. Then he picked up the length of cord and shook it out, holding on to one end.

"What are you gonna do?" I asked, my voice barely audible. "Are you gonna tie me up?"

Dad didn't answer. He took my left hand and wrapped the cord around and around my wrist.

"Where's Mom?" I asked, beginning to shake. *I must have done something terrible . . .*

He pulled my left hand behind my back, twirled me around to wrap the cord around my waist, and wrapped it, once again, around my wrist. I dropped the chalk from my right hand as I was whirled around. It hit the hardwood floor and broke into pieces.

"It's time for you to learn the correct way to write," Dad said as he tied the cord snugly, tugging at it to check for security, as if I were a prisoner who might try to escape. "It's time for you to change hands. You'll be off to school this fall. We can't have you still writing with your left. You want to be like everybody else, don't you?" He picked up a piece of the broken chalk from the floor and put it back in my right hand.

I nodded but didn't really see why it mattered if I wrote with my left instead of my right, as long as I could read it. Besides, I knew I wasn't like everybody else. Not like the other girls, anyway. I was smaller. And when I looked in the mirror, the face that looked back at me didn't have nice cheeks and a round chin. It was thin and long and squirrelly. If Dad could change that, I'd willingly let him tie me up.

"I'm gonna write your name for you," Dad said, picking up another piece of the broken chalk, "and you copy it, using your right hand. By the time school starts you'll know how to spell your name and you'll be using the correct hand to write with."

He wrote my name on the chalkboard, using all capital letters. Mother and Alice had already taught me how to write my name with big and little letters, how to count to ten and the colors of the rainbow.

I tried to copy what my father had written, pushing up on the chalk rather than pulling down, sometimes making the letters backward. He erased the entire word and made me start over. My head buzzed. I thought I'd never be able to think straight again. By the time we finished the first lesson, white specks floated in my eyes, swimming around inside my eyes like tadpoles in the creek.

"We'll do this every evening until you've got it," Dad said, erasing the letters I had worked so hard on with one quick brush of his palm.

One evening, just days before school started, I worked on the chalkboard for an hour, with Dad giving instructions. I was still making letters backward, sometimes the whole word backward. Every time I started to write with my right hand, it felt like my brain would pop—like opening a Mason jar—everything I knew spilling out into the air, never to be seen again. After Dad untied the cord holding my left hand behind my back, I went outside and sat on the steps. I wanted to cry but knew better than to cry around him. He'd say, "If you're gonna cry, let me give you something to cry about." Even Mother disliked for us to cry; crying was permitted for real injuries only: a cut foot or falling down on skinned knees. There was something about tears that made them both uneasy, almost fearful, so I held my tears, but they were thick and teeming in my chest. I propped my arms on my knees, sank my face into my hands and thought about the only time I had seen Mother cry.

It was before I started to school. Mother was having another baby. I had been waiting for this new baby, not particularly anxiously but with curiosity. John was not a baby at all, not to me, anyway; he could walk and talk a little, too. And Willie and Doris Ann were certainly not babies, even though Mamie called them that when she talked to my mother. A baby smelled pretty and let you hold it in your arms like a doll; it didn't cry or tear at your hair.

Mamie came over while Mother had gone to the clinic and dressed me in my only good clothes. All of us were dressed in our good clothes and placed on the couch in the living room, in order of birth, like a row of ornaments: Alice, Stewart, David, me, Willie, Doris Ann and John. We sat for what felt like a long time waiting for Mother to arrive with the new baby. Mamie went home. Finally a car drove into the yard. We all ran to the door. Mother got out of a taxi, alone. She had a small suitcase but no baby.

"Where's the baby?" Alice and Stewart asked simultaneously, pushing open the screen door.

"The baby died," Mother answered, moving through the sea of children, gently pushing us aside with the suitcase and creeping toward her bedroom.

"Where's Dad?" Alice asked, turning from the screen door, directing the question to Mother's back. Mother didn't answer. The screen door slammed shut.

Later that evening, after Dad had come home and gone back to the bar, I heard squeaks, like a caught mouse, coming from my parents' bedroom. I sneaked to the door and peered into the darkness, expecting to see the cat with a mouthful of fur. Instead, I saw my mother sitting on the edge of the bed rocking back and forth, crying bitterly, a pillow held tightly over her face to muffle the sobs.

Alice told me later, under the quilts in the dark, her warm breath in my ear, what she had overheard Mother telling Mamie: that Dad had buried the new baby girl while Mother was still in the hospital; he was drunk and could not remember where he had buried her. She heard that this baby was a blue baby. *A sky-blue baby to hold, to play with, to show off to Mamie. We would surely have had the only sky-blue baby had she lived.* Alice also heard that Dad had been watching when this baby died, that this baby had hair the same color as mine, that her name was Mary Louise.

❧

I watched an army of ants march across the step below me, lifted my feet and scooted up a step so they wouldn't be blocked. Mother came out and sat down beside me. She smoothed her skirt and ran her fingers through her hair.

"The writing lesson over?" she asked. I nodded. She watched the ants march across the steps. She picked up a leaf and placed it in the path of the ants. They marched across it without pausing.

"It's foolishness, you know, you writing with your right hand when God gave *only you* in this family the ability to write with your left."

I nodded my head, unable to speak. Mother did not look at me; she watched the ants and dropped another leaf in their path. This time they moved around the leaf rather than over it.

"Why don't we make this writing with the right hand a game," she said, almost whispering. "When you're around your father, you write with your right hand. When he's not home and when you're at school, you write with your left hand. It'll be our secret, okay?"

I nodded again and put my face down on my knees, a flood of relief in my chest, barely able to hold back the tears. Mother patted my back and stood up. She looked about the yard as if searching for something, ran her hands into the side pockets of her dress and began to whistle a tune. She walked slowly back inside the house, her soft serenade lingering in my ears.

After that day, the right-handed writing no longer made me seasick. It was a game and I was good at games. I got better and better at it, no longer making letters backward. Dad would smile at me, so pleased with his teaching. I was so delighted to be smiled upon by him that I worked even harder, perfecting each letter, each number. With each writing lesson, I hoped for my father to smile at me, to shake me gently as he untied the cord on my left hand as if he were tickling me, to swat at my bottom just as I moved out of his reach.

After six months Dad threw the cord away. My first-grade year was half over. As far as he knew, I was like everyone else. We continued practicing on the chalkboard once a week, moving from block letters to cursive. I began to notice that my right-handed writing was completely different from my left-handed writing, angular and sharp rather than curved and flowing, perfect lettering but not having the grace and rhythm that the left-handed writing possessed. It was as if someone else had written it.

My father's disappearance made my mother very unhappy. She didn't sing the way she usually did, her sweet soprano filling the house as she washed the dishes. She didn't want to read to us from our favorite book or play hide-and-seek, indoors, just before bedtime. She filled her days, silently, with housekeeping: stacks of dishes, mounds of clothes sorted into jeans, colors, whites and diapers, washed with a scrub board in the double kitchen sinks, hard Lava soap rubbed across the cloth leaving marks like a plowed field. When she wasn't working, she sat on the porch waiting for the mailman or stared out the window as if expecting Dad to drive up with boxes of groceries.

Within days of Dad's departure, there was nothing left to eat. Nothing. Mother harvested edible wild greens from the ditches using a stick to whack the brush and frighten away the snakes before walking into the tall weeds.

Stewart suggested we catch the snakes and sell them to the snake handlers at the Holy Roller church down Mudd Street. We hadn't actually been to this church but we had heard from the kids at school about the snake handlers, wrapping rattlesnakes around their arms and necks to pray. If the snake bites you and you die, then your belief in God isn't strong enough to keep you alive. But Mother said they liked to find their own snakes.

"Besides," she said, "I think there's something wrong with those people, using snakes to worship God. I've read enough of the Bible to know it doesn't say anything about torturing a poor snake or yourself to get to heaven. If that's what it takes to get to heaven, I'll just stay right here."

We tried to help Mother find the greens by walking along the edge of the ditch, picking what we thought she was picking.

"No, not this, you can't eat this," she said, taking the weeds from our hands. "Dandelion greens look like this, the curly ones, close to the ground with the yellow flowers."

*　　　　*　　　　*

Our neighbor, Mamie, brought Mother catfish on a line of rope. We had known Mamie since we moved there. Dad had often gone fishing with her husband, Buck.

Mamie and Buck had more children than my mother, ranging from almost grown to babies. The older ones helped care for the younger ones so Mamie could work and fish. In the afternoons, Mamie ironed clothes for white people for five cents apiece. In the mornings, she fished. She claimed she had to, "to feed all them young 'ens," but she really just liked to sit on the red clay bank with a can of worms and not hear a single child's voice. She fished in the pond that stood between our house and hers. Nobody knew who owned the land the pond was on. It had gone unnoticed for years, fished only by those few who had stumbled upon it. It was swarming with the biggest catfish you ever saw. They churned the water when I threw in cracker crumbs.

I loved to go fishing at the pond with Mamie and this she allowed as long as I did not speak, not one word. She tapped lightly on the back door just as the sun lit the sky. If I was ready to go, fine, if not, she went on without me. She would ask me how I was doing in school or something like that, but I knew that once we broke into the path toward the pond, I had best not speak, or even sneeze. Mamie could get on to you something fierce.

Mamie would sit right down with her big rump on the hard ground, her cotton print dress spread across her knees making a valley in her lap for extra bobbers, a foil package of chewing tobacco and a fan with an advertisement from the local funeral parlor. She wore a hat with two dozen handmade fishing lures knit into the tight straw, fished with a long cane pole and a round red-and-white bobber, sometimes red worms. She could catch more fish than anyone I knew, even Dad or Buck. Anyone. "Don't let your shadow get in the water," she'd say. "Fish ain't stupid, you know."

Mother didn't tell Mamie that Dad was gone, that we had nothing to eat, no money to buy anything. Mamie brought catfish because she liked Mother and knew she appreciated the fish. She showed Mother how to skin a catfish with a razor blade, how to keep from being horned when cleaning them.

"A catfish has a needle-sharp spine on its back. If he sticks you with it, the wound almost always gets infected," Mamie said to Mother as she held a squirming catfish with a pair of pliers. "Then you'll have to burn the infection out by packing gunpowder into the wound and striking a match to it." Mamie showed us the black round flat scars on her hands from being horned by catfish.

Mamie had no way of knowing that the few flopping catfish, lips strung through a rope, were all we had to eat some days. Three or four catfish, fried in a cast-iron skillet and divided between eight people, was not enough food for an entire day. If Mamie didn't stop by, there was nothing to eat at all.

❧

As if a school bell had rung, we filed back into the kitchen and claimed the same places we had occupied before, Alice pushing for more than her half of our shared kitchen chair. Mother had begun cooking the corn and beans. The aroma made me dizzy, and even though my stomach was empty, I thought I would vomit. I put my face against the kitchen table and watched Mother's back, the curve of her thin shoulders, the red curls of wet hair licking the back of her neck. I wanted my hair to be curly and red like hers instead of dark and wavy like my father's. I wanted to be able to stand at the stove and wave my wooden spoon and make hot delicious food from hard little seeds. I fell asleep.

I awoke to the sound of rustling paper. Mother was tearing a piece of paper from a brown grocery bag. Stewart came back into the kitchen with one of his short yellow school pencils and gave it to Mother. She wrote on the brown paper: letters and numbers. First-grade letters and numbers that even I could read.

"This is your Aunt Janet's address and phone number in Birmingham," she said to Alice, placing the paper in her held-out hand. "I'm going to eat the corn and beans now. If I get sick, you call your Aunt Janet from the gas station and tell her to come and get you. Throw the rest of the corn and beans into the outhouse before you leave, so none of the kids eat any of them. The directions for calling collect are written right here." She pointed to the bottom of the brown paper. "Can you do this?" she asked.

"Yes, ma'am," Alice answered, wadding the paper into her fist.

"If I'm not sick in two hours, we'll all eat the corn and beans. Okay?" She looked at the seven faces around the table. We nodded.

"Tomorrow, I'm sure we'll receive some money in the mail from your father," she said as she picked up John, who was wet and fussing, and left the room. We stared at each other. Stewart shrugged his shoulders. Alice grimaced. Mother returned with the baby in a dry diaper and the wind-up clock from her bedroom. She stood John in a kitchen chair and wound the clock, placing it in the middle of the table, the bright yellow face turned so everyone could see it.

"When this hand reaches the three, if I'm not sick, you can eat." She walked to the stove and scooped corn from one pan, beans from the other. She put the plate on the table and sat John in her lap. She ate. Slowly. Taste and wait. Taste and wait. One bean at a time, one kernel of corn at a time, her hands shaking. Finally she spooned the corn into her mouth and chewed, cheeks puffed and eyes closed. Just watching her made my mouth fill with saliva, my lips kiss together.

We watched Mother for what felt like an eternity. No one spoke. I could hear David breathing, in and out, in and out, as if he were keeping time by breaths, his arms spread across the table like the hands of the clock. Mother played with John's toes and seemed to have forgotten we were there. Her blue eyes were unfocused and weary and she seemed to be drifting farther and farther away. *Are her lips turning purple? Is she still breathing?* No one moved from their chairs; the tick of the clock enclosed the room. *Maybe we should touch her.* Still, no one moved. I could hear Alice's stomach rumbling loudly and I knew she could hear mine, fierce hunger in our bones. Without taking her eyes off Mother, she gently walked her fingers over my leg and put her hand on top of mine.

Suddenly Stewart slapped the table with his palms, knocking over the yellow-faced alarm clock, and shouted, "Ten more minutes!" Mother jumped in her chair, ransomed back to the present by the noise, finally focusing her eyes on what was truly visible.

John fell asleep before the ten minutes were up. Mother carried him to the living room, laid him on the couch and covered him with an afghan from the rocking chair. We never took our eyes from her; we were wide awake now, voraciously hungry and smiling.

In the time it took Mother to put John down, Stewart had passed out spoons. Alice had a stack of chipped, mismatched saucers in her arms. Willie, Doris Ann and I were squirming a dance in our chairs, spoons in hand, while David pretended to conduct our dance like a choir director. There was a sense of excitement, of celebration, in the air.

Mother scooped equal portions of corn and beans onto each saucer. Falling into the spell of David's choir-directing, she hummed a song we had learned in church. She made a saucer for John, covered it with another saucer turned upside down and put it at the back of the stove. She put our saucers on the table, asking us not to begin eating until everyone was served and the food blessed. She put down the last saucer and sat between Willie and Doris Ann. After the blessing, she opened a book and began reading aloud.

"Alice's Adventures in Wonderland," she read, "for Alice, because she has been so brave. Alice was beginning to get very tired of sitting by her sister . . ."

We ate. We laughed. We kicked one another under the table, told on each other, lined the bright yellow kernels of corn in rows, spelled our names with them. We counted the corn kernels as we put them on our tongues and, because we liked corn better, we devoured them all before starting on the beans. Then we ate the sweet white navy beans, spearing a bean onto each tine of the fork like little shoes, licking the bean juice from our saucers, chins dripping.

"Down, down, down," Mother read. "Would the fall never come to an end? 'I wonder how many miles I've fallen by this time?' Alice in Wonderland said aloud. 'I must be getting somewhere near the center of the earth.'"

After dinner we went outside to watch the stars peep out of the deep Alabama sky, one at a time like tiny sparks from the fire. Alice and I twirled around, making the stars spin until they had tails, imagining that we had fallen to the center of the earth like the Alice in the story. We picked up imaginary bottles and drank from them. We threw our hands over our heads and grew tall like a telescope, then squatted on the ground, growing small again. We splashed around as if swimming in tears and then fell to the ground and waited for the stars to stop spinning. I caught one, a red twinkling dot, and made a wish. I wished for a sailboat. We had been given coloring pages in first grade and I had kept the one of the sailboat. I colored the boat blue with a yellow sail; and, as part of the secret I shared with my mother, I traced my left hand in red onto the sail—holding the crayon in my right hand. I smiled when I gave her the drawing. She taped it on the refrigerator door for Dad to see; it flapped like a kite every time the door was opened and closed.

The next morning we got out of bed, pulled on our clothes and went to sit with Mother on the front porch to wait for the mailman. We played a game called "I spy," where someone picks something that the others can see, tells what color it is, then everyone has to guess what the person picked. "I spy something red."

"That stop sign?"

"No."

"Is it Toot-toot's shirt?"

"Stewart's shirt is yellow, Doris Ann. It has to be red."

"Oh."

"A red bird."

"What red bird? You have to be able to see it."

"There was a red bird by the tree."

"The red sign on the gas station?"

"No."

"Mom's hair."

"Yes!"

The sun drifted from our faces to our knees. The baby whined and we were tired of the game. Stewart asked Mother to read to us but she shook her head.

"Not right now, a little later," Mother said, tapping the toes of her shoes on the step. She brushed two ants from John's leg and picked him up. The toe-tapping becoming a bounce, a pony ride. We went back to our game.

Mother spotted the mailman before any of us and stood up, handing the baby to Alice. She watched him, a hand over her eyes, walk slowly up the hill, sorting his letters. She smiled when he handed her the letter from Dad. Waiting for the mailman to walk back down the hill, she looked carefully at the letter in her hand, at the return address, at the postage, the handwriting.

She opened the letter, not tearing the flap, and slid the letter from the envelope. Folded neatly in a sheet of white paper were two one-dollar bills. Mother dropped her hands to her sides, sucking in a quick sharp breath, the two dollars in one hand, the envelope in the other; the white paper fluttered down like a badly folded paper airplane, coming to rest on the bottom step.

Mother stood in silence a moment, then abruptly walked down the steps. We followed. Alice gave John to me and ran after Mother; Stewart and David followed her. I was pulling John by the arm, trying to keep up. Willie and Doris Ann fell behind and Doris Ann began to whimper. Mother stopped in front of a thick bed of daylilies on the north side of the house, fire-red, tall and straight, in full bloom. She stood for a long time, not moving. We all stood perfectly still, not attempting to move any closer to her. She stared at the lilies.

"They're so beautiful," she said, touching a frilly petal with the corner of the envelope. "I just wish we could eat them." She burst into tears, crushing the envelope and the two one-dollar bills to her face.

An hour later Mother took the crumpled brown paper with Aunt Janet's phone number on it and the two one-dollar bills to the gas station at the bottom of the hill and called her sister in Birmingham to come and get her starving children.

Anniston, Alabama

1990

"And the sins of the fathers shall be visited upon the heads of the children, even unto the third and fourth generation of them that hate me."

> Well, then, I hate Thee, unrighteous picture;
> Wicked image, I hate Thee;
> So strike with Thy vengeance
> The heads of those little men
> Who come blindly.
> It will be a brave thing.
>
> —STEPHEN CRANE

Alcoholic's Purgatory

*M*y father believed he was the master of his fate. He did exactly what he wanted to do and, by manipulation or force, made those around him do what he wanted them to do. He inflicted pain recreationally, both physical and emotional. It was his hobby, his pastime. We marched before him like tin ducks in a shooting gallery, a mother duck and her eight ducklings, to be shot through the heads and hearts, only to pop up again and go around once more.

Now, staring at him in his casket, it still holds true. He is handsome: black suit, salt-and-pepper hair slicked back, a VFW hat folded neatly on his chest. I lean forward, searching for the round dark spot on his lower lip where he held a cigarette for sixty years, still visible even through the layer of fleshy-pink paint that covers his lips.

"What are you staring at?" my brother David asks. He's standing next to me in front of the casket, pulling at the neck of his choke-tight dress shirt.

I touch the same spot on my own lip to show David. "The spot on his lower lip."

Standing next to David is my oldest brother, Stewart—who is tipping back a half-pint of Jack Daniel's. And next to him is Alice, my oldest sister. She has one hand around her rib cage and with the other holds the sleeve of her dress away from a patch of shingles on her left shoulder. She drops the sleeve, reaches into her dress pocket and pulls out wallet-size school pictures of us when we were kids. She flips through them, studying each one. She has them in birth order, and when she flips to mine, I cringe. In the photo she has chosen—the only school picture I ever had made—I am an innocent third grader, aware that my face is less than perfect, peculiar, even, but so *unaware* of how much worse it will get. The camera caught my hopeful expression: that the flash might erase the flaws, reshape the bones in my face. I have my father's hazel eyes, but in this picture, they are dark pools like eyes behind a mask.

Alice flips through the remaining pictures and slides them into Dad's breast pocket.

Janet, our youngest sister, joins the line, squeezing in next to me. She looks so like our baby: sweet and a little lost. I put my arm around her waist. My three other younger siblings, Doris Ann, Willie and John, form a second line behind us, leaning into our backs. Janet reaches out and gently rubs Dad's fingers. "He doesn't look like himself at all," she whispers. "They should have put his glasses on him." David and I look at each other and almost smile. Stewart raises his eyebrows. In a businesslike tone, Alice says, "He didn't wear glasses."

"Yes, he did," Janet says emphatically. "He's always worn glasses."

Doris Ann brushes damp, dishwater-blond hair away from her swollen eyes. "He didn't wear glasses."

"Come on, now," says Willie. He hates for us to fight or even disagree.

John adjusts the lapel of his military uniform. "Hell, yeah, he did. He started wearing glasses about five years ago."

Janet looks at me, then Alice. "Five years ago! I'm twenty-two and he's worn them all my life!"

There's a long silence while everyone considers this. Janet hates the gap between her memories and ours. She's the youngest, with eight years between her and John, who was heralded as "the baby" for those eight years. And even though we've tried to tell her what she missed was hell, she still hates it when we talk about places and events that she knows nothing about.

Alice nods her head and we drop the subject.

John rubs his eyes and sighs. "I haven't been really scared since I left home. The Infantry, the Airborne, Air Assault School, French Commando School and now serving as drill sergeant—nothing I've done in my military career has been half as scary as living with Dad. I don't have nightmares about being killed in combat; I have night-mares about Dad coming home at three in the morning."

I nod. "Same here. I still wake up every morning at three A.M., look at the clock and spend the next two hours sifting through the past, trying to think of what I could have done differently; well, more like what I would do *now* if I had it to do over again."

"Me too," John says. "It's pointless as hell, but I can't make myself stop thinking about it. Sometimes I feel like trying to understand life with Dad's about like fuckin' around with a big picture puzzle that's been chewed on by a dog."

Alice looks at John. "Yeah," she says. "That's just what it's like. Sometimes I feel like I'm gonna come unglued."

Janet twists away from the line. "I'm gonna go say hello to Aunt Janet and Mom." She's a tall strawberry blonde, and even in the staid dresses she wears to teach high school, she's very curvy. Several of Dad's American Legion buddies are sitting in the first pew. They turn to watch her leave the viewing room, but even a beautiful young woman can't restore the color to their ashen faces. Their world has been badly shaken. They sit like a row of gray stone statues, speechless.

"He used to stand in my yard, long after I'd left home, and scream obscenities," Alice says, staring down at Dad. "I lived in the projects, and the little black kids would cry and run for cover when they saw his car coming down the street." She hugs her rib cage tighter and her shoulders slump. She is so small—five feet five inches and 102 pounds. There's gray hair edging around her temples but she looks like a thirteen-year-old. Her head shakes with the nervous tic that developed when she was in her teens.

I sneak away from the line and follow Janet out of the viewing room. I want to say hello to Aunt Janet, check on Mother and make sure Janet is not angry with us again. Doris Ann catches up with me. "Hey," she says. Last night she and I sat on Mother's porch and talked for hours. We talked, then cried, then talked.

She grabs my arm and pulls me into the women's rest room. Her hand is rough and tanned, a sharp contrast against my pale arm. She has on a dark gray pantsuit and black loafers. She leans against the lavatory and, with one deft motion, twists her shoulder-length blond hair into a knot and pins it with a barrette. Her hair has a permanent crease just above her ears from wearing a hard hat every day. Several years ago she hired someone to clear some land next to her house. They showed up with a backhoe and a bulldozer, worked for two days and never returned, leaving the equipment sitting in her yard. A month later she found out it had been repossessed by the bank. She took out a loan, bought the equipment and started a demolition business. She runs the wrecking crane. I've seen her down a small building with that same deft movement she used to pin up her hair.

"Where are you going?" she asks.

"To talk to Janet, make sure she's not mad."

"You know she's mad. We embarrass her. She's corrected my English three times today. I love her, but Jesus Christ, sometimes I wish that girl had never got an education."

I laugh and suck in a deep breath. "I know. She came into this world and she was everything to us. We watched her sleep for hours, ran home from school to play with her, and took her everywhere we went from sunup to sundown. But she doesn't remember that. And now, she's so far ahead of us—so beautiful and clean." I stop abruptly, aware that I've said too much. Doris Ann looks at me with surprise. I brush away tears that are suddenly spilling down my cheeks.

Us kids sat on the living room floor smashing Silly Putty against the Sunday comics to transfer the colored pictures. I sat with my Easter basket in my lap, watching as David stretched a reversed Spiderman into the shape of a drinking straw. He laughed and squashed the crime fighter into a ball. I wanted to see what Rex Morgan's dark-haired nurse, June Gale, looked like with a stretched face. If the beautiful June Gale's face could be stretched to look like mine, then it seemed there ought to be a way to unstretch my face so it looked like hers. But I didn't break open my plastic Silly Putty egg. I waited until David traded comics with John, then I tore the Rex Morgan strip from the top of the page.

"Hey!" John cried. "That's got Barney Google on the other side!"

"All right," I said and slapped Rex Morgan down on the floor. "Do Barney Google. But hurry up—and don't tear it 'cause I want to save Rex Morgan."

"What for?" John asked.

David bit the ears off of a chocolate Easter bunny and mumbled, "She's in love with Rex Morgan." I started to protest, but decided that was a safer explanation than the truth.

While John transferred Barney Google, David got bored and wandered away. A few minutes later, Willie and Doris Ann went to look for tadpoles down at the creek. John peeled his Silly Putty from the comic page and ran after them. Alice and Stewart had skedaddled as soon as we came home from church and Mom had already settled onto the couch with a book. As soon as I was alone, I slipped Rex Morgan and the beautiful June Gale into my basket, sneaked to the bathroom and locked myself in.

June Gale smiled from the middle of the comic strip. I tore her out and laid the square of newsprint on the back of the sink while I rummaged through the green plastic grass in my Easter basket for the things I'd hidden: Alice's liquid makeup, mascara, eye shadow and lipstick, Mom's pressed powder, an almost empty roll of duct tape and the Silly Putty egg. I lined them up beside June Gale and sat the basket on the edge of the sink.

Before we left for church that morning, I had also hidden Dad's footstool under a pile of dirty clothes in the bathroom. I raked away the clothes, pushed the stool in front of the sink, stood on it and taped June Gale to the lower left corner of the mirror. I studied her perfectly shaped face: cheeks, chin, lips, eyes, teeth and hair. Then studied my own reflection, running my fingers over my forehead, nose, cheeks and chin. *It's not that bad. If I just look at my hair, or my ears, or my eyes. My eyes are kinda nice. But my mouth is too far down, or the space between my nose and mouth is too long, or maybe the cheeks are too long. Something. 'Cause my upper lip won't cover up my gums and teeth. It's like a Silly Putty–stretched face.* I tapped my front teeth with my index finger. *These teeth are too big and pushin' everything around, especially my chin; it's pushed into my neck, all the way to nothin'* . . . I leaned into the mirror, jutting my chin out as far as it would go, then relaxed it. Tears welled up in my eyes. *It doesn't look like a real chin, even when I poke it out.* I pulled a washcloth from the towel rack, buried my eyes in the rough fabric to dry the tears and thought about the time that Dad took us to the Birmingham Museum.

It was at a time when he was trying hard to be nice. He loaded us all up and took us to the museum to see the Remington Collection, bronze sculptures of cowboys roping cattle and busting horses. In the next room was a mummy sealed in an airtight glass case. The sign said the woman had fallen from a cliff and crushed her face. You could see the distortion in her bony jaw. Some of the ancient material wrapped around her entire body was peeling away from her skull. Her teeth protruded from the withered binding like a set rattrap. She looked like a dried-out camel. She looked like me. Afraid that David, Willie and Doris Ann would also see the resemblance, I ran into the next room and called for them to come look at a full suit of armor.

I held the washcloth over the bridge of my nose, revealing only my eyes, and leaned toward the mirror. *If I was a girl from India, nobody could see this stretchy face. Just my eyes. My eyes are kinda nice. I'd wear black veils that cover up everything except my eyes and I'd look just like all the other girls around. I'd wear dark eyeliner and eyebrows, and those jingle things on my ankles—and the boys would think I'm beautiful.* I pulled back from the mirror and smiled underneath the washcloth, but could see only the narrowing of my eyes. I twisted my mouth, opened it as wide as I could and jutted out my chin, but saw only a pair of hazel eyes with dark curly lashes. *How easy it would be to hide this face! Nobody would ever know!* I lowered the washcloth to study my distorted mouth and chin, held the washcloth up again, then down, up, and down, exhaling a long sigh.

But I'm not a girl from India. I'm American—like June Gale. I stared at June Gale for a second, dropped the washcloth into the sink and went to work.

June Gale wore her dark hair chin-length, poufed out on the top and flipped up on the ends. I pulled Alice's hairbrush from underneath the straw in the basket and began to tease my shoulder-length hair, pushing the brush toward my scalp the way I had seen Alice do it. The back of my hair already had knots in it from rocking myself to sleep at night, so it held the tangles better than the sides. Once every inch of hair stuck out in a huge ratted ball, I smoothed the top layer and tried to make it flip on the ends, turning my head back and forth to view the back. It flipped in several different directions, but it still looked good.

I plastered the bouffant with Alice's hair spray, which I'd hidden along with Dad's footstool in the dirty clothes. The mist blew into my right eye and it watered as I rubbed it with my fist. I splashed water in it and dried it on my shirt. The water made my eye bloodshot and caused it to sting worse; I closed it for a minute and worried about how long I would have before someone knocked on the door. With my ear to the door, I listened, but didn't hear anything.

I pulled the damp shirt off, dropped it to the floor, pulled one of Alice's bras—32A—from the basket and slipped it on. My chest registered zero, flat as a pancake, so I fastened the bra, adjusted the shoulder straps and stuffed the cups with toilet paper. Rummaging through the dirty clothes, I found one of Alice's nightgowns and pulled it over my head. The toilet-paper breasts poked proudly from the slinky pink gown. I shoved my chest forward and turned back and forth. *Perfect.*

Alice's liquid makeup was a shade too dark for me, but it covered the big dark moles around my nose. I smeared several layers over them, dotted it around my puffy eye and then patted my whole face with Mom's light powder. Next came blue eye shadow, mascara and lipstick. Whenever Alice was gone, I played in her makeup. Even though she yelled, told on me and occasionally smacked me, I considered these hazards simply the price of beauty. And I'd gotten pretty darn good at applying mascara and lipstick. I fluttered my coal-black lashes, smacked my rose-colored lips together and listened again for noise on the other side of the bathroom door. It was quiet, so I glanced at June Gale one more time and popped open the Silly Putty egg.

Silly Putty smells like school glue, the thick pasty kind that comes in jars with a smearing stick attached to the lid. I had tasted Silly Putty before, but it had no flavor at all; just a smell. I squished and stretched the pink putty until it warmed in my hand, then rolled it into a ball, punched my thumb into it and hollowed it into a small bowl shape, flattening the edges and sculpting the tip. June Gale seemed to be smiling at me from the corner of the mirror and I smiled back as I worked the putty and studied her face: round jawline, slightly square chin. Pushing my thumbs on either side of the putty, I squared the shape. After holding it up to the comic strip, I slipped the pink putty over my nub of a chin.

It was too long. I shoved it with the palm of my hand to shorten it. With a little adjusting, it fit my chin like the rubber tip on a cane, but it wouldn't stick. I pushed it on tight and leaned my head back, but as soon as I let go, the Silly Putty chin fell off. I had anticipated this. Silly Putty wouldn't stick to newspaper, so I figured it wouldn't stick to me either. I had heard Dad say that duct tape would stick to anything, so I had confiscated the end of a roll. I placed the sculpted chin on the sink, peeled off a small strip of duct tape, rolled it into a loop— sticky side out—and stuck it to my chin. I pressed the putty chin against the tape and let go. It held.

I stared at my reflection in the mirror. The face that looked back was still freakish. My front teeth were still too big and crooked, and the break between the Silly Putty and my skin was obvious—like I was a coloring book page that had been colored outside the lines.

But if I squinted, squinted my eyes until they were almost closed, I could see a fair resemblance to the beautiful June Gale.

I wipe my tear-wet hand on my hip and stare into Doris Ann's eyes in the women's rest-room mirror. "No matter what I do to myself, I feel like it'll never be enough."

"I know," she says, leaning against me, shoulder to shoulder, hip to hip. "Sometimes I feel the same way. Like I'll never catch up with everybody else."

"Would we rather have it the other way," I ask, "to have had Janet live through what we lived through? Dad *without* glasses?" The answer is no. I push away from the sink. "I'll catch you later."

"You want me to go with you?"

"No. You go watch that crew," I say, pointing toward the boys, "and I'll take care of Janet."

I find Mother, Aunt Janet and Janet in the waiting room next to the chapel. My taciturn mother is sitting on a pale blue love seat next to Doris C., holding her hand and listening to her recount the story of Dad's death.

Doris C. is Dad's widow. He had to marry someone named Doris because that's my mother's name, except she spells hers with two *r*'s. My parents were married for thirty-five years; and when Dad got

drunk, he'd call my mother's name in a mournful wail until she'd
come and soothe him like a baby. After they divorced, he went
through several nice old women before he found another one named
Doris. I don't think she ever knew he wasn't calling *her*. Doris C. really
is a nice woman—too good for Dad—but I couldn't stand to go to
their house.

To remain married to Doris C., Dad had to behave: no drinking,
no cussing. Of course, he did drink occasionally, but on those nights
he staggered in at Stewart's house, trying to pick fights with whoever
was available, eventually passing out on the floor or the couch, never
making it home. At home—his home with Doris C.—he sat pleas-
antly in the La-Z-Boy rocker wearing a smoking jacket and slippers,
smoking a pipe filled with apple-blossom tobacco. Doris C. had a
miniature poodle named Miffy, adorned with a pink bow between its
ears and pink polish on its toenails. When we visited, that dog
hopped in Dad's lap and yapped at us like we were burglars. The first
time I saw Dad all decked out and lounging in that La-Z-Boy, I
wanted to snatch him up and beat him with a stick. *How dare he act
like a civilized human being with her, when he treated our mother and us
so badly. How dare you! And that dog! When we were kids, if we happened
upon a dog that didn't fit his ideal, he waited until we loved it and then
shot it. He wouldn't have even considered Miffy a dog. To him, a dog was
big, ferocious and hard-hearted and would eat that poodle for lunch!*

I eventually calmed down, got used to it; I was even thankful that
he wasn't living alone in that ratty apartment anymore, spending his
time and money at the American Legion drinking with that tattered
group of alcoholic war buddies. If Doris C. could keep him out of the
bars, it was more than we could ever do.

Mother's suit is the same powder-blue color as the love seat and she
fades into it like the Cheshire-Cat in *Alice's Adventures in Wonderland*.
Like the Cheshire-Cat she smiles when she sees me, acknowledges me
with a nod and disappears back into the story she's being told. Aunt
Janet and Janet are sitting in stuffed high-back Victorian chairs at the
other end of the long room, staring out the window. I pull up a chair
just as Janet is saying that she and I cried when we heard the news
about Dad but Mother did not.

"Well, she never has cried about anything that she should have cried about," Aunt Janet says as she reaches up for a hug. I pull my chair as close to hers as possible, noticing how young she looks, even at seventy-five.

"I got the prettiest nieces in the world," she says. "Barbara, are you still going to church?"

"Yes, ma'am," I answer. "But it's not as much fun going to church in Iowa as it is in Alabama. The preachers don't preach. They're afraid they might offend someone."

Aunt Janet laughs and pats my knee. "Keep going anyway; it can't do you no harm. Don't let your mama's truancy set an example." We fall silent and stare out the window. Aunt Janet looks troubled. After a few minutes she says, "Y'all probably don't know nothing about this, but your grandmama died of kidney failure when your mama was but two years old. Dorris was just learning to talk good when Mama died. After the funeral, Daddy couldn't get Dorris to talk anymore. She'd just lay across our laps like a rag doll. Daddy took her to the doctor several times, but he said there wasn't nothing wrong with her physically. He said she was grieving the loss of her mama and there wasn't nothing we could do; she'd have to decide for herself to join this old world again." Aunt Janet looks up. "Does she ever mention her childhood at all?"

Janet shakes her head.

"She's told me quite a bit," I say. "Only because I badger her about it. She's told me a lot since I started working on our family tree. She doesn't remember her mother."

Aunt Janet stares out the window. "Yeah, I know," she says. "She didn't start to talk again until she was five years old. She scared us all nearly to death. We thought we'd lost our baby. She's still that way, you know; don't say much. She's a loner. Don't want nobody to know nothing about her, most of all how talented she is.

"I know she loves me as much as she loves anybody in this world, but she never calls me, hardly ever comes to see me. She just locked herself away long ago and stayed that way.

"When we was teenagers we had this book with a story in it about a woman who left all her family and friends and went to live by herself in a shack on a mountain. Whenever your mama would just disappear from us emotionally, me and your Aunt Lola would kid her;

we'd say, 'Dorris is gone off to the mountain.' She didn't care. She just wanted to be by herself, I guess, which is kind of a sad joke on a woman with eight kids and a worthless husband."

Janet starts to cry and Aunt Janet pats her folded hands. "I'm sorry," she says. "I shouldn't've of said anything ugly about your daddy."

Janet wipes the tears from her cheeks. "It's not Dad," she says, "it's Mom." Tears fill my eyes again. I look out the window and watch a robin hopping on the lawn. As unreachable as Dad was, lost in the disease of alcoholism, Mother is just as far away. I have a cup sitting on my mantel that Aunt Janet gave me when I was a teenager, a china cup that her mother-in-law had given her long ago. Inside the cup are my mother's curls, in various shades: auburn-red, auburn-red mixed with gray and pure gray. Curls that I have collected at different times over the years, the first one when I was about twelve years old. Mother always cut her own hair, snipping curls from around her face and dropping them to the floor. I often watched and when she wasn't looking I'd snatch one for myself, tuck it inside a matchbox and hide it away in the large cardboard box that held all of my prize possessions.

I've heard my mother complain recently about her missing photographs: photographs of her when she was in the U.S. Marine Corps, of her and Dad, of her holding us as babies. Her photographs are missing and she speculates on who took them, speaking in a tone meant to rebuke should the guilty party be listening. But we are all guilty. I have slipped several of them from her trunk myself, when she's not home or when she's asleep. Like the curls, they are pieces of her to possess, as much of her as I can get.

"You already looked at your daddy?" Aunt Janet asks.

"Yes," I answer. "He looks good for a man who smoked and drank for seventy-three years."

"Well, God didn't bring him into this world smoking and drinking," Aunt Janet says dryly, twisting her mouth to a frown.

I laugh. "Yeah, he probably didn't start until he was five." This makes Janet laugh and we smile at each other.

"I'm gonna go see for myself," Aunt Janet says, patting my knee again. "Then I'm gonna sit with your mama some more." Janet and I go along with Aunt Janet, walking side by side. We are the same height and about the same weight, but Janet is fuller, less angular, more healthy-looking.

She has Mother's full, round lips and thick curly hair. She has a perfectly shaped face. I'd hate her for it if I didn't love her so much.

We walk with Aunt Janet back to the viewing room. She's wearing a dark dress with a white sweater draped across her shoulders and a black pocketbook strung over her crossed and locked arms. She walks up to the casket next to Alice. "How's everybody doing?" she asks.

Alice wraps her arms around her. "We're fine, Aunt Janet."

"You ol' beautiful thing," Aunt Janet says. Alice blushes. Then, in order of birth, skipping me and Janet because we've already been hugged, Aunt Janet hugs Stewart, David, Willie, Doris Ann and John. "Y'all the prettiest bunch of babies," she says, patting John's back, "but you're all too thin. I guess I need to invite you to dinner more often than just Thanksgiving." She wobbles a little and John steadies her. She glances at Dad and mutters, "He never deserved a one of ya." She takes a step toward the casket to study Dad. "Yep, that's him." She grimaces. "I can't believe he's dead. I thought he'd surely outlive us all." She pats Alice's arm and turns to leave. "I'll be with your mama." We watch her walk away. David and Willie frown, offended.

"You can't blame her," Alice snaps. "He certainly caused her enough grief. She's had to bail us out of trouble our whole lives." She looks down at Dad. "He had no right to live as long as he did." She glances at each of us—in case any of us want to dispute her claim— then stares down at Dad again.

John leans into my back and whispers in my ear, "Are you sure *she* didn't kill him?" I don't want Alice mad at me and nudge John away. He pulls me backward against his chest. I know he's smiling. I relax and let my back rest against him, resisting the urge to laugh, fearful that it would turn to sobs.

Stewart takes another swig of whiskey. "He was a tough ol' bird. I half expected him to outlive me."

As a matter of fact, we had all expected Dad to outlive Stewart. Stewart's been trying to drink himself to death, from morning to night, on the job and off. His supervisor at work has sent him through detox three times. Even drunk, he's the best welder they've got. But his drinking has started to affect his performance. He fell out of an armored tank last year, bumped his head on the gun tube and landed on the caterpillar track, breaking his nose and cheekbone. It's gotten to the point where his drinking is affecting everyone in the family, even me and I live in Iowa, a thousand miles from Alabama. Stewart told me on the phone recently that he's started getting up at 3 A.M. to slug down whiskey, that his body has an uncontrollable craving for it. "It's like I been taken over by a demon," he said. "There's hardly any of *me* left."

Alice is still staring at Dad. "He was a mean ol' son of a bitch. I'm not glad he's dead, but I'm not real sad about it either." Her head tics to the right and she slouches as if trying to roll herself into a ball.

David fidgets and clears his throat. "He wasn't really mean," he says. Alice turns around to face David and her mouth falls open. She straightens her shoulders and puts her hands on her hips. "Where the hell were you living?!"

"Let's don't talk bad about him now that he's gone," David says, shifting his weight uneasily from one foot to the other. "I'm sure he did the best he could."

Alice's eyes narrow. "That was the best he could do?!"

"Let's don't talk about this," Willie says, waving his hand in the air like a referee. Alice turns around and places her hands on the edge of the open casket. Her head tics as she glares at Dad.

"The best he could," she fumes.

"The best he could," I whisper, letting the words settle into my brain. Stewart tips back his whiskey bottle.

"It's not fair to blame him for the bad stuff," David says. "He didn't remember hardly anything he did when he was drunk." We fall silent, contemplating this. I close my eyes and wonder if he really didn't remember or if it was just an act, a refuge for bad behavior. How easy—and convenient—not to remember the sins you've committed. Did he use that excuse when he had to explain himself to God? Or did God send him straight to hell?

Even though I know Alice is right, I can't stand the thought of him being in hell. My eyes squeeze tighter as I try to think of where else he might be. Maybe God has a special place for dead alcoholics—like the Catholics' purgatory—for the alcoholic who didn't beat his kids (not all the time, anyway), just forgot to feed them (so the bones in his daughter's face grew like a thin pine tree).

A purgatory for the alcoholic who forgot to buy his children shoes and clothes and other useful things, and carelessly gave one of two hogs the family raised to the American Legion for their yearly picnic, which he didn't take his family to, not even his wife. A special place. He didn't, after all, kill anyone (not exactly) or leave marks that could be seen (not exactly), so a place less than blistering pelting burning screaming hell, yet always fearful. Maybe reincarnation—reincarnation as the child of one of his own children—where the sins of the father have been passed on to the son.

Birmingham, Alabama

Sweet Elixir

We had never even seen a Coke machine before we moved to Birmingham and moved in with Aunt Janet and Uncle David. Then we discovered the sweet, sweet elixir to which we became immediately addicted. We found it—the cure to all our childhood woes—right across the street from Aunt Janet's house. "Murphy's Dry Cleaning," the sign read, "Five Dress Shirts for a Dollar." There was a Coke machine just inside the front door. (In the South, it's a Coke: not a pop—not a cola—not a soda.)

The oldest couple I had ever seen owned the cleaner's. They were both thin and gray and road-map-wrinkled. Mr. Murphy had a long white mustache that he tugged on when he was thinking. They both wore glasses and, if the sun was shining, straw hats, even indoors. Mrs. Murphy was the English teacher at the elementary school we attended and Mr. Murphy worked all day at the cleaner's.

Willie, Doris Ann and I spent our free time scouting the neighborhood for empty Coke bottles to sell to Mr. Murphy. We staggered in with our arms full of dirty bottles and lined them up on the floor. We had been putting the bottles in the wooden case by the machine, but Mr. Murphy had caught on that we didn't always bring ten bottles for the dime he handed over, so he made us line them up in the middle of the concrete floor to be counted.

"Count 'em," he said, as if he wasn't sure we could count. We pointed to the bottles, hopping our fingers from one to the other. "Out loud," he scoffed, tugging on his mustache.

"Onetwothreefourfivesixseveneightnineten," we counted—as fast as we could. If we had more than one set of ten, we had to line them up in two rows of ten or three rows of ten.

"Now what's three times ten?" Mr. Murphy asked, holding his hand over the three dimes as if he didn't have to give them to us if we didn't know the answer. If Mrs. Murphy was at the cash register, we had to spell to get our money.

"How do you spell *deposit?*" she asked, pushing her glasses up on her nose with her index finger.

"Spell *Birmingham.*"

At first we groaned, but after the first few times she gave us words that were worth learning to spell: *devious, powwow, zombie, albino, bloodthirsty, angelic, witchcraft, belfry, diabolical.* And she gave us the meanings, sometimes in a story that lasted longer than our Coke. We clung to her words, hoping she would use our name in the story. "Once there was an albino dog named Snow," Mrs. Murphy narrated. "Most people were afraid of Snow. But not John," Mrs. Murphy said, fixing her eyes on John, whom we'd dragged along because he was just three and Mrs. Murphy thought he was *adorable.* John blushed, smiled and hiccuped.

We couldn't leave the cleaner's without a deposit bottle, but sometimes we didn't take one on purpose, just so we could hear a story. But if Mrs. Murphy wasn't there, we lined up on the concrete-block wall under the big glass picture window and slowly sipped from the thin-neck bottle, an RC Cola (*only* an RC Cola), making it last, making that sound Dad made when he took the first swallow from a beer. *Aahhhhhh!*

When we couldn't find any empty Coke bottles to satisfy our RC habit, we thieved our cousin David Junior's U.S. coin collection, punching the copper pennies out of the little blue books ten at a time.

Like my oldest brother, Stewart, David Junior had been named after his father. To avoid confusion, most people called my dad "S.K.," for Stewart Karl, and my brother "Stewart." Mother was the only person who ever called my dad Stewart. When they were both in the room, she called Dad "Stewart," and my brother "Stewart Junior." Doris Ann had been named after Mother, Dorris, dropping one *r* and adding Ann. But the way we ran it together, it sounded like *Darsan.* David Junior was called David Junior all the time. That's better,

Stewart explained, than being called just Junior, as if you didn't really have a name.

On our first night at Aunt Janet's house, Stewart and David were moved into the already cramped room with David Junior and his younger brother, George. They walked into the small white house, dropped their clothing-stuffed pillowcases on the floor next to David Junior's bed, and began casing the house like burglars about to make a heist, rummaging through every drawer, closet, and shelf. I followed behind them, awestruck at the things they found. There were so many things we had never seen before: television, running water, binoculars, model cars and airplanes and a U.S. coin collection. David Junior followed them, taking things that were his and putting them back where they belonged. He didn't care if we prowled in George's stuff as long as we left his alone.

George was the same age as Willie, seven—ten years younger than David Junior—and had had polio as a baby. He was small and cute with eyes as round and dark as chocolate cookies and walked with a lilt to the left, then a lilt to the right, that we tried to imitate. Aunt Janet called him Sweetpea. We picked it up like a flock of mynah birds: *Sweetpea, Sweetpea.* Sweetpea had a wheelchair next to his bed and an extra pair of metal braces propped against the wall. He let us take turns riding around the room in his wheelchair until Mother came in and told us to leave it alone. "That's not a toy." The metal braces on Sweetpea's legs both frightened and fascinated us. We followed behind him to see how they fit onto his legs. We wanted to try them on, but Mother gave us *that look* before we got the request out of our mouths.

David Junior had just graduated from high school. He was tall, towering over everyone; he had pale blue eyes and strawberry-blond hair. I had a crush on him from the moment I first saw him. The crush became more pronounced the day after we arrived, when he loaded a canvas bag of *The Birmingham News* onto his white Cushman Eagle motorcycle and flew off to deliver them like a knight on a horse. But the crush was somewhat dampened when he smacked me right on my behind with a rolled-up newspaper for climbing the apple trees in the backyard. He frowned and yelled, "Get down from there. Every time you climb up there, it knocks down a dozen apples!" So we threw his rolled newspapers into the branches, snapping limbs and knocking down ten times as many as before.

David Junior was also displeased with the mattress Willie, Doris Ann, John and I slept on; it covered the entire living room floor. We had to roll it up and push it against the wall every morning because it was impossible to get to the bathroom without walking on it. There were so many of us that we took up all the room wherever we were: inside or out. When we were all in the house—as at suppertime—there were twelve people in the living room/dining room at once.

David Junior wiggled his shoulders as if he were being suffocated and left as soon as he could get away, only to find when he returned that we had been prowling through his things again. He complained when we played with his model airplane collection, claiming we broke off propellers and wings. He and Uncle David got a ladder and hung them by fishing line from the ceiling so we couldn't reach them. I liked to sneak into the room with the broom—while David Junior was out delivering *The Birmingham News*—and stir the planes with the broom handle, filling the air with soaring fighter planes, the wings crashing into one another.

Within a few weeks of our arrival in Birmingham, David Junior packed his duffel bag and left for Auburn University, leaving his U.S. coin collection covered with old underwear in his dresser drawer. (As if we wouldn't look under tattered jockey shorts.) We began thieving the pennies; we held too much reverence for the silver coins ever to think of stealing them: the 1947 half dollars with Liberty on the front walking into a sunset cradling an armful of flowers, and on the back, a bald eagle. They were too glorious to spend. Besides, we thought pennies wouldn't be missed when there were full books of Liberty silver dollars, Mercury dimes and buffalo-head nickels.

One day Katie, the Negro woman who took care of Sweetpea while Aunt Janet worked all day for the Telephone Company, caught me punching the pennies out of the little blue book. I had already punched out ten for myself and dropped them into my pocket and was punching out enough for Willie when she caught me. She shouted, "What?!" so loud I dropped the book to the floor, scattering the pennies everywhere. She made me pick them up and put them back in the book, then made me sweep the living room and dry the dishes. She walked behind me with a hickory switch, shaking her head disgustedly, her dark eyes glaring. Finally she let me slip out the door. I ran to the grove of apple trees behind the house to meet Willie.

"I only got enough for one Coke," I panted, fishing the ten pennies from my pocket. "We'll have to share."

We had pilfered all the pennies from the little blue books for 1948, 1949 and 1950 when David Junior came home for the Thanksgiving holidays. He took the remains of his coin collection back to Auburn with him, swatting us with a newspaper as he went out the door.

Without the coin collection, we had to become more inventive to acquire our daily RC fix. Willie was the most creative. He was seven, a year younger than me. We were the same size and shape, skinny dark-haired rogues, except my hair was just wavy, while his was wildly curly. Willie's left foot curved in slightly and his right eye was crossed, giving him an impish appearance. We were all small for our age—and wiry.

Willie was the mastermind behind the slug. He figured out, all on his own, that you could take one of Uncle David's files from his toolbox (a toolbox we had been warned never to touch), and file a penny down to the size of a dime. Just the right size to fit in the Coke machine.

He taught Doris Ann and me how to make them: "You hold the penny with the pliers," he said, using the same teacher voice Mrs. Murphy used when she taught us how to diagram sentences. "Now, file away from your body against the little rim of the penny; keep turning it in the pliers so it files down evenly. Work both sides. When the rim is gone, hit it a lick around the edges and it'll be the same size as a dime."

I followed Willie's instructions to completion, then held the copper dime in the palm of my hand; it even had the weight and feel of a dime! It took a lot of effort to turn a penny into a dime, but a dime was hard to come by. I had had only one dime in my life: the year before, in first grade.

🦎

Every day at Eastaboga Elementary School all the students lined up at 10 A.M. and walked to the cafeteria for ice cream, except for those who didn't have a dime to buy ice cream: me and my brother David and my brother Stewart and my sister Alice. It was embarrassing to be the only kids in school who never got to line up for ice cream. It wouldn't have been so noticeable except you had to sit in the classroom by yourself until everybody came back from the cafeteria—laughing, smacking their lips and looking at you from the corners of their eyes. We had to pretend every day that we didn't notice how everybody looked at us—every day, because we never got a dime for ice cream. I had tasted it before and knew how good it was. I walked home from school every day with Sonja; sometimes she stopped at Pace's for a strawberry cone and gave me a lick.

Jim Wheelbanks, the boy who sat across the table from me, always had a dime for ice cream. Everybody else in first grade got a dime from their parents too, but Jim Wheelbanks was the meanest about it. He had a book satchel and a real rubber raincoat, big thick erasers on his pencils and a smooth wooden ruler with black lines to draw by. He showed everybody his pencils with the name of his father's drugstore written on them, and made fun of whatever you had that wasn't as good as what he had. He wore blue jeans that were still dark blue and little round glasses that he said cost a lot of money.

I wore a new pair of shoes to school one day, white patent-leather buckle shoes. They weren't really new. Mother had gotten them at the Blue-Eye Creek Baptist Church rummage sale for five cents. From the top they looked brand-new, but they had one round hole in the bottom of each sole; not hard to repair. Mother had me stand on a piece of cardboard while she drew the outline of my shoe with a pencil. Then she cut out the foot shapes with scissors and tucked them inside my shoes to keep my socks from getting wet or dirty.

Right after roll call, I raised my hand and told the teacher that I had new shoes and pointed down to them. Before Mrs. Wilkerson could say anything, Jim Wheelbanks shouted from across the table, "Them shoes ain't new; they got holes in the bottom. I seen the holes when she was going down the slide on the playground before the bell rang." Just like that, in front of everybody. I looked at the floor and Mrs. Wilkerson told everybody to turn to page fifteen in their spellers. She never said anything to Jim Wheelbanks about speaking out of turn or being rude—something she would have done if it had been me speaking up instead of him.

Later that morning, at the 10 A.M. ice-cream lineup, Jim Wheelbanks was in such a big hurry to be first in line, he dropped his dime. It rolled across the floor and the kids scattered everywhere trying to grab it. They bumped into each other and knocked chairs around. Jim Wheelbanks's dime rolled right under my chair and before anybody could see it, I put my foot on it. I wiggled that dime right into the hole in the bottom of my almost-new shoes, sat up straight in my chair and let them look for it. Mrs. Wilkerson moved the chairs out of the way, then the table. Finally, it was past time to go, so Mrs. Wilkerson said Jim Wheelbanks would have to stay in the classroom until everybody got back. All the first graders lined up to go to the cafeteria and I got at the end of the line.

"Barbara," Mrs. Wilkerson asked, "did your mother give you ice cream money today?"

"Yes, ma'am," I lied, "she did." I didn't care; my face burned hot, but I could feel that dime snug inside my shoe. Mrs. Wilkerson stood watching me for a minute, then marched the class down the hall for ice cream. Mrs. Wilkerson was leading the way and I was last in line, so nobody saw me slip the dime out of my shoe. It shone like a jewel in my hand, thin and light as a feather. I squeezed it tight to make sure I didn't drop it too.

As we walked to the cafeteria, I thought about what the preacher had said in church the Sunday before—about sin and going to hell. I thought I might go to hell and slowed down, letting the line get ahead of me. Then I remembered that it says in the Bible, "An eye for an eye and a tooth for a tooth." Jim Wheelbanks had pushed me into a swing the very first day of school and knocked out my front tooth. Blood ran down my chin and dripped onto his new shirt.

Mrs. Wilkerson took us both inside. She put a soaked paper towel on my gum, then she rubbed and rubbed Jim's shirt. When I tried to tell her what happened, she told me to "hush." She didn't punish Jim Wheelbanks at all! He didn't have to sit in the coatroom in the dark like I did when I turned over the fishbowl. He didn't have to read extra pages in the reading circle like I did when I spun the "not-to-be-touched" globe of the world; and he didn't even have to stay in from recess and clean the erasers. Now we were even.

I caught up with the class and marched into the cafeteria. I examined the dime one more time, then placed it right in the middle of the lunchroom attendant's palm. I got an ice cream sandwich: vanilla ice cream in the middle, with chocolate cookie on both sides. It was the smoothest, most delicious thing I had ever put in my mouth. I licked the ice cream between the two slices of chocolate cookie until it began to melt down my fingers; then I held it up and let the soft cream drip onto my tongue.

At recess, Mrs. Wilkerson asked my brother David if Mother had given us ice cream money that day and, of course, he told her "no." But he was proud of me when she told him I had stolen Jim Wheelbanks's dime; Stewart too. It felt so good walking home with my older brothers pushing me and laughing.

"Stole Jim Wheelbanks's ice cream money. Girl, I tell you what!"

I walked home so happy, licking the sweet cream left between my fingers.

❧

We couldn't use our copper slugs at Murphy's Dry Cleaning because Mr. Murphy would have known exactly who put them in his Coke machine, so we went across Tenth Avenue to the one at the coin-operated laundry, Susan's Wash and Dry.

We went in, cased the joint, put the empty deposit bottle in the wooden crate, dropped the slug into the machine and pulled out an RC Cola. Then we popped off the top and took the bottle down to Randolph Park to sit with the bums while we drank it. In Birmingham the bums congregated around a huge oak tree and staked out their territory with bags and blankets on the north side of the park, where a fire burned constantly in an oil drum. They stood around the fire even when it wasn't particularly cold, sipping from a bottle, warming first one side of their bodies, then the other. How careful they were when they happened upon a pint of whiskey or a bottle of wine, passing it, calculating how much liquid was extracted with each swallow, making the day evolve around a bottle. We imitated the bums.

We found a spot in the park close enough to the bums to watch their every move, but far enough away that we didn't feel compelled to share our bounty. We were familiar with the dance of a drunk: the slight lilt of step, the stagger, the drunken stupor. So familiar—from living

with Dad, breathing the peril—we were comfortable among the dere-
licts in the park, knowing instinctively when danger came into play,
when to move farther from the oak tree, when to leave the park alto-
gether. Often a familiar vagrant would throw up a hand in welcome. We
did likewise but never moved into their circle. We had suffered enough
bumps and bruises in our young lives to be painfully aware that a drunk
can hurt you in an instant and not remember it the next.

We secured a spot on the tattered grass, sitting cross-legged in a
circle, and passed around the RC. Occasionally we found a brown
paper bag on the ground, the kind the liquor store puts wine bottles
in, and dropped the RC in the bag, just for effect. As the bottle was
passed around the circle, each of us watched the other to make sure
nobody's Adam's apple bobbed twice. Timing was everything. The
bottle would move into my hand and I would hold it, contemplating
the thickness and weight of the glass, the taper of the neck and
admiring the type printed on the bottle's round surface. I filled my
mouth as full as I could without swallowing and let it slowly trickle
down my throat, burning my eyes and nose to the point of tears.
Then I passed the bottle to Willie. He did the same and passed it
down. When the liquid in the bottle was partially gone, we took turns
blowing over the opening, creating ghostly hollow sounds that
frightened away the squirrels and birds. The bums circling the oil
drum imitated our call, blowing over the opening of a wine bottle and
sending out a deep-pitched, vacant sound.

When the Coke was gone, we walked downtown and slipped
inside The Birmingham Library. We had to go in one at a time
because the woman at the front desk said we were "disruptive." She
had caught us playing hide-and-seek inside the library. We had
pushed the oversized books to one side and slipped into the book-
shelves to hide. One day Doris Ann climbed up to the third shelf—
which was against the rules of the game—and fell out the back side,
sending a dozen big books down on some woman's head. The librar-
ian had escorted us to the door and told us not to come back without
our mother. We waited a month, then came up with the plan to go in
one at a time; if the library was busy, we'd each follow on the heels of
a woman going in, pretending to be her child. I went first. Willie
counted to five hundred, then walked through the glass doors,

through the aluminum flip gate and up the stairs to meet me in the section that housed the medical journals; then Doris Ann counted to five hundred and followed.

The medical journals had pictures. Colored pictures of bodies. Pictures with transparent overlays of intestines—we called them "gopher guts." Transparencies of lungs, kidneys, stomach, heart and, of course, genitals: *girl stuff* and *boy stuff*. There were pictures of pregnant women from the time of conception to delivery, with cut-out sections of the stomach to show what the baby looked like inside the womb, *frogmen that turn into see-through babies*.

After looking at the guts and unborn babies, we went to the art section. Most of the art books were oversized and heavy. It took two of us to get the best books down from the shelf. We'd spread each one out on the floor and lie on our stomachs to flip through the pages, placing the empty RC bottle in the fold when we reached a picture we wanted to study. I had already decided to become an artist, so these books were my favorites. I ran my index finger through the shapes and figures, pretending to draw them: John Singer Sargent's painting of *The Pailleron Children*, the pouts on their faces and fancy clothes painted as if you could reach into the picture and touch the buttons on the little girl's dress; Henri Rousseau's *The Sleeping Gypsy*, a lion licking at a sleeping man cuddling a guitar; and Pablo Picasso's *Woman Ironing* that looked like Mother, long fingers and thin arms, ironing our school clothes every night before she went to bed. Willie and Doris Ann liked George Bellows's paintings of boxers. They said the best one was *Dempsey and Firpo*, where Jack Dempsey, the "Manassa Mauler," knocks Luis Firpo, the "Wild Bull of the Pampas," out of the ring into the first row of spectators. Doris Ann was a tomboy.

Our mother triggered this interest in art. She had taken drawing classes when she was in college at Birmingham Southern. Later she had taken the American Artists correspondence course. She still had the four huge books on how to draw and paint. Book number one taught drawing: cylinders and cones, human figures, dogs, cats, elephants and horses. There were chapters on shading and shadows, muscles and bones and linear and aerial perspective. The books progressed through color charts, oil painting and stretched canvas. I loved every page. I took the picture pages out of the five-ring spiral clip, one at a time, put them against the window and traced Norman Rockwell's *The Saturday Evening Post* covers, Robert Fawcett's charcoal nudes and Al Parker's romantic couples.

I put my drawings in a cardboard portfolio that held Mother's old pencil drawings, which were brown and dry as tobacco leaves. Some of them had tracing paper overlays with red pencil corrections and notes of encouragement and suggestions from the correspondence-school instructor. I followed the directions in the book and gave my drawings to Mother to grade. She placed waxed paper over my images and made corrections with a red crayon.

For my birthday that December, Mother gave me a paint-by-number set of two collie dogs. The plastic buckets of paint and the spaces within the drawing were numbered; number 5 blue went in all the little spaces marked with a 5, mostly sky and clouds. Number 3 brown and number 4 yellow went on the dogs, but also on the trees in the background. I pulled everything out of the box and spread it out on the kitchen table while Mother and Aunt Janet cooked supper. Stewart came over to show me how to apply the paint and took over, claiming it took a steadier hand than mine to paint the eyes and mouth of a dog. I had to beg just to paint part of the fur on the dog's back and a few of the number 5 clouds. Mother and Aunt Janet were so pleased that we enjoyed the paint-by-number set that everyone began to get them for birthdays until the walls were cluttered with paint-by-number ships, clowns, horses and birds. Before long we were sneaking into Modern Drugs on Tenth Avenue to admire the larger paint-by-number sets like Edgar Degas's *Ballet Rehearsal*. Whenever we completed a painting, we signed and dated the back so we could keep track of who painted what, smearing our names in block letters with the last of the oil paint.

We didn't really need to sign them. It was fairly easy to tell who painted what—Alice's were the best: neat and clean, the colors blended where they touched. Stewart's were all clipper ships, some with bright clear skies, some with dark stormy skies, the paint smooth and crisp. The rest of us smeared the paint or painted inside the spaces so carefully that the lines showed when the painting was finished; and sometimes we confused the numbers, painting the horse's eyes orange and the bird's feet bright purple.

❧

If we didn't have a bottle for deposit, we drank our slug-purchased RC Cola sitting in the pink plastic chairs at Susan's Wash and Dry so we could drop the empty bottle into the wooden crate next to the machine when we were finished. We slid the bottle around the table, leaving a stream of condensation in its cold wake, and watched the speeding traffic on Tenth Avenue, hoping for a minor collision to keep our adrenaline flow at its usual accelerated level.

Each time we were ready to drop a slug into the machine at Susan's Wash and Dry, we carefully checked out everyone inside to make sure Susan wasn't there. We were very thorough, each of us checking a part of the L-shaped room while Willie discreetly dropped the slug into the machine. We liked it best on the rare occasion when there were no women around at all, no one who might be Susan.

One day a seedy old man was sitting at a table reading the newspaper when we came into the laundry. He had on a billed cap pushed to the back of his head, work boots and a dirty T-shirt, a pack of cigarettes in the T-shirt pocket. He ignored us when we came in and we ignored him.

We spread out inside the building. I checked the washer area, Doris Ann checked the dryers. Willie checked the tables set up for folding clothes, since the Coke machine was in that area. We were in luck—there were several dryers running, but the old man was the only person in the place. We gathered around the Coke machine while Willie dropped the filed-down penny into the slot. Just as he pulled an RC from the line of colored bottles, the old man grabbed him by the arm, slapped his face and shoved him into the Coke machine.

"I've got you now!" he shouted, spreading his arms wide and dancing back and forth to keep us from running away. "I thought it was you'uns." Willie covered his cheek with the palm of his hand and jumped protectively in front of Doris Ann and me, while I tried to shove Doris Ann ahead of me and she tried to climb me like a pole, crying, "Mom!" as if she would just appear and save us.

"Sit down on the floor!" the old man shouted. His skinny body trembled as he towered over us. We sat down on the linoleum and pushed our backs against the wall by the dryers. Doris Ann and I scooted close together, burying our faces in our shirts. The old man reached over and unlocked the money box on the Coke machine and stirred the change until he found the slug. We pressed together, our bodies flattening into one, knees rattling and teeth chattering.

"There she is," he beamed, exposing cigarette-stained teeth. He pinched the slug between his fingers and waved it in our faces. "See how it's a penny filed down to the size of a dime," he said, as if we hadn't seen it before.

"Now, what should I do with these juvenile delinquents? Do I call their father and have him pick 'em up here, or call the police and have 'em put in jail for life?"

We were terrified. Not of Dad, he was still missing—and even if he wasn't, nobody ever knew how to find him—but of going to jail. We had heard stories from Dad about how they treat you in jail: "They put you in a filthy room that hasn't been mopped in years, with a bunch of drunks that piss on the floor.

"You're lucky if they remember to feed you at all. One time I was in for three days and all I got was a pack of Saltines and a Coke. I hadn't done anything wrong. Oh, I'd had a beer or two, but I was driving the speed limit, a long way from drunk. And they don't let you out until they feel like it, whenever it suits 'em. Best not to say nothing. Then they can't keep you longer for being a smart-mouth. They can keep you there until you rot if they get the notion."

We would never see our mother again. Whenever we wandered off too far, Mother sent Stewart and David to look for us. They always found us, but we were sure they wouldn't find us if "Susan" called the police and had us put in jail. Mom wouldn't think to look at the jail for anyone other than Dad.

The old man put the slug in his T-shirt pocket just in front of his cigarettes. We could still see the outline of it through the cotton shirt. He pulled a table and a pink plastic chair closer to us and sat down, lit a cigarette and drummed his fingers while he stared at us, taking in every inch: shirts, shorts, thin legs, wild hair, bruised elbows and skinned knees.

He looked directly at me and I drew myself up even tighter. I recognized the look on his face. I had seen it on the playground at school, a sneer that curled a boy's mouth just before he tormented me. My permanent teeth were coming in—huge, white kernels—too big and crooked. My face had always been askew somehow, but now it grew beyond itself, twisted and knurly. Around other kids, I stayed close to Willie and Doris Ann for protection, safety in numbers. But most adults tried not to look at me, or looked through me. I hid my face in my shirt and tried to be invisible.

The old man crushed out the cigarette, reached in his pocket for another and tapped it against the table to pack the tobacco. He reached out and ran the cigarette down my thigh to my knee. "You're a scurvy thing," he said. I covered my face as much as possible as Willie hunched up and slapped at the cigarette. The old man laughed and booted him in the chest back to the floor. He reached down and picked up the RC that Willie had dropped in the scuffle, stood and leaned toward the Coke machine just far enough to open the bottle. It had been shaken and drops sprayed in our hair and across our faces, as if we'd been spit on. He sat back down, tipped the bottle back and, without closing his eyes, guzzled the whole thing. He laughed again, plopped the bottle on the table with a loud thud and wiped his mouth with the back of his hand. He studied us for a minute, then inched his dirty work boots a little closer to us, hesitating between moves and chuckling. Finally he picked up his newspaper, snapped it in front of his face, shifted in his chair to get comfortable and began to read. He was reading every page from top to bottom while we huddled in the corner. We relaxed our grip on each other and murmured plans to escape.

"He smells like rotten eggs," Willie whispered in my ear. "Let's make a run for it. When he's about halfway through the next page let's take off for the door. I'll count to three and we all run at the same time."

Just as we were about to make our break for the door, an old woman came in carrying a stack of folded clothes. Her knee-length navy dress was flecked with lint and multicolored strings from the dryers, and her white hair was pulled tight into a ponytail tied with a rag. Her body was thick and square like a refrigerator and dark purple veins bulged from under stockings that were rolled down just below her knees. The collar of her dress stood up on one side and pointed toward a red sweaty face with a clenched mouth, as if her lips had been glued together. She was old but her walk was brisk, rapid and loud. We could hear her forced heavy breathing as she crossed the room snorting like a bull. This must be the real "Susan"! She was far more frightening than the old man. We resumed our clutch on one another and prayed she wouldn't kill us before the police had a chance to lock us up.

"What are you doing?" she yelled in a croaky voice as she crossed the room, knocking chairs out of her way with her hips. Our hearts leaped into our throats and Doris Ann and I both cried for Mother.

"I've been doin' all the work by myself all morning. Where the hell have you been?" she barked at the old man.

"I caught 'em kids been puttin' slugs in the machine." The old man stood up, dropping the newspaper to the floor, and dug into his shirt pocket.

"Here, right here." He held up the slug for her to examine. She dropped the folded clothes on a table and marched closer, her face turning purple and her glasses sliding down her nose. She glanced briefly at the filed-down penny, stuck out her tongue and slapped it out of his hand.

"I don't give a damn about no ten cents," she screamed. "I done lost thirty bucks with you sitting on your ass all morning. Who do you think has to do all your work while you're . . . ?"

We didn't wait for his answer. When the old man turned to follow the rolling slug, we ran, screaming and crashing through pink plastic chairs, out the door, across speeding traffic on Tenth Avenue, all the way to Thirteenth Avenue before we stopped to catch our breaths. We were so shook up, we didn't have an RC for two days.

Homecoming

Oh listen, sister.
I love my mister man—and I can't tell yo' why.
Dere ain't no reason why I should love dat man.
It must be sumpin' dat de angels done plan.
—Oscar Hammerstein II

Aunt Janet's small smoke-stained kitchen was a separate room just off the dining room, but the dining area and living room joined, divided only by the abrupt end of the black-and-white checked linoleum. We were sitting at the table eating corn flakes for supper, twisting around, trying to watch "The Beverly Hillbillies" on the TV in the living room, when the door was casually opened without even the hint of a knock. "Dad! Dad!" we shouted, dropping our spoons into our bowls and clamoring from the table. He brushed a wisp of glossy black hair from his eyes and smiled, acting surprised by our shouts—as if he had just gone to the store for a pack of smokes, instead of off on a three-month excursion in Pennsylvania.

Soundlessly, as if he were afraid of waking a baby, he closed the door behind him. We cornered him there, with his army duffel bag on his brawny shoulder, a fresh cigarette jutting from the corner of his cocksure mouth, smelling of tobacco and Old Spice shaving lotion. "Dad! Dad!" we screamed, shoving one another, trying to get his undivided attention as everybody talked at once.

John wrapped his arms around Dad's legs and held him prisoner, continuously screaming, "Dad! Dad! Dad!"

"Dad!" Stewart said. "Aunt Janet had to come and get us and load all of our stuff in her station wagon. We had to leave most of our furniture."

"Look, Dad!" David shouted, popping him on the shoulder and pulling up his sleeve to show his muscle. "I've been lifting David Junior's weights! I can lift almost fifty pounds . . ."

"Dad! Dad!" I shouted, jumping up and down. "Dad, look at my cheeks. Look at my ringworm scars! Remember, I got them from you before you left . . ."

"Dad, listen!" Willie cried, "Listen! I had to learn this at school. 'We the people of the United States, in order to form a more perfect union, establish justice—' Dad, listen!" he yelled, starting over because Dad wasn't paying attention. Doris Ann was shaking his arm, one hand over her ear to block out Willie's preamble, shouting "Look, Dad! Look at me! Mom cut my hair! Dad, look!"

I started over, jumping into the air, pointing at my cheeks and shouting, "Dad, look! Dad, look!" but it was impossible to catch his eye.

Spot, Sweetpea's black-and-white terrier, was barking frantically, leaping from the couch to the coffee table, to the chair, and back again, knocking everyone's schoolbooks to the floor. Alice and Sweetpea remained at the table, staring. Alice—her spoon frozen in mid-air, a piercing bitterness in her eyes—glanced at me briefly, then returned her gaze to Dad without lowering the spoon. I stopped jumping and backed away until I bumped into a kitchen chair. Dad worked the cigarette with his lips from one corner of his mouth to the other. He cupped a hand over John's head, ruffled his hair and tried to pry himself loose.

He quieted the group with a soft "shhhhh," brushing his lips with his right index finger and then catching the cigarette between his fingers. He reached behind his shoulder and pulled the duffel bag forward, dropped it to the ground and began untying the knotted cord. Voices trailed to whispers. Only the television continued to chatter. Even Spot, his tail and ears spiked, hopped onto the back of the couch and stood frozen, a low growl rumbling from his throat. I watched Dad's hands move in and out of the duffel bag—rough, callused hands, knuckles permanently stained with engine grease, thick, grooved nails trimmed with a pocketknife—searching for whatever he had brought us.

He finally found what he was searching for and the clank of coins against metal rang like a tambourine, bringing unanimous cheers. Stewart and David applauded. John let go of his legs and clapped too, dancing in a circle. Dad booted the duffel bag against the wall and put the cigarette back in his mouth so he could pry open the metal box. He tugged at the lid with his grease-stained fingernails and puffed fat smoke rings into the air. John and Doris Ann jumped to stick their fingers inside the fading loops. David whisked them away with the palm of his hand. A large pale halo floated over my head and I slipped my hand through it like a bracelet, watched it widen and disappear.

The top popped from the metal box and we caught our breath as a dozen copper coins rained to the floor, popping like firecrackers and rolling in circles. I leaped forward, snatching two of the pennies that rolled my way as Willie, Doris Ann and John, laughing and bumping into one another, seized the others. I ran closer and grabbed a few more. Dad laughed and shook more pennies onto the floor for us to chase. Stewart and David sidled up to Dad, laughed and pointed at us, pretending to be too big for pennies. Dad wiped the corner of his eye with a grease-stained knuckle and dumped the rest of the pennies on the living room floor at Stewart's feet, covering the tips of his shoes with the blazing copper coins.

"Divide those up equally among the crew, Stu," he ordered, handing the box to Stewart. "Make sure you include Sweetpea," he added as he caught the cigarette between his fingers again, fixed his eyes on Mother and waltzed confidently toward the kitchen. Alice's head moved in a slow semicircle as he walked by without even noticing her. She dropped her spoon into the cereal bowl, splashing milk onto the plastic tablecloth, and turned her head in the other direction to continue watching Dad. She had been so sure he wouldn't return.

"He's gone and he's not coming back. Mother will take care of us and we'll get to stay here in the city forever," she had said as we walked home from school the day before.

I walked over to the mound of pennies, my attention shifting from my father to my brother. I bent closer to the pennies, to keep count, to make certain justice was served. I glanced up long enough to see Aunt Janet and Mother standing in the kitchen doorway.

Aunt Janet stood with her hands on her hips, scowling, working a striped kitchen towel laced between her fingers. Mother leaned against the doorframe, her eyes round and lips slightly parted, her fingers caressing the buttons on the front of her cotton dress. She straightened as Dad approached, like a puppet whose strings were drawn tight: her chin lifted, her jaw became rigid and her lips pressed together. Her hand moved to her mouth as she sucked in a jagged breath, but her liquid blue eyes did not spill a single tear.

3 A.M.

"The one that figures out the answer first wins a dollar," Dad said, folding a crisp bill and placing it on the kitchen table. He took a drink of his beer and wiped his mouth with the back of his hand. "Now this riddle is for *the boys*: Brothers and sisters I have none, but this man's father is my father's son. Who am I?" Stewart and David— the two of Dad's four boys who were considered *the boys*—jotted down the riddle, asking him to repeat it again, which he did.

"Now you kids," he said, pointing to the rest of us, "figure this one out: As I was going to Saint Ives, I met a man with seven wives. Each wife had seven sacks, each sack had seven cats, each cat had seven kits. Kits, cats, sacks and wives, how many were going to Saint Ives?" He sat at the table, lit a cigarette and repeated the riddle as we wrote it onto notebook paper. Before I had completely written the riddle down, John fell asleep in his chair. *Good. One less competitor. I'm gonna smoke the others, win that dollar and buy ten chances on the radio raffle at the school Fall Festival. This one is easy!* I was already adding sevens in my head.

"Hey, there, Miss Sinister," Dad pestered, tapping my paper with his finger. *No! He's not gonna send me for something! I'll lose!* I looked up, hoping my expression conveyed my annoyance. He ignored me. "Run in the other room and get your old man the Bible." I dropped my pencil.

"Make everybody stop till I get back."

Dad took a sip of his beer, then a draw from his cigarette.

"All right. Everybody stop till Southpaw gets back." Pencils clattered onto the table and they all frowned at me. I dashed into the living room, returned with the big family Bible, shoved it in front of Dad and jumped back into my seat. Everybody picked up their pencils and went back to work. We knew what was coming. There were places in the Bible that made no sense to Dad and sometimes, while we worked out the problems he assigned us, he read the passages out loud and puzzled over them. He opened the Bible toward the back of the book and studied the pages a few minutes. I added sevens: seven wives, seven sacks, seven cats, seven kittens.

"Twenty-eight!" I yelled. "The answer's twenty-eight!" I pushed my paper toward Dad and smiled triumphantly. Stewart looked up, rolled his eyes and went back to his problem.

"Nope," Dad said, squinting as he read. I pulled my paper across the table and stared at the numbers. *How could it not be twenty-eight? Seven wives, seven sacks, seven cats, seven kittens. That's twenty-eight!*

"Now, if you want a real problem to figure out, figure this out," Dad said, running his finger along the familiar passages. "Romans 8:29 and 30. 'For whom he did foreknow, he also did predestinate to be conformed to the image of his Son, that he might be the first-born among many brethren. Moreover, whom he did predestinate, them he also called: and whom he called, them he also justified: and whom he justified, them he also glorified.' Now," he said, pausing for effect, taking a draw from his cigarette, "how can we have a free will if we're predestinated? That's like a rigged crapshoot . . ."

Sacks don't count! Sacks aren't alive! I subtracted seven from my total and pushed the paper in front of Dad again. "Twenty-one!" Dad ignored me. "Dad, it's twenty-one!" He shook his head, opened his mouth and let smoke drift into the air like idle sheets on a clothesline.

"Look," I said, lifting my paper. Dad shook his head. I glanced at Stewart and he shook his head. Doris Ann and Willie smiled. I sat back down with a dejected thump. Dad closed the Bible and opened it at the beginning. Willie stopped writing, watched him a second, then looked at me. *This is it!* He and I had been waiting for Dad to read Genesis ever since the zookeeper came to Anna Stuart Dupuy School three weeks earlier. I sat forward in my chair and waited; adrenaline rushed through me.

"Here's a good riddle; Genesis 4:16," Dad said with a smirk. He took another sip of beer, studied the passage and then read, " 'And Cain went out from the presence of the Lord, and dwelt in the land of Nod, on the east of Eden. And Cain knew his wife;' There! Right there!" He pointed to the passage. "There was no wife for Cain to marry! There was only Adam, Eve and Cain on earth. So who did Cain marry?" He paused once again, for effect. "He married a monkey, that's what. He married a monkey and that's where Negroes came from, from the monkey. Monkeys have dark skin. That's why Negroes have dark skin."

My chest tightened as I blurted out, "The skin on a monkey is pink." Everyone looked up. Dad lowered the Bible onto the table, took his cigarette from his mouth and looked at me. I swallowed and raced on. "At Dupuy School, a man came with a baboon and a spider monkey and three chimpanzees—and we got to pet them; and we brushed the hair backward and the skin was pink." Everyone was still staring. "Second and third grades went together; me and Willie," I added, pointing to him.

"It was pink all right," Willie confirmed. Dad glanced at Willie, took a draw from his cigarette and studied the Bible passage again. He lifted the book closer to his face, ran his finger up and down the page, flipped to the previous page and back again.

"It was pink all right," Willie repeated. He pulled up his shirtsleeve to the elbow and tapped on his arm. "Just about the same color as my arm."

My heart jumped in my throat as Dad rocked forward in his chair and put the Bible back on the table. He leaned over the large leather-bound book and began reading the passages, running his finger down the page and moving his lips as he read. He blew a cloud of smoke and it curled off the open Bible into the air.

"Pink?" he asked, knitting his brow.

"Pink," I answered.

Walk the Golden Streets

S.K.

School had been out for the summer of 1963 long enough for us to be bored. We complained to Mother that there was nothing to do. It was Saturday. Dad was going to visit Uncle Jake and we wanted to go along.

When my father returned from his trip to Pennsylvania the previous October, Uncle Jake, one of Dad's older brothers, had come back with him. He brought his wife and five kids and rented a house just outside of Anniston, Alabama, a small town an hour from Birmingham. A farmer owned the house they rented. The soybean fields sloped away from the small white house in all directions as far as you could see.

Our cousins were older, practically grown, and weren't interested in playing with children. But there were two barns filled with old abandoned furniture and machinery, a pond, a huge oak tree with a tire swing and Uncle Jake. Uncle Jake wasn't as tall as Dad, nor was he as lean, and he didn't have the grace that—when Dad was sober—made people stop and watch when he walked by. Uncle Jake didn't really have anything Dad had: height, hair, build or elegance and he knew it; he made smart-aleck remarks like: "Only men who never get laid have a full head of hair and only men who don't know how to drink stay so thin." Uncle Jake was five feet eight inches, two inches shorter than Dad, with a round chubby face instead of the sharp bones that framed Dad's face. Instead of Dad's creamy olive-toned skin and hazel eyes, Uncle Jake's complexion was ruddy and his eyes were a watery blue, surrounded by spiderweb wrinkles from smoking short smelly cigars and drinking too much whiskey.

He began each morning with a toddy, a cup of hot tea and two tablespoons of Southern Comfort, and ended each night with a shot. He told jokes and funny stories; he laughed out loud and sometimes made Dad laugh, too. He always hugged us when we came in, calling us by our nicknames, Dave, Southpaw, Will and Darsy. And he always gave us Cokes and a bag of Oreo cookies to devour while we played in the yard, leaving the men to talk business.

Mother ignored our pleas to go with Dad to visit Uncle Jake, telling us to go out and play. She didn't like Uncle Jake (I once heard her tell Alice that he was dangerous), but what she liked even less was the way Dad changed in his presence. He would do anything for Uncle Jake, regardless of how stupid, and imitated his every move, matching him drink for drink and dollar for dollar in his get-rich-quick schemes that never panned out. In the past Dad had invested in a worm farm and a bait shop, both located at Uncle Jake's, neither making enough money for Dad even to get back his investment. Uncle Jake would show him the books, spreading them out on the table and spilling handwritten cash receipts for minnows and worms all over the floor, but never did there seem to be a record of a profit.

Pleading with Mother to go to Uncle Jake's hadn't worked, so we pleaded with Dad, waiting until Mother finished shaving him—just before he burst into an old Irish ballad. He pulled on the shirt Mother handed him, buttoned it from the top down and tucked it into his jeans as we begged, "Oh, please, oh please," folding our hands together as if praying.

"Yas can all go," he said as he buckled his belt and flipped the end through the loops.

We cheered and scrambled to find our shoes, wash our faces and comb our hair so Dad would deem us presentable. Mother frowned and made a feeble attempt to argue, but we knew she would be overruled. Dad said we could go, and what he said, she abided by, even if it was against her better judgment and even if it put our lives in danger.

Alice refused to go and Stewart was out on his paper route, but David, Willie, Doris Ann, John and I piled into the station wagon— David, at eleven, demanding his place of honor in the front seat next to Dad for the hour drive. Mother stood on the porch and waved good-bye as we pulled from the curb, a slight look of disapproval clouding her face.

"See ya this evening, Gravel Gerty," Dad shouted, catching the cigarette from his mouth and hanging it out the window. He blew a couple of smoke rings then quickly exhaled the rest and flipped the cigarette to the ground as we turned toward the highway.

As soon as we turned onto Highway 78 toward Anniston, I noticed a group of Negroes walking along the shoulder. I turned and watched them until they were out of sight. David saw them too and looked over his shoulder. As we traveled farther, there were more: men and women, all walking slowly, carrying bags and blankets, some with small boxes tied to their backs or balanced on their heads. Willie, Doris Ann and John saw them too, and their heads turned along with mine and David's to watch the slow migration in silence.

"Sweet Jesus," Dad said, lighting another cigarette and tossing the match out the window. Our heads turned, synchronized like the gears in a watch, to stare at him. "They're walking on Washington," he explained, puffing hard on the cigarette.

"They're gonna walk all the way to Washington from here?" I asked skeptically.

"Washington, D.C.," Dad said, shaking his head in disbelief. We were still staring at him. He glanced at David and let out a long sigh. "You remember a while back when the Negroes stopped riding the buses? The city bus boycott?" We stared. I didn't know anything about it and I didn't think the others knew. David nodded his head, not because he knew but because it was a way to get Dad to continue. "Well, that started it. Now they're walking all the way to Washington, D.C., for a rally. There's thousands of 'em going. Their leader is that Negro preacher Bull Connor had in the Birmingham jail for a while; name's King. They want to end segregation—you know, be able to go in public places, shop in stores, eat in restaurants."

He took a long draw on his cigarette and glanced in the rearview mirror, catching my eye. I blushed and looked at the floor. Until that moment, I didn't know they couldn't eat in a restaurant. I knew the older boys in the neighborhood had been picking on the Negro boys who sold Popsicles from hot-ice boxes mounted on company bicycles. They pushed them from the bicycles and took the money and ice cream. I also knew that when Katie brought her daughters to Aunt Janet's house, we had to play inside; she was afraid to let them go outdoors. I had even heard about several Negro churches being bombed, but I hadn't put the pieces together.

"Ya can't blame a man for wanting a decent life," Dad said, taking another draw on the cigarette and blowing the smoke out, keeping his eye on the road instead of staring at the stream of black figures as we were. "Makes no sense," he added, almost to himself, "they got no place to stay, nothing to eat once they get there . . ."

I perked up. "Can we give them a ride?" David and I turned to watch four young Negro men wearing worn military boots and cut-off blue jeans fade into the distance. They raised clinched fists and looked straight ahead. Before they were lost from view we passed an old man and woman pulling a wooden wagon.

"How we gonna give 'em a ride?" Dad asked, exasperated. "We couldn't fit more than one or two in here. There's thousands of 'em. The migration stretches from here to Washington, D.C.!" He took another draw from his cigarette and blew it out. "Besides, they don't want a ride; they're with their families, walking together. We'd only separate 'em—if we could even get 'em in the car, which I doubt."

I curled my legs under me so I could see better and leaned on the back dash, watching the Negroes shrink to silhouettes against the bright blue sky like antebellum cutouts, only their clothes were rags, not finery, and their parasols were tattered umbrellas. I watched a woman walking along the shoulder of the road with a pair of old work boots tied to her feet with frayed rope. A step ahead of her was an old man with the same kind of rope tied around his waist for a belt. Before they were out of sight, a group of young women came into view. They wore bell-bottom jeans with black peace signs the size of saucers painted on both thighs and their hair bushed around their heads like the halos on Gozzoli's painting *Angels in Adoration.* One of the women held the hand of a girl who looked about ten, my age. She was the youngest person I had seen so far.

"Where are the babies?" I asked. "There aren't any babies or little kids."

"I imagine they left 'em home with somebody," Dad said, "out of harm's way."

We drove on in silence. Once we passed a woman carrying a small child. "Why are they taking the baby?" Doris Ann asked. We turned our heads to look at Dad again.

"Maybe they couldn't find a babysitter and Grandmother wanted to go to Washington, too," Dad answered. We turned back to the flow of dark figures. After watching for a while, I began to recognize groups as families: grandparents, parents and older children, walking together, an occasional bicycle or small cart wobbling alongside. We even passed a woman pulling a red Western Flyer wagon with two small boys in the bed and a goat tied to the back. But most of the processional was made up of men about the same age as my father. Their shoulders curved like boards left in the rain and they stared at their feet as if counting the steps. Occasionally someone—usually a teenage boy—would catch my eye and hold my gaze as we flashed by, hold it until the horizon split it like a knife.

Uncle Jake, the stump of a cigar stuck in the corner of his mouth, pulled Coke bottles from the refrigerator as we ran into the house. He popped off the caps with a wide-mouthed Aunt Jemima bottle opener attached to the cabinet and handed them out, laughing and roughing us up as we grabbed the cold bottles. David snatched the bag of Oreos from the kitchen table, tore it open with his teeth and handed out four chocolate cookies to each of us, hoarding the rest for himself. I parked myself at the table and eyed the bag, counting to see how many more cookies I could rightfully claim, and began the traditional sliding of the cookies apart and licking the white icing from the middle. There weren't enough chairs at the small Formica table for all of us, so Uncle Jake sat John on his lap. Dad lifted Willie out of his chair and stood him at the corner of the table, smiling at him good-naturedly as he took over his chair. Willie smiled back, unafraid, and licked his cookie. I smiled, too. That was one of the reasons I liked to go to Uncle Jake's; Dad treated us nice—special—as if he liked us. At home he would have just yelled for Willie to move.

I looked around the small kitchen and admired the new refrigerator. There were several new Band-Aids on the wall above the stove. Uncle Jake often got drunk and shot his pistol into the wall. He tried to conceal the holes by covering them with flesh-colored Band-Aids.

"Where's Aunt Nina?" I asked, thrusting the toes of my tennis shoes against the rose-patterned linoleum to make them squeak.

"She's gone shopping, spending all my money, and the kids have gone to do whatever it is that teenagers do," Uncle Jake said. He hopped out of his chair, turned John like a sack of potatoes under his arm and jumped to make him laugh. He trotted to the refrigerator, bucking like a horse, and opened it wide to show off new bottles of Jack Daniel's, Southern Comfort and Wild Turkey whiskey, and two six-packs: Pabst Blue Ribbon and Falstaff. That's all the refrigerator held, except for Coke, a jug of milk and a carton of orange juice, and ketchup, mustard and mayonnaise stashed on the bottom shelf of the door.

"Pick your poison," he said.

"I'll have a Pabst Blue Ribbon," Dad said, rubbing his lips with his fingers.

"Ah, ya coward," Uncle Jake said and tossed him a beer. He pulled the bottle of Southern Comfort from the shelf and kicked the door shut. "You'll never grow hair on your chest with that stuff. You need mother's milk!" he shouted playfully. He planted the huge bottle of whiskey in the middle of the table. "You know, Southpaw, your Dad's the baby boy," he said. "The baby of eleven kids. He was spoiled!"

Dad thumped the top of the beer a couple of times to quiet the fizz and pulled the tab, holding it toward David and me. He chuckled as it sprayed us.

"Here," he said, handing me the tab, "don't say I never gave you nothing." I laughed and muttered a sarcastic "Thanks." But I had a cigar box full of his beer tabs, some he had given me, saying exactly what he had just said, and some I had taken from the station-wagon ashtray. They were precious somehow, because he had held them between his fingers; so I saved them. I felt that in this way I had something of him, too.

"He's just the spoiled baby," Uncle Jake said again as he broke the seal on the Southern Comfort bottle. Dad ignored him. He took a sip of his beer and placed it gingerly on the table, not looking at Uncle Jake or any of us. He tilted his head slightly to the left and held it there. Other than when Uncle Jake made him mad, the only time I saw that tilt of his head was when the police were on him for something.

When I was very small, we lived in a dry county and Dad ran moonshine. I could tell whether he was hauling or driving the pace car by the car that was parked in the front yard. If it was a beat-up old wooden-slat pickup, he was hauling; if it was a shiny new Studebaker, he was the pace. The pace car sped down the road to attract the police and the truck full of moonshine came along a few minutes later. Occasionally the police came to our house searching for moonshine, shining flashlights into the attic and poking fingers into boxes of Christmas decorations. Dad would tilt his head and hold it there, restraining his temper, something I thought he ought to do when he was mad at Mother. There was never any real reason for Dad to get mad at Mother; he was mad at her because there was nothing to get mad at—mad because she was so good and he was so terrible. So he turned everything backward and made it out as if it were her fault he did terrible things. She should have gotten mad about all the stuff that he did, but she didn't. She just pretended it didn't happen: cleaned up the broken dishes and furniture, hid bruises, took him aspirin and breakfast in bed and kept us quiet and out of the way. She smoothed everything over, like putting icing on a charred cake.

"He's Irish," she would explain. "Not just Irish but *black* Irish. Your father's father was a typical Irishman—blue-eyed and ruddy. He and your grandmother had eleven children—all with fair complexions that burned and freckled in the sun and pale blue eyes. Except your father. He was born with dark brown hair, almost black, and hazel-green eyes. That's known as *black* Irish.

"There's an old Irish folktale that the black Irish came from the sea; that the fishermen married seals and that's how the dark hair got into the Irish blood. So beautiful! But, *oh*, they have a temper! All Irishmen have that temper. Your grandfather had that temper. Why, he beat one of the boys with barbwire once. And when your grandmother died—when your father was just seven years old—his father sent him to live with his older brother in Canada. He wasn't much safer with his brother; he had that same Irish temper. And your father has it, too."

Mother told the story of Dad's ancestry as if it were a story from our red leather storybooks, to keep us quiet for a while, but it was the thought of being beaten with barbwire or being sent to live in Canada that really kept us on our tiptoes and speaking in whispers.

"All right," Uncle Jake exclaimed, dropping John on the floor, "Dave, Southpaw, Darsy, all of yas, out the door, so your father and I can talk business." He pulled a shot glass from the cabinet and sat it on the table.

We hustled from our chairs, taking our Cokes and cookies with us, arguing over the remaining cookies as we slammed out the back door. I was glad Aunt Nina was gone. She was a strange, pear-shaped woman, not shaped like a woman at all, and she wore round circles of reddish-purple rouge on her cheeks like painted doll cheeks, and her lipstick was smeared all around her mouth as if she had put it on while riding a horse. On the visits when Mother came with us, Aunt Nina talked to Mother, but if she wasn't with us, Aunt Nina talked to me. Mostly, she told on Uncle Jake: how much he drank, how much money he blew, how badly he treated her. It was all true, but she said it as if I should do something about it. She followed me from room to room, whining in my ear. After every sentence she asked, "You know what I mean?" I'd nod, but I didn't always know what she meant.

I was overjoyed that she wasn't home. With Aunt Nina out of the way, we could do whatever we wanted. She wasn't there to tell me the bad things Uncle Jake did, or to tell us to stay out of the barns or out of the snake-infested pond. Dad and Uncle Jake would sit right where they were until dark, never bothering to see what we were up to.

We sat on the back steps until the Coke bottles were empty and the last crumb fell from the cookie bag, listening as Uncle Jake told Dad about the rich man who farmed the land around his house and how he got rich in the first place. It was an old story and we had heard it before, so we tossed our empty bottles into the wooden crate on the back porch and ran for the barn. David sprinted ahead to get there first.

The barn was stuffed with old furniture and farm equipment that belonged to Edson Tucker, the "rich farmer" Dad and Uncle Jake were discussing inside the house. Edson Tucker wasn't just a farmer, he was also the deputy sheriff. This made him twice as alluring; and even made his junk in the barn more alluring—*touching objects that belonged to a deputy sheriff.* But we had long ago rummaged through all of the drawers in the dressers and desks, finding scads of dried-out ink pens, paper clips, boxes of metal "I like Ike" buttons and a box of clear condoms that we used for a water-balloon battle. David had made up the rules for the water-balloon fight: If you got hit directly with a water-filled condom, you were pregnant and *it*. But we were no longer interested in the contents of the smelly old furniture; we were interested in the tractor, a green 1959 John Deere, used to plow, plant and harvest the fields of soybeans that surrounded Uncle Jake's house. Edson Tucker lived a mile away and Uncle Jake's barn sat a city block from the house. We could drive the tractor and never get caught.

David threw open the double barn doors and climbed onto the seat of the John Deere as the rest of us climbed onto the tires and hood.

"I think this thing runs just like Uncle Jake's pickup," David said. He examined the gearshift and touched the key hanging from the ignition. "Everybody get off and let me figure out how to drive it," he said. "Then you can get back on." We wiggled in our spots but didn't get down. "Move!" David yelled. We flinched but held our ground. "I've gotta learn how to drive it first!" he yelled, swinging his fist at us until we jumped to the ground, mumbling that we were going to tell on him. "You can get back on in a few minutes, dammit! You're such brats!"

Willie, Doris Ann, John and I stood just outside the barn with our arms crossed, pouting, while David tried to crank the tractor. He pushed in the clutch and turned the key. The engine turned over and died several times before it jumped to life, huffing and puffing thick black smoke. Grinding the gears, he put it in reverse and let the clutch out. The tractor jumped a foot and we jumped farther out of the way, scared but happier. David jumped the tractor out of the barn a foot at a time, forced it into first gear, and began driving slowly around the barn, the tractor coughing a constant put-put-put. We ran behind the tractor as close to the huge heavy-tread wheels as we dared, sucking in the puffs of diesel fuel, licking the taste of coal from our lips.

By noon we had taken turns driving the beat-up green tractor around and around the barn, popping the clutch and grinding the gears until it coughed to a stop, out of fuel, halfway around the barn. "Let's just close the barn doors and leave it there," I said, after we had searched, unsuccessfully, for a gas can.

"Yeah," David said. He walked over and slammed the barn doors, "Edson'll think Man did it." Man was Roscoe Mansfield. He worked for Edson Tucker driving the tractor. We had heard stories about him, just as we had heard about Edson Tucker, but we had never actually seen him. Dad and Uncle Jake said that Man was crazy.

We spent the rest of the afternoon paddling around the pond in two leaky boats, using boards for oars. David and Willie took one boat, the one that didn't leak as much, and Doris Ann, John and I took the other. We tied the boats together and pushed out into the muddy, bug-spotted water.

"Do you think Man ever killed anybody?" Willie asked, hopping into the boat as it inched away from shore.

"He'd be in jail if he killed somebody, you idiot," David said, slapping the surface of the water with the board to splash Willie.

"Then why do they say he's crazy?" Doris Ann asked.

"You don't have to kill somebody to be crazy," I said, holding my paddleboard over my head and jumping into the boat. I climbed to the front, taking the best seat, and dipped the board in the water. "Look at Crazy James, he just goes around Birmingham pushing a wheelbarrow full of old newspapers and talking to himself all day long. Everybody knows he's crazy, but he didn't kill anybody."

"That's right," Doris Ann said, taking the other seat, "and the Donut Man. That fat guy that comes by all the time trying to sell donuts."

"He's not crazy," I said. "He's retarded."

"What's the difference?" John asked, sitting on a bucket and dangling his feet in the water.

David smirked, "Retarded is somebody who's dumb enough to put their feet in a pond with five hundred water moccasins." John flipped his feet out of the water.

"I'm not retarded. You're retarded." We laughed and splashed him with water.

"Man must be like Crazy James," Willie said. "Uncle Jake said he gets the tractor stuck in the mud about five times a season; and he said they have to tell him to stop plowing if it starts to rain hard 'cause he's too dumb to figure it out himself."

"Yeah, but that's not *crazy*, that's just dumb!" I said. "What's the difference in crazy and dumb?"

"Dumb and crazy are sort of the same," David explained. "Kinda like you and John." John and I wailed in protest and threw water at David. Doris Ann and Willie laughed, so we threw water at them, too. "Crazy is worse," David continued. "Man is crazy because he . . . I don't know, maybe he eats dog sandwiches."

"They eat dog sandwiches in Korea," I said. "Is everybody in Korea *crazy?*"

"Only if they eat dog sandwiches." David laughed. He tossed a tin can to Willie. "Bail some water before we sink."

"You think you're so funny," I said, pushing the board deep into the water and pushing out, causing the boats to bump together. I tossed a tin can to Doris Ann and pointed toward the water seeping in around our ankles. "Maybe he hears voices," I said. "That's supposed to be crazy." David and Willie rolled their heads around and stuck out their tongues.

"I'm hearing voices," David said.

"I mean voices that aren't really there, ratfink! Maybe he thinks he's Old Blood and Guts." Everybody laughed. General George Patton was a standing joke at our house. Shortly after Dad returned from Pennsylvania, he took us to the drive-in theater to see the movie *Pat-*

ton. It was the first movie we had ever seen and we were very excited, but Dad got drunk and ranted about Patton, MacArthur and World War II through the entire movie. The assistant manager, a young man in slacks and a white shirt, was sent out to solve the problem, but when he got close to our car he stopped, glared at Dad as if he were a rabid dog, turned around and went back to the concession stand. After repeatedly shouting for him to "Shut the hell up," the people parked on either side of us cranked up and moved farther away. About halfway through the movie, Stewart came up with the idea of slipping out the back window and sitting on the ground at the front of the theater to watch the rest of the film. Mom was in the front seat listening to Dad's ranting. She didn't say a word when we sneaked away.

"Maybe Man thinks he's MacArthur headed for the Philippines," David said, wrinkling his brow and pretending to hold a pipe in his mouth. "I shall return."

"I think you should be removed from command," I scoffed.

"It's hot out here," Willie complained.

"Hey, let's have a water battle!" David said. He crawled over, untied the boats and pushed them apart. "Let's get closer to shore," he said, shoving the board deep into the murky water. Doris Ann and I paddled behind him. "Now," he said, "we splash water until one of the boats fills up and starts to sink. Whoever sinks first is Man for the rest of the day: c-r-a-z-y!"

By the time my boat began to sink, it was getting late. We were hungry, sufficiently scraped and bruised and ready to go home. We used the tin cans and emptied as much water as possible from the boats and tied them back to the dock, their rears still heavy with water. We ran back to the house, stopping at the outside spigot to wash our faces, hands and feet, then barged back inside, tracking water from the porch to the kitchen. I dashed into the bathroom and brought back towels. We dried off as much as possible and dropped the wet towels on the floor to mop up the puddles.

Just as we had expected, Dad and Uncle Jake were still sitting at the table drinking, but Dad was no longer drinking beer. Uncle Jake was pouring whiskey into his shot glass as we gathered around the table again.

"That's good," Dad said, placing his palm toward the glass. "That's good."

"Drink up, goddammit," Uncle Jake barked. He filled the glass until it spilled onto the table, then he filled his own to the white dotted line.

I walked up to the table, smiled and in my most pleasant voice said, "It's time to go home, Dad."

"We'll go home when I get good and goddamned ready," Dad said, staring down at his drink. Uncle Jake raised his shot glass in toast. "I'm goin' back to the wagon; these shoes are killin' me." He laughed, slammed the shot and hammered the glass against the table, and said it again: "I'm goin' back to the wagon; these shoes are killin' me!" I backed away and rolled my eyes at David and Willie. Dad was plenty drunk and showing off and Uncle Jake kept repeating that stupid saying that nobody understood. We could be there all night and we knew it. I went to the refrigerator, took out the orange juice, sat on the floor in front of the refrigerator and passed the carton around.

"I'm telling ya, S.K., he come close to getting his liver cut out," Uncle Jake said. "One more move and I'da nailed him. He'da been a dead son of a bitch!" Uncle Jake popped his arms out like a jack-in-the-box and scratched the chair against the linoleum. Dad chuckled and lifted the overfilled shot glass, spilling whiskey onto the table.

"Goddamn, S.K., don't waste the mother's milk!" Uncle Jake shouted. Dad took a sip of the whiskey and put it down, then wiped his wet fingers on his pants. David passed the orange juice carton to me. I took a drink and passed it to Willie. We finished the orange juice, only half-listening to Uncle Jake's tale of near death, and tossed the carton into the trash by the stove. David brought the fan from the back porch and plugged it in. We took turns holding our wet shirts in front of the fan to dry. We sat for another forty-five minutes playing the hand game Rock, Paper, Scissors. David spit on his fingers and whacked our wrists blue until we cried "Uncle." We were starving, so I pulled the jug of milk from the refrigerator and looked in the cabinet for crackers. There were several cans of sardines and two cans of tomatoes, but no crackers. I sat back down, took a drink of milk and passed it to Willie. Willie took a drink and passed it to Doris Ann.

John took the jug of milk from Doris Ann and peeked inside as if he might find mashed potatoes and gravy in there. "But I'm hungry," he whined. Dad turned and looked at John. We tensed and waited, trying to read him as if he were a storm cloud that could possibly rain, snow or blow over. He nodded as if in agreement and glared at each of us as if surprised to find us there. He pushed his chair back and stood, wobbled, put his hands on his hips, cleared his voice as if he hadn't spoken in a long time and said, "I better get these kids home." Before he could change his mind we jumped to our feet and ran to hug Uncle Jake good-bye. Doris Ann and I grabbed him around his neck and shouted, "Bye, Uncle Jake; we had fun!" just as he shouted, "Before you even finish your goddamned drink!"

We climbed into the station wagon, tired, damp and hungry, happy with our visit. But for Dad, the visit with Uncle Jake had gone badly. There was something about the way Uncle Jake talked to Dad, a certain voice, a way of putting him down that was hard to put your finger on, but you knew it when you heard it. And, from the look on Dad's face, I knew it must have been like that all day. He had that tight, explosive look and he started yelling before he pulled out of the driveway.

"Goddammit, sit still and roll those windows up!"

He was really drunk, reeling when he walked to the car, but we had seen him a lot worse; he could still drive. He slumped in the seat a minute with his foot on the brake, cleared his throat, pulled onto the road and eased down the street at a snail's pace. David leaned over, pretending to tie his tennis shoe, and looked at the speedometer. He casually threw his arm over the seat and flashed five fingers three times: fifteen miles an hour. I was riding directly behind Dad, so I already knew how fast he was going and preferred it that way. It would take forever to drive the sixty miles home, but at least we would get there. We had been with him when he decided everybody on the road was trying to prove how much better their car was than the station wagon. He'd slam the gas peddle to the floor and weave and bob down the highway at ninety miles an hour, honking the horn and yelling out the window, "You can't make a silk purse out of a sow's ear!"

Dad slowed down even more when we came to the curve in the road that joined with Highway 78. As the car inched around the curve, the headlights shone on the stream of Negroes walking in the twilight, an eerie dark procession alive with the hum of soft gospel music. "We're march-ing to Zi-on, Beau-ti-ful, beau-ti-ful Zi-on. We're march-ing up-ward to Zi-on, The beau-ti-ful cit-y of God." Ahead, just off the highway, two Negro men were shaking hickory nuts out of a tree and a group of Negroes were picking them up, dropping them into pockets, aprons and paper bags. Several people kicked at the grass and leaves in search of more. Dad put his foot on the brake and lowered his window. A rush of fear climbed up my back and flooded my chest. From the front seat, David shot me a look of complete dread.

"Dad," David said, reaching toward him. Dad ignored him and leaned out the window. He threw his arm out and started banging on the door of the station wagon.

"Get a goddamned job!" he shouted. "Get a goddamned job, you lazy sons a bitches! Get a goddamned job!" Adrenaline rushed through my body and I dropped onto the seat. David did the same. Willie and Doris Ann followed, pulling John down with them. Someone threw a hickory nut and it hit the car like a shot. Doris Ann and I screamed and covered our heads. Dad's foot slipped from the brake pedal and we lurched forward. John fell onto the floorboard, bumping his head on the door handle as he fell. Dad stomped on the brake, tossing us in the other direction, slammed the car into park and leaned farther out the window.

"You goddamned lazy bastards! Get a goddamned job!"

Hickory nuts pelted the station wagon like a torrent of hail, popping against the metal, a sharp staccato on the windshield. I slid from the seat and hunkered down on the floorboard. The others did the same. John crawled over Willie and rolled into a ball against my legs, calling for Mother.

"Get a goddamned job!" Dad shouted. The Negroes retaliated with ferocious, warlike whoops and cries: "Goddamned honky!" "Crackers!"

"Drive on!" David pleaded. "Please, Dad, drive on!" We all began to plead.

"Let's go home, Dad!"

"Push the gas pedal, Dad!"

"I want Mom! I want Mom!"

"Let's go, Dad! Let's go home!" But Dad was so involved in his ranting that he couldn't hear us. I covered my ears and hoped the angry crowd wouldn't pull him from the car and kill him, or, if they did, they wouldn't kill us because of his stupidity.

"Shut up, Dad!" we shouted. "Shut up!" But our pleas were drowned out by the battle. A hickory nut sailed in Dad's open window, ricocheted off David's closed window and plopped onto the backseat. Others followed. Dad was pelted with the nuts; they bounced about the inside of the car like popcorn, ricocheting off windows and dropping onto our backs. They rolled onto the seat and bounced to the floorboard, collecting into a pool at our feet.

"Shut up, Dad!" David shouted. Willie echoed the plea, "Shut up, Dad!" "Roll the window up, Dad!" I cried, holding my hands over my ears and dodging the bouncing nuts. Finally, he began to roll up the window, still hanging his head out, ignoring the hickory nuts that pelted his face, screaming obscenities, until the rising glass forced his head back inside. He brushed hickory nuts from his lap, then leaned over the steering wheel and went into a fit of coughing. I lifted my head and peered out the windows. Angry shouting Negroes surrounded the car. Many who had already traveled on down the highway were now running back. I was trembling. I was afraid they would pull Dad from the car and kill him. We were doomed. The hickory nuts continued to pop against the car like fierce hail. Dad lit a cigarette and tossed the match on the floorboard. He coughed again and leaned his face into the window, pressed his nose against the glass.

"Goddamned sons of bitches! Get a goddamned job!" He coughed and took another draw from the cigarette. The black faces were now close enough to the car for us to see them clearly; and they could see us. Several men rocked the station wagon back and forth. John started to cry. I leaned over him and began to pat his back. Doris Ann and Willie were moaning, almost in tears. We were all about to cry when suddenly, as if inspired by a breeze, the angry group stopped rocking the car and backed away to the edge of the road.

A heavy black woman with her hair wrapped in a yellow cloth held up her arms and began to sing. Her voice was deep, stronger and more powerful than any I had heard in church before, even in the men's choir. Several of the men and women dropped the hickory nuts from their fists and locked hands, joining her. They began to sway back and forth in the darkness. More people dropped the hickory nuts and joined them. The angry cries faded as the crowd gathered into a massive choir, returning to the song that they had been singing earlier: "The hill of Zi-on yields a thou-sand sa-cred sweets. Be-fore we reach the heav'n-ly fields, Be-fore we reach the heav'n-ly fields, Or walk the gold-en streets, Or walk the gold-en streets."

3 A.M.

"Get outta that bed," Dad shouted, spraying droplets of beer and saliva across our sleeping faces as he pulled the blankets from our bodies. "Get up! Get up; all of yas!" We lumbered from our beds and wobbled sleepily to the kitchen table, dropping into our usual 3 A.M. chairs as if they were assigned seats: Alice, Stewart and David on one side of the table; me, Willie, Doris Ann and John on the other. Mother stood behind Alice with her hands on the back of her chair.

"I want this place spotless!" Dad shouted, waving one hand while holding a beer in the other. "This place is a pigsty!" He stumbled backward, bumped into the kitchen sink and dropped the beer to the floor. He turned around and steadied himself, cleared his throat, then turned back to face us, shoving the dish rack full of clean dishes onto the floor as he turned. Shattered bits of glass pierced my bare legs and I sat up with a jerk. John slid from his chair and ran under Mother's arm. I straightened up and put my feet on the floor, as did the others, in case we needed to run. David rubbed a cut on his foot and wiped the blood on his T-shirt. Mother breathed an exasperated sigh, wrapped her arms around John and dropped her shoulders into her numb, impervious state.

"It's a disgrace!" Dad thundered, kicking the pile of smashed dishes and sending a cracked bowl whirling across the floor. "This house hasn't been cleaned up since the day we moved in. I work like a dog to rent a nice house and nobody even bothers to sweep the floor. Now get up and clean it up!"

He slapped the table with the palm of his hand. "Now!" We

jumped to our feet and moved, to put as much distance as possible between him and us. David left a trail of bloody toe prints across the kitchen floor. Doris Ann and I furtively picked the slivers of glass from our legs as we straightened the kitchen chairs around the table. It was pointless to clean the house ahead of time; no amount of cleaning could ward off the 3 A.M. ritual. In fact, it was better left slightly a mess; then he could see our progress.

Mother pushed John toward the doorway, telling him to pick up toys in the other rooms. Willie followed. Mother dropped a dish towel over the spilled beer, knelt and began picking through the dishes, stacking the whole and chipped ones to the side and tossing the badly damaged ones into a brown grocery bag. She pulled a broom from the closet and knelt again, searching for more keepers. I tiptoed across the floor and filled a plastic bowl with water and added some laundry detergent to wash the woodwork. Doris Ann tiptoed to the sink and practically climbed inside the cabinet while she looked for rags. I wanted to climb under the sink myself. I could feel the anger climbing up my cheeks and was afraid it would be noticed. *He didn't find this house; he didn't rent it; he didn't do anything!*

The day Mother rented this house, Dad was nowhere to be found. She brought the key home from work, borrowed Aunt Janet's broom and mop to clean the floors, then gathered us kids together to help move down the street. The house was a duplex, three rooms on each side, with a hall in the middle, but Mother rented both sides. She forced open the painted-shut hall doors and turned one of the kitchens into a bedroom. After the floors had been cleaned, we marched the two blocks from Aunt Janet's to our new house with our belongings balanced on our heads like acrobats in a circus parade. Lamps. Pillows. Books—lots of books: red leather-bound children's storybooks, twelve black leather biographies of Jesus' apostles, the huge family Bible and fifty or more novels Mother had read over and over again. Mother followed behind pulling Sweetpea's Western Flyer wagon loaded with a large cardboard box of whatnots and dishes wrapped in newspaper.

The last items moved were our prized possessions: Dad's light-up, three-dimensional picture of Leonardo da Vinci's *The Last Supper* and Mother's wooden trunk. Dad had bought the light-up picture of *The Last Supper* as an anniversary present for Mother. It was two feet by three feet, in a deep, heavily gilded frame. When plugged in, it came to life. Jesus sat at a long table with the disciples on either side. The disciples radiated: fleshy bronze skin, onyx eyes, thick muscular shoulders draped in chocolate brown and rich indigo, their bodies leaning obsequiously toward Jesus. Jesus, clad in burgundy and soft blue, cast his doe eyes downward, glowing reverently. Everything looked remarkably real. Even the loaves of bread looked within reach, touchable. Dad might have bought the light-up picture for Mother, but he was the only one allowed to plug it in. And he reserved even that for whenever he brought home a drinking buddy.

"Isn't it immaculate?!" he said. (Dad used the word *immaculate* to describe anything he thought was particularly fine: a car, a pig, a light-up picture.) "There's not another one like it in the entire U.S. of A. Move your head back and forth just a little and see how the disciples look like they're talking. So lifelike," he said, pausing while the buddy attempted to focus. "I bought that in Philadelphia, Pennsylvania. It was expensive, but worth it. There's not another one like it in the country. It's a collector's item. By now it's probably worth a fortune, but I'm not gonna sell it, just gonna hold on, let it get more valuable."

The other prized possession, Mother's trunk, was made of cedar with thick leather straps and brass buckles. It was filled with things we were never supposed to touch. We knew what was inside because whenever there was an opportunity we went through the trunk anyway.

"Don't touch anything," Alice commanded as she took the items from the trunk and placed them on the floor in a long row. She wound Mother's wooden metronome and tapped the stick, filling the room with a slow ticktock, swaying a little as she studied the items. Using two fingers, she held up a black lace swimsuit that looked like a dead animal, shivered and dropped it back into the trunk. She walked back to the line and picked up a black-lacquered jewelry box and held it out so we could see inside. Ghosts of heavy bracelets and pearls embossed the red velvet lining, but now it held only Mother's broken jeweled watch and her wedding ring, worn almost to the breaking point where the thin gold had rubbed underneath her finger. Alice held the box for us to rub our fingers over the smooth velvet before she closed it and put it back in the trunk. Then she picked up Mother's Marine Corps uniform, slipped her arms into the jacket and placed the hat on her head. It covered her eyes and she pushed it to the back of her head.

"Mother was wearing this uniform the first time she met Dad," Alice explained. "He was sitting at her desk reading the paper. His arm was in a cast where he got shot in the war and he had scabs on his forehead. He was very handsome and she was very pretty." She took the hat off and passed it around so we could try it on, then put it back in the trunk. She put her hands on her hips and studied the line again. Keeping time with the metronome, she marched to the large photo album and sat on the floor. We scooted around her. She opened it and read the captions under each picture.

"Night school in Omaha," she read, pointing to a sepia-toned picture. It looked like the four people in the picture were taking a test, but Mother was leaning back against the wall in her desk and she was laughing. Everybody else was intent on their work. We looked at the picture and laughed. *Our mother was acting up in school.* The next picture was of Mother standing beside another woman in uniform. "Dorris and Betty," Alice read.

"That was Mom's best friend?" I asked, examining the picture.

"Yep," Alice answered, "they used to stand side by side when they sang in the Marine Corps choir and they shared clothes and lipstick."

"If that's Mom's best friend, how come she never comes to see us?" Stewart asked. Alice shrugged her shoulders and turned the page. After carefully returning the photo album to the trunk, she thumbed through the stack of sheet music looking for the songs we had heard Mother sing while she was ironing or washing dishes.

"This," she said, "is 'Dearest, believe.' 'Haste then and save Him ere he die.'" She placed it on the bottom of the stack and held up another. "And this is 'Beautiful Dreamer'; you know that one." She straightened the music stack and flipped through the pile of programs, choosing a small yellowed program with several deep creases on the cover. "A White Christmas Program," she read, "presented by The Fortieth Street Methodist Church, Sunday, December 20, 1942, five P.M." She opened it carefully. "Program," she read. She scanned the printing until she came to Mother's name. "Solo: 'Jesus, Joy of Man's Desiring,' by Dorris Robinette." She scanned it again until she came to a familiar name. "Second reader: Janet Robinette. That's Aunt Janet," she said. She continued the search until she came to Mother's name again. "Solo: 'Cantique De Noel,' by Dorris Robinette. Then the choir sings eight songs and Mom's in that, too."

The bottom of the trunk held a layer of ticket stubs and a few things that belonged to Dad: a German beer stein, a small box of World War II medals and a wooden box containing a .38 pistol. Alice opened the box of medals and passed them around. I took the Purple Heart out of the box and held it in the palm of my hand.

Stewart leaned closer. "He got that for getting shot," he said, tapping the front of the heart. "That's George Washington."

"I know," I said. "He's on the wall in the principal's office at school."

"And this pin with the stars tells how many battles he was in; four battles."

"George Washington was in four battles?" David said, pushing to see better.

"Not George Washington!" Stewart yelled. "Dad!"

Even though Alice didn't touch the box containing the pistol, we knew it was there. We had seen Dad dig it out before, shoveling Mother's things into a heap on the floor, then gently placing the wooden box on the table as if it were made of the most fragile glass.

Mother and Stewart moved the light-up picture of *The Last Supper* and Mother's cedar trunk from Aunt Janet's house to our new house, placing them in the middle of the living room floor with our other belongings. The pile didn't seem big enough to turn this house into *our* house and I thought for the first time about the furniture we had abandoned in Eastaboga: the cool blue kitchen table and white chairs with slender deerlike legs; the squeaky wooden rocking chair where Mother had rocked the babies to sleep; the bed that Alice, Doris Ann and I had shared, the springs broken so badly we rolled together like pigs in a blanket. The boys had also shared a bed, but theirs was larger and had a dark headboard that slanted forward. Mother knew when we were jumping on their bed because the headboard would whack against the wall. There was also a large dresser that matched the slanting headboard. Mom and Dad had a dark wooden bed like the boys'. But instead of a matching dresser, they had a white vanity with square movable mirrors on both sides and a small bullet hole in the top left drawer. Even though I was very small when it happened, I could still remember how the bullet hole got there.

It was late at night and we were all in bed in the Eastaboga house. Doris Ann, Willie and I held our hands over our ears and rocked our heads back and forth to drown out Dad's voice. He had been yelling at Mother for a long time. Stewart and David had climbed onto the end of our bed and were sitting against the wall with Alice, staring at the closed bedroom door. Suddenly the shouting stopped. After a couple of minutes, I uncovered my ears and propped up on my elbows to listen; Willie and Doris Ann did the same. Nothing. No shouting. No crying.

"Bang!"

Alice screamed at the gunshot and ran for the door. We followed her, frantic, crawling over each other and chirping like birds. Alice threw open the bedroom door and ran through the house to our parents' bedroom, screaming, "Mom! Mom!" Mother—already on her way to our bedroom—met us just outside their bedroom door.

"It's all right," she cried, running toward us on her tiptoes. "Shhh, shhh, shhh. It was just an accident. Everything's all right." She rounded us up, corralling us with the skirt of her dress. "It was just an accident." She held her skirt out to the sides to keep us from seeing into the bedroom as she herded us back to bed, but we could still see him as we walked backward, shuffling and bumping into one another. We could see him sitting on the edge of the bed, holding the pistol in one hand and covering his face with the other.

The next morning Mother took Dad breakfast in bed and asked us not to disturb him. When he finally got up, he walked through the house in his sock feet, placing them on the floor as if there were blisters on the bottoms. He said he had shot at a rat that was trapped in the drawer.

Later, Stewart went into their bedroom to examine the vanity. We circled around him, and Alice watched from the open door in case either parent came in that direction. He stuck his finger into the hole, opened and closed the drawer, looked underneath, and ran his hand along the bottom.

"I don't see how a rat could have gotten into that drawer," he said.

But that vanity was long gone and I'd never see it again. In fact, we had hardly any furniture for our newly rented house. Studying the things that were piled on the floor, I began to miss other things: the highchair we had all sat in as babies, the coffee table where we colored pictures and did our homework, the shelf where Mother displayed the porcelain ducks Dad had bought her for Christmas one year.

Why had we left all of our furniture behind?

Cautiously, even reluctantly, Uncle David wheeled the brown station wagon up the steep driveway the day he and Aunt Janet came to get us in Eastaboga. Aunt Janet sat next to him; Sweetpea was in the backseat with his dog, Spot, who leaped gleefully from the car, but snapped when we tried to pet him. Uncle David walked around the yard with his hands deep in his pockets, kicking stones while Mother and Aunt Janet packed. Mother stuffed our clothes into the pillowcases from our beds. Aunt Janet put toys, tennis shoes and Dad's fishing gear into a cardboard box. They stopped occasionally to discuss what should be taken, what should be left behind. Mother skipped over most items without giving them much consideration, but paused at a box of record albums. Some of them were recordings she had made, "long before we were born."

"Just keep the ones that you recorded, Dorris," Aunt Janet said, picking up a thick paper-covered album and sliding it from the jacket.

"There's no need to keep them," Mother said. She handed the entire box to Stewart and told him to take them outside. We followed him into the yard to play catch with the records. Stewart read the labels before sailing them into the air. "The Benny Goodman Orchestra." "Frank Sinatra sings 'One for My Baby and One More for the Road.'" "Dorris Robinette sings 'I've Got You Under My Skin.'" As the car got closer to being fully packed, we started throwing the records at the oak tree in the front yard, smashing them to pieces. By the time Mother called us to get in the car, there was a pile of shattered records around the tree. Stewart threw the last one out the back window of the station wagon as we drove away. It landed unbroken in the driveway. As the car moved toward the street, the record looked like a black hole in the dry red clay.

Mother and Stewart stood beside the trunk and stared at the small pile of possessions, too.

"Why didn't we go back for our furniture when we left East-aboga?" I asked.

"Where would we have put it all?" Mother answered. "Your Aunt Janet had already done so much. Just don't think about it."

By that time Dad had been back from Pennsylvania for eight months. He had a job working construction, but still hadn't rented a house for us. Most of his paycheck got spent down at Ruby's Bar on Tenth Avenue. He would have let Aunt Janet and Uncle David keep us forever if Uncle David hadn't come home one day and, needing a tool that we had broken, demanded that we all get out of his house. In one minute I heard more words come out of his mouth than in the entire eleven months we had lived there. He was quiet; his voice was deep and soft and it seemed as if he whispered rather than talked—when he talked at all. But he didn't whisper that day and even threw in a few cuss words as he stormed into the house. We were stunned into silence. Alice cried and wanted to call Mother at work, but Aunt Janet wrapped her arms around Alice's shoulders and told her it was news that could wait until Mother got home.

I was glad we would have to move from Aunt Janet's house. I loved living there, but I slept every night on the mattress in the living room with Doris Ann, Willie and John. I didn't mind the company, but I had begun two nighttime transgressions that disturbed and embarrassed me: rocking my head and wetting the bed. I had always rocked my head at night, back and forth, back and forth, as did Willie and

John. It was a comfort, like rocking in the old rocking chair, a steady, dependable rhythm. But lately it had gotten worse, more frenzied, and the bedwetting horrified me. Mother never mentioned it. She washed and dried the covers every day and put the mattress outside in the backyard to air whenever possible. My face flushed crimson and my ears burned every time she pulled the mattress out the back door. It was as if everyone in the world was being told about my problem, as if they could see through my skin and bones to my heart, where control of this life had slipped away. *Wets the bed, at nine years old!* I was sure that if we had our own house it wouldn't happen; all I needed was a house. I was sure of it.

Mother was working as a secretary for an investment company and when she wasn't working, she was occupied with Dad. So after we moved into the duplex house on Thirteenth Avenue, I took control of everything I could take control of, which was Willie, Doris Ann and John. I told them when to go to bed at night and when to get up for school, where they could go and where they couldn't, when it was all right to go barefoot and when they had to wear shoes. I regulated the afternoon housecleaning, throwing out commands like a general: "John, pick up the toys! Willie, take all the dishes to the kitchen! Doris Ann, pick up the clothes and papers and hold the dustpan!" I dominated the lower ranks and miraculously the bedwetting stopped. But the head-rocking, "bumping," as Dad called it, got worse. So did his nighttime sessions of abuse. He shouted with rage and I rocked my head in response—back and forth, back and forth, shaking away memory. He screamed for me to "stop that goddamned bumping!" But, as soon as he left the room, I rocked harder, blurring thoughts, blurring sounds.

As if in conspiracy with my unsightly, tangled face, my hair twisted into tight, ratty knots, impossible to comb.

Mother cut the tangles from my hair, snapping the scissors around my ears and dropping the hair onto the floor in great wads. A bob, she called it. Short like a boy's at the back, a little longer on the sides. I wanted long hair like the other girls in school. Not just for the beauty of it, but for protection: I could drop my head and hide behind it when other kids teased me about my face. But I didn't want long hair as much as I wanted to rock my head, purge the demons from my thoughts, and still the *haint* that rattled my bones. I grew thin and pale. Protruding, crooked teeth parted cracked, bitten lips. Mouth breather. Tongue-thruster. The epitome of a guttersnipe. My hazel eyes made only the briefest contact with other eyes before darting back to the floor.

Doris Ann and I tiptoed around the broken dishes and sneaked out of the kitchen into our bedroom. We quickly picked the remaining glass from the backs of our legs, shook the bloody slivers onto a discarded homework assignment and wadded it into a ball. Then we pulled on our tennis shoes and ran back to the kitchen before we were missed.

Alice took the broom from Mother and began furiously sweeping the broken dishes. She walked across the glass and held the dustpan secure with her bare bloody foot. She picked it up, dropped half a bowl and half a plate back to the floor, shattering them further, and dumped the remainder of the dustpan into the paper bag with a crash. Mother took the dustpan out of her hand and stooped to hold it for her. The dishes disappeared into the trash. Alice began pushing the broom, recklessly swatting whatever was in her path, rapidly accumulating a pile of dirt, paper, clothes and toys. Doris Ann and I crouched in the far corner of the kitchen and began slopping soapy water onto the baseboards with a sponge and drying them off with a rag.

"And Stewart, I want that grass cut!" Dad shouted as Stewart and David tumbled out the back door and slammed the screen. "You can't see your knees for the weeds in that backyard. And David, pick all that trash up along the fence and use the machete on those high weeds while Stewart cuts!" Dad lurched to the right, then to the left and wormed his way to the table, where he had left a six-pack of Pabst Blue Ribbon.

"How about some food around here? I haven't eaten in so long my stomach thinks my throat's been cut." His mouth twisted into a crooked smile as he jerked a beer from the plastic ring and pulled the tab.

Mother stacked four chipped bowls on the table, pulled a pot from the cabinet, filled it with water and put it on the eye of the stove. She always made spaghetti when she had to cook in the middle of the night. It was quick and easy, and usually all that was available. Spaghetti and canned tomato sauce. If there wasn't any tomato sauce, she'd use a can of tomato soup and put a dash of oregano in it. She opened the cabinet above her head and brought out a box of spaghetti and a box of salt, poured a mound of salt into her palm and sprinkled it into the water. She opened a drawer next to the stove and pulled out a flashlight.

"Barbara, will you take this out to Stewart so he can see what he's doing out there?" she asked, holding out the flashlight and returning the salt to the shelf at the same time.

I dropped the soapy rag into the bowl and grabbed the flashlight without answering. Sometimes, if Dad didn't hear your voice, he forgot about you. Lately, I had been on a lucky streak. He had not fully directed his anger at me since last summer. I had been forced out of bed at 3 A.M. plenty of times since then but had not been hit for a while, not more than a clip, anyway, not since the time he got Willie, Doris Ann, John and me out of bed and beat us. He beat us—not because we had done anything wrong—but to get at Alice.

When Dad wasn't torturing Mother directly, he tortured Alice, which was the same as torturing Mother—only worse. She didn't mean to, but Mother loved Alice best and Dad knew it. After Dad returned from Pennsylvania, Alice, a ninth grader at Woodlawn High School, stopped doing her school work; her grades dropped from straight A's to C's, then plummeted to F's. Within a short time, she refused to go to school at all, claiming the teachers hated her and she hated them.

"You *will* go to school, goddammit! You sorry thing!" Dad berated her, slamming his fist on the table. "You make F's 'cause you hang out with that bunch of worthless scum! Those lowlifes! But then, you're about as worthless as anything I've ever laid eyes on!"

Dad screamed that Alice was no good and she believed him. She fought back like a Kamikaze pilot, sidestepping Mother and throwing herself into the path of his rage. When she became numb to his assaults about her schoolwork and friends, he invaded her privacy: pulled the clothes from her closet, threw away rollers and lipsticks, demanded to know whom she was seeing and if she was sleeping with them.

"You're a goddamned lying whore!" Dad shouted, slapping her onto the floor and kicking her. "You sorry thing!"

"Stewart, that's enough," Mother said, dancing between them.

"What about *you?*" Alice spat.

"Alice, don't say another word," Mother coaxed. "Stewart, why don't you sit down and I'll fix you something to eat."

"She drives me to it, Dorris! She drives me to it!"

When he wasn't smacking Alice, he was smashing her *things*. He smashed her record player and the records she had borrowed from her friends. He bought her a radio for her sixteenth birthday, only to smash it with a hammer the next weekend. He ranted about her makeup and clothes: short skirts that inched upward with every slap to her face. One evening, he held her by the hair for half an hour, forcing her to watch as he burned her skirts in the backyard.

Alice—being much smarter than Dad—stayed ahead of him in the conflict, got back at him by stealing money and cigarettes from his pockets and—when he passed out on the floor—swiped his keys and took her friends for joy rides in his car. His car. Not our car.

A used 1962 Cadillac, antique gold with leather seats and power windows. He traded the Chevy station wagon, four hundred dollars and his father's Union Civil War rifle for it. He talked about it as if it were the only car like it in the world, reciting the same speech he gave about the light-up picture of *The Last Supper,* except it was the leather seats that were *lifelike* rather than the disciples. "It's immaculate," he said. And certainly not to be touched by this ragged brood, unless, of course, it happened to be dirty. The immaculate gold Cadillac was then washed in the backyard, in the dark, during the 3 A.M. housecleaning ritual, and waxed to a high shine.

As luck would have it, he never caught Alice borrowing his car, and she often let us go along in exchange for keeping our mouths shut. Just to make sure we wouldn't tattle on her for smoking, she forced us to smoke one cigarette each. We sat with the cigarettes stuck haphazardly in our mouths and lowered the magical power windows so the breeze would burn the cigarettes as she drove the streets of Birmingham, picking up the tattered, smoking, cussing teenagers that filled our house during the day.

I liked my oldest sister on those occasions, but sometimes I hated her. And hated Dad, too. And for the same reasons. They both held Mother prisoner. She was so busy soothing Dad and protecting Alice that she was absent from my life. I felt invisible. And I made things worse by resenting Alice. I resented the money Mother gave her for makeup, plastic rollers, bobby pins and *True Confession* magazines. I resented the clothes she made for her and the time she spent teaching her to walk, pacing back and forth in the living room with a book balanced on her head: "Let your hips carry your body." I followed behind and diligently practiced everything Mother begged Alice to do. I learned to waltz, fox-trot, eat with the correct fork, shake hands properly and walk with a book balanced on my head—a head that held a book, Alice informed me, because it was *flat*. I might as well have been walking on my head. Mother was amused but uninterested in my accomplishments. There were times when I felt so abandoned, consumed by jealousy and anger, that I wanted to slap my sister, too.

Once, I found a pack of cigarettes in Alice's purse and showed them to Dad, tattling. He put them in his pocket and went to the bar. Later that night as I rocked myself to sleep, Mother came and sat on the edge of my bed. I was startled and stopped rocking. There were no good-night rituals in our house; she never looked in on us at night. I immediately imagined she was concerned about me and my heart leaped with happiness. She leaned over until I could feel her breath on my face and whispered, "If you ever tell on Alice again, I'll beat you within an inch of your life." Then she walked away. I rocked, rocked harder, wept and hated them even more, including Mother. A red-hot, hungry hatred.

I handed the bowl of soapy water to Doris Ann and took the flashlight out to the backyard. I stood in the darkness, holding the flickering beam on the lawn mower while Stewart pulled at the starter cord. "Dammit," he muttered and kicked the ground each time the motor stalled. The lights were on in the houses on both sides of us and I knew our neighbors were watching. They always turned their lights on to let us know we had disturbed their sleep. They themselves were standing in one of the dark rooms with their faces pressed against the screen of an open window, watching and listening—too afraid to walk over and say anything to Dad. No, they'd wait for the light of day, to complain to us; with sneering faces they'd demand that we stop him from waking them, demand that we stop him from using foul language, demand that we stop him from ruining the neighborhood with his drunkenness—as if we had that power. The people across the street and down the block wouldn't speak to us at all— except to tell us to get out of their yards. I stared into the indigo night counting the stars in time with the sound of David whacking at the weeds, as if I were knocking the stars from the sky with each blow, bringing the long night to an end. It was the middle of summer but I shivered; the beam of light danced in the darkness.

When the house had been sufficiently cleaned and the grass cut, Dad called us back to the kitchen. It was just beginning to get light outside. We sat around the table watching him smoke cigarette after cigarette, pressing the charred butts into a jar lid. He was silent for a long time. He rapped his knuckles on the chest of anyone who dared to fall asleep, demanding that he or she sit up straight and pay attention. Finally he told us that Mother was pregnant again. He slurred, "One more to make up for losing Mary Louise," as if the baby had died on purpose and he couldn't get to her to give her a good cuff. We turned to stare disbelievingly at our mother. She sat with her arms crossed, her fingers softly working the flesh on her upper arms; she had that vacant look on her face, that unreadable, unfocused stare.

Shed No Beam
upon My Weak Heart

Dorris Robinette, USMC

When Mother was well into her ninth month of pregnancy, one of her girlfriends from college came by our house. They had gone to Birmingham Southern together, both majoring in music, and later joined the Women's Marine Corps on the buddy system.

Due to her advanced pregnancy, Mother was no longer working

when her friend knocked on the door. While Mother had been work-ing as a secretary, she had managed to secure some of the luxuries we had become acquainted with while living with Aunt Janet: an inside bathroom, running water and gas heat. But with Mother out of work, we relied on Dad to pay the bills, and only a fraction of his weekly paycheck actually made it home. The gas had been turned off.

Mother's friend was not expected company. Toys and clothes were scattered everywhere. The only decent piece of furniture we owned was a huge rocking chair Dad had bought at an auction. The auction-eer had claimed the black-lacquered, claw-foot rocker was from China. Shortly after Dad brought it home, Mother had pulled the rotting upholstery off and re-covered the seat and back with the same kind of material as the original: red velvet. It was wide enough for two kids to sit in at once, and often, when my face swelled with one of my chronic toothaches, I slept in it—curled into the extra-wide seat, dangling one foot so I could rock myself through the night. Dad had also purchased our couch at the auction, but it was just an ordinary, secondhand couch; the Chinese rocker—like the light-up picture of *The Last Supper*—had the feel of riches.

When Mother's friend arrived, Willie, Doris Ann, John and I were piled on the shabby couch wrapped in a quilt. We were drinking Kool-Aid from jelly glasses and watching cartoons on a battered TV set. The dog, an English sheepdog Uncle Jake had given us, was asleep beside me with his head in my lap. Mother was sitting in the rocker reading *The Agony and the Ecstasy*. She wore a red skirt, a pink blouse and a white sweater that wouldn't stretch far enough to but-ton. The blouse would button, but the buttonholes were tightly drawn, exposing her belly. When she answered the door, she held a hand over the most obvious triangle of flesh and opened the door just wide enough for her friend to slip through, apologizing for her appearance before the woman was inside.

The friend was introduced to us as Betty. She had curly brown hair pulled back in a ponytail and was the same height as Mother. They could have been sisters. She wore a long black coat with a fur collar and her sweet perfume filled the air when she walked.

After hugging her friend, Mother pushed the dog off the couch and told David to put him outside, brushed away the dog hair and sat on the warmed spot, offering the rocking chair to her friend. Betty started to remove her coat, realized it was cold in the room and removed only her gloves and tucked them into a large leather purse. As she pulled the rocker closer to the couch she said, "Oh, my, this is a lovely rocker."

"It's from China," I beamed. She smiled at me, dropped her purse onto the floor and sat down with a deep sigh.

"Well, Dorris," she said, touching Mother's arm. "You look wonderful . . . and pregnant." They laughed and Mother dropped her head.

Except for Dad, Mother didn't have friendships. We had seen pictures of her with friends, but had never actually met one. Occasionally, some women from church would come into our house offering the possibility of friendship, but Mother wouldn't say much when they came and sighed in relief when they left. We knew she was afraid they might cross paths with Dad. But more than that, she didn't want her time to be taken up by anything other than Dad. She seemed to crave him as much as he craved alcohol.

Betty reached into her purse and brought out a small box of chocolates and six photographs for Mother. She reached back in and brought out bright green bubble pipes and small jars of soapy liquid for Willie, Doris Ann, John and me. We blew bubbles into the air, catching those that didn't instantly pop, on the ends of our pipes, and begged Mother to blow on the iridescent spheres until they burst. Then we gathered around to listen while Betty told us stories. She put her arms around us, an unfamiliar demonstration of affection, and I blushed self-consciously, feeling too old, at twelve, to be hugged, but I didn't move away.

"Your mother was so much fun in college." Betty laughed. "We were in the Art Club and the Drama Club and, of course, Choir. We were both music majors. We had this voice instructor—he wasn't part of the college curriculum, but we were taking lessons from him anyway—and he was just crazy about your mama. Not because she could sing so well, but because she could recite poetry, and he secretly hoped to be the next Walt Whitman." Betty and Mother laughed. "He used to write poetry sitting at the counter at the dime store and then make us read it out loud before our lesson every week. He loved your mama because she could recite almost any poem on request. Oh, he thought that was something. I've always been good at it myself, but nothing like your mama. When we were in the Marines, we'd go out and show off." Betty and Mother laughed again. I joined in, but didn't really know what they were laughing about.

"Once," Betty continued, "a G.I. bet fifty dollars she couldn't recite 'Thanatopsis.' He lost, of course." Betty patted my back. "Did you know she could recite just about anything?"

Of course I knew. I could recite many of those poems myself and so could the other kids. Along with the other books Mother owned and carried with her from place to place was an old tattered poetry book. It was our source of entertainment before we moved to Birmingham, before TV, radio and RC Cola. Mother had read poetry to us almost every day: while we ate our pancakes on Saturday mornings, as we sat on the back steps and watched the sun go down in the evenings and by candlelight during storms with the whine of a distant tornado in the background. She had repeated the same poems so often that we chimed in to help her through the lines. With Mother's help, Alice had directed numerous plays using the poem book as a script, making notes in the margins: *Stewart will read this, Barbara will say this, David will read this for Easter, Mom will make the babies listen.* Stewart could recite "The Village Blacksmith" and "The Rum Tum Tugger." Alice could recite "Hiawatha's Childhood" and "Dream Fairy Dear," and insisted that the latter be part of the Christmas play every year; she said that fairies were elves without their Christmas outfits on.

The Christmas play began with carols selected in the order of favorites according to birth: Alice's favorite, Stewart's favorite and so on. Then Alice read the Christmas story from the Bible: Luke 2: 1–14. Then it was time to recite poems. Alice recited "Dream Fairy Dear," then anyone could recite, even the babies if they could talk. I usually recited my favorite poem, "The Tale of Custard the Dragon" by Ogden Nash. We all knew several of his poems; they were funny and some of them were short enough for the little kids to learn. The play ended the same way every year, with everyone singing "The Twelve Days of Christmas," including the audience: our mother, her sweet voice remaining ever so low as not to drown out the voices of her children—except for the part about the five golden rings, which she had to sing all by herself.

*   *   *

We were still living with Aunt Janet for our first Christmas in Birmingham. Stewart realized we didn't have a gift for her, so he talked with Mother about doing a short play just for Aunt Janet. Mother helped him pick out poems for each of us to recite, familiar poems we almost knew by heart already. Alice wouldn't have anything to do with Stewart's play; she had, after all, just turned twelve and now had *real* friends to play with. Stewart liked that better anyway; he wanted to be the boss, to decide how the play would unfold. He wanted to direct this play because he had learned a new Christmas song at school and he wanted to be the one to teach it to us; he knew Mother and Aunt Janet would be impressed.

The brand-new Christmas song was "The Little Drummer Boy." Stewart's fifth-grade teacher had copied the words off the radio and taught them to her class. Stewart lined us up in order of birth and taught us the words: "Come, they told me, pa rum pum pum pum. Thy new born King to see, pa rum pum pum pum."

"This song doesn't make any sense," David complained.

"It doesn't have to make sense!" Stewart shouted, waving the handwritten script in the air. "It's a Christmas song!"

Stewart worked on us for over a week, giving pop exams on our recital piece any time of day. We began to avoid him. Finally the time came to present the play to Aunt Janet. Mother held John on her lap and sat on the end of the couch, presenting the center seat to Aunt Janet. She sat down, her dish towel still on her shoulder, adjusted her glasses and straightened her housedress. We sang "The Little Drummer Boy" first and Stewart sang louder than the rest of us.

"Oh, my," Aunt Janet cooed, clapping madly. "I heard that on the radio at work yesterday. Isn't that a beautiful song, Dorris?"

After praise for the opening number had subsided, we recited poetry. Our instructions were to take two steps forward, keeping our arms by our sides, recite directly to Aunt Janet, and take two steps back into line. Stewart was first, of course. He stepped forward and recited "O Captain! My Captain!" by Walt Whitman. David was next with "The Charge of the Light Brigade" by Alfred Tennyson. I was after him. I stepped forward to recite "The Donkey," by G. K. Chesterton, a poem about the donkey that Jesus rode into Galilee. But

I couldn't get out a single word. I sputtered and made no sound at all, blushed and dropped my head. Stewart glared at me, then began the first line, slowly, waiting for me to catch up.

"When . . . fishes . . . flew . . ."

"And forests walked," I recited, a little too loudly. "And figs grew upon thorn. Some moment when the moon was blood, then surely I was born. With monstrous head and sickening cry and ears like errant wings. The devils walking parody on all four-footed things." I finished the poem and stood like a stone, shocked by how clearly the beautiful words described the sadness of feeling unsightly and less worthy than others. David pulled me back in line.

"She did just fine," Aunt Janet said, wiping her eyes with the dish towel.

Willie stepped forward and recited "The Modern Hiawatha," by George Strong. Then he quickly—impromptu—recited his favorite "Little Willie" poem: "Willie saw some dynamite, couldn't understand it quite; curiosity seldom pays: it rained Willie seven days." Stewart glared at him and Willie jumped back in line.

Doris Ann was last. She stepped forward and, holding her straight blond hair away from her face as if it interfered with her voice, screamed, "Algy met a bear. The Bear was bulgy. The bulge was Algy." Everybody laughed. Stewart had to straighten out the line and tell us to "shut up" before he could finish the play.

He ended with a poem that Mother had told us was by Aunt Janet's favorite poet, Stephen Crane. He took his time, dramatically emphasizing, "For truth was to me a breath, a wind, a shadow, a phantom, and never had I touched the hem of its garment." David rolled his eyes and we smiled to each other. But it *was* the best way to recite. Mother had taught us to read and recite poetry with emotion and fervor, a practice that helped David win the Alabama State Poetry Festival the following spring with the poem he had learned for Aunt Janet's Christmas present. He won first place, and his picture, along with the two other winners', was on the front page of *The Birmingham News*.

When our play was over, Stewart took a bow. Mother applauded. Aunt Janet wept into her dish towel, then clapped her hands and whispered, "Thank you so much." She hurried into the kitchen and busied herself cooking supper. From the living room, we could hear her sniffles among the clatter of pots and pans.

"Why is she crying?" Stewart asked.

"She's remembering," Mother explained. "After our mother died, your Aunt Janet—who was eight years older than me—helped take care of me. She used to read those same poems over and over to me, just the way I've read them over and over to all of you."

Betty asked Mother if she would recite something for us, but she said, "No, not now," and Betty patted her arm.

"We had great fun in the Marine Corps. All the men wanted to go out with your mama because she didn't drink and they could have her beer tickets. Do you remember that, Dorris?" Mother laughed again, but this time it sounded like the anxious laugh she used when she talked to the landlord or the insurance man.

"And she has the sweetest voice I've ever heard," Betty said. "We sang in the Marine Corps Choir and your mother was our soloist. Oh, she sang like an angel, and she looked like one, too." She pointed to the photographs she had brought along. I reached out and lifted a photograph from Mother's lap. She was singing, holding an open songbook. The photograph was black and white, but had been hand-painted. Bright red-orange shaped Mother's full mouth and her per-fect curls were tinted a deep burgundy-brown. Teardrop diamonds dangled from her ears. She wore a robe, black ankle-strap heels with a V-cut toe and the watch hidden in her jewelry box. Her fingernails and toenails matched her red lips. I stared at the photograph, aston-ished. My mouth fell open like the one in the picture. I could tell it was Mother, but not the one I knew. I had never seen lipstick on her lips nor her lashes tinted dark, and had never seen her wear jewelry at all. It was as if this photograph had been taken of a movie star who looked like my mother: uniform curls, dark spidery lashes, perfect white teeth and dimples.

I lifted another photograph from her lap. It was of Mother and Betty sitting on the floor in their bras and panties. Betty was shaving Mother's legs with a razor and they were laughing as if at a joke. Mother took the photographs away from me and put them back on her lap underneath a photograph of her and Dad. I leaned forward to study it. They were wearing their Marine Corps uniforms and standing on a city sidewalk in front of a barbershop. Dad looked almost the same to me: tall, dark hair, eyes that spoke danger. He was offering Mother a taste of his ice cream. They were smiling.

"I took that shot," Betty said, tapping her polished nails on the photo, "when we were stationed in Philadelphia. My, S.K. was handsome. Is he still as wild as he used to be?" She giggled and patted Mom's knee.

I tried to see the other pictures, but Mother stacked them together and crossed her hands over the stack. I could tell by the way she pinched her mouth together that she didn't want this woman to be in our house, couldn't wait for her to leave, didn't want the chocolates, photographs or bubble pipes. Betty apparently understood, too; she left and never returned. She didn't get to see Dad, nor did Mother mention that a mutual friend had stopped by. She had learned to say as little as possible to Dad about visitors or simply not to mention them at all. The smallest incident could lead to accusations, fits of rage and slaps to the face. Mother often stared into space, but she never cried. Tears had become an emotion she denied herself and, consequently, denied her children.

After Betty left that day, Mother sat in the Chinese rocker for what seemed like hours pretending to read her book, never turning the pages, her mind drifting like the fragile bubbles from our bubble pipes, as if expectantly waiting to snap into nothingness.

Sentinel

Janet

Once again, Mother came home from the hospital in a taxi, and we ran to the curb to help her out of the car. Tears filled her eyes and I was afraid that, once again, the baby had died. But when I looked through the open car window, the baby was lying on Mother's lap.

"Her name is Janet," Mother said, trying to smile. "Janet Lynn, after your Aunt Janet." Stewart opened the door and pulled a small suitcase from the backseat as Mother handed the taxi driver a few bills. He refused to take the money and tears spilled down Mother's cheeks. We escorted her and the baby into the house, silently, pretending not to notice when she wiped her cheeks with her palm. We were so astonished by Mother's tears that we forgot about Janet until she began to murmur like a kitten. Stewart slid Mother's suitcase into the middle of the floor and we gathered around to meet our new baby sister.

"Does she have ten fingers and ten toes?" I asked, as Mother eased herself onto the couch. Earlier in Mother's pregnancy, I had overheard her tell Alice that she was afraid there would be something wrong with the baby, "I'm forty-five, too old to be having babies."

Mother placed the new baby on her lap. "Of course she has ten fingers and ten toes. She's perfect." David elbowed me in the ribs and Stewart frowned. I slipped the receiving blanket away from her small pink fists and checked for myself. Ten perfect fingers with ten perfect fingernails.

"Can we look at her feet?" David asked. Even though he had elbowed me, he had overheard the same conversation and also wanted to see for himself. He gently plucked the socks from her feet and wiggled her toes. She smiled and clicked her tongue on the roof of her mouth. We cooed back, smitten.

Mother let each of us hold her for a minute, then put her in the secondhand crib that sat in the middle of the living room floor. We walked around and around the crib as if watching an exotic animal at the zoo, keeping an eye on the occasional tear that trickled down Mother's cheek. After Janet fell asleep, we climbed onto the couch with Mother and told her what it had been like to be without her while she was in the hospital.

"Dad cooked breakfast this morning," Stewart scowled. "Eggs. They were terrible."

"Why didn't Barbara cook them?" she asked, only partially listening.

I shrugged. "He wanted to do it. They were scorched, but he was real happy about cooking 'em."

"Yeah, he was," Stewart said. "We didn't tell him they were terrible." Doris Ann patted Mom's knee and said, "The grits were worse than the eggs."

"Lumpy and not done," David explained, sticking out his tongue.

"And the toast was black." John frowned. "And he made us eat it anyway."

"I tore mine in half," Willie added, "and put it in my pocket and threw it out on the way to school." Mother giggled and wiped her nose on her sleeve. We perked up, aware that the idea of Dad's cooking for us had somehow cheered her. We launched into a full account of dinner the night before: chili (made with macaroni instead of beans!) and Yankee cornbread (cornbread with sugar added to the batter). We described him wearing her yellow apron and singing "Wild Irish Rose" as he cooked in the wrong pans and served in the wrong bowls. She laughed out loud.

Eventually Stewart and David went to pick up the newspapers for their paper routes and the others went out to play, but I stayed inside the rest of the day. Mother thought it was the new baby that held me there, but I was watching my mother, waiting to see if the tears returned, afraid that if she ever once really began to cry, she would never stop.

Sweet as Honey in My Mouth

The spring I turned thirteen, Mrs. Lawrence from the Fresh Air Farm came to see Mother. She spread color pictures of the summer camp for underprivileged children across the coffee table, explaining that we qualified to attend. We would receive free checkups, shots and dental work while learning to swim, hike and camp. I could hardly contain my excitement. I took a close look at the photos, visualizing myself as the cute girl in the archery picture, the girl paddling a canoe downriver, cooking on an open fire, swimming in water that wasn't polluted with sewage.

For me, even more exciting than the campfires and canoes was the opportunity to see a dentist. I had two decayed molars that ached and swelled. But I didn't care about the painful teeth, it was the teasing that hurt. My teeth were growing more and more crooked and they protruded so badly it was hard to swallow. I was desperate to have them attended to before school began in the fall and the kids began heckling me again, calling me "bucktoothed beaver." I was so happy to be going to camp and most of all to be on my way to the dentist, I smiled when I rocked myself to sleep that night, imagining straight white teeth and smooth lips that touched sweetly together, imagining myself to be as cute as the girl in the camp pictures.

I was also delighted with the chance to play, to have no responsibility. Mother had gone back to work and for months my free time had been spent taking care of Janet. Alice, who no longer attended high school, took care of her during the day, but as soon as I got out of school, she became my responsibility.

Not that I minded taking care of her. My new baby sister was the only thing that made being *out* of school better than being *in* school. Most of the kids picked on me, but at least at school I had heat and lunch. When the bell rang, I ran home to Janet. She was so small that taking care of her made me feel strong and gave me a sense of control. I took over her life with the same despotic rule I forced on the other kids. And they were more than happy to go right along with me, carting Janet around as if she were one of the dolls the girls in my class got for Christmas—the kind we didn't get.

Of course, as Janet's caretaker, I made mistakes. Twice I pinned the diaper through the skin on her hip, discovering the problem only when she continued to cry after I picked her up. I also skated with her on my shoulders. I held her hands and sang her favorite songs as I scratched up and down the sidewalk on metal skates clamped to my sneakers—skates redeemed by mail with Dad's Raleigh cigarette coupons.

By far the most dangerous thing I did while she was in my care, though, was to take her under the streets of Birmingham by way of the storm sewers: huge round concrete pipes that tunneled under the city, catching the rainwater that flowed from the streets.

Willie pried open the heavy round metal cover with a stick and jumped down into the pipe. The pipes were large enough for us to stand up. I was the tallest, so I had to be careful; if I straightened completely, the concrete scraped the skin off the top of my head.

Once Willie was secure inside the pipe, I held Janet over the hole and dropped her into his arms, then jumped down myself, followed by Doris Ann and John. Willie carried a broken handle from a broom to whack the manhole covers off from below whenever we wanted to climb out. After the cover was loosened and pushed out of the way, Doris Ann and I boosted Willie through the opening, then threw Janet up until he caught her, usually on the first toss. If we couldn't get the covers off the holes or if we got lost, we followed the path of the water—the pipes emptied into Village Creek, two blocks south of our house.

We kept a collection of box turtles and snappers, crayfish and tadpoles found inside the drainage pipes or along the creek bank. We ran across snakes, but left them alone. We were never quite sure which snakes were poisonous. We knew for sure that the diamondback rattlesnake was deadly. Whenever we chanced upon the rattlebones, we backed away and ran home to brag about how close we had gotten to it. But the other snakes didn't have a music box tied to their tails. We couldn't tell the difference between a copperhead and a cottonmouth. We did know that the coral snake was poisonous and the scarlet snake was not, but we never remembered which way the rings were supposed to go.

"It's a scarlet snake," Willie said, sliding his broom handle into the coiled body of a brightly colored snake and lifting it into the air. "Red, black and yellow rings."

"That's a poisonous coral snake!" I said, squeezing Janet with one arm and shielding Doris Ann and John with the other. "Red, black and yellow rings. The scarlet snake has black, yellow and red rings."

Doris Ann pushed against my arm for a closer look. "I thought the poison one had yellow, black and red rings."

We stared at the beautiful limp snake that dangled from the stick.

"It's a scarlet snake," Willie said, but with less conviction. He held it another minute while we all, simultaneously, gave our expert opinion on poisonous snakes.

"Shut up!" he shouted and tossed the coral/scarlet snake back into Village Creek.

One day, when there had been no rain for some time, we came upon a bum sleeping in the dry round pipes. Doris Ann and John stepped over him. Willie leaned on his broomstick as if it were the staff of Moses.

"Is he dead?" John asked, poking the man's shoulder with his toes. The bum jerked awake, pressed his arms against the concrete pipe and stared at us as if we were a band of angels come for his soul. Willie and John had on shorts, but no shirts. Doris Ann and I had on shorts and T-shirts. Janet had on only a diaper and ruffled plastic pants. We were all barefooted. The bum pointed at Janet, who was propped on my hip, as if she might be a cherub with her wings pinned back and asked, "Is that a real kid?"

"He's not dead," John said with disappointment. Willie and I stepped over him and kept walking. We were in a hurry to get home. John had a small box turtle in each pocket and we wanted to put them in the sink in the boys' bedroom with the crayfish and tadpoles we had caught the day before. For three city blocks, we could hear the echo of the man running through the pipes, rumbling and receding like thunder.

While Janet was in my care, we kids played catch with her. Literally. We stood in a circle and tossed her around like a ball, delighted by her squeals, never once considering the possibility that we could drop her. We talked baby talk, acted like clowns, danced, whistled, clicked, sang and clapped. Anything to make Janet laugh. We dressed her in hand-me-down clothes Aunt Lola sent, and paraded her around, avoiding any kids who weren't kin because—regardless of how well we tried to conceal our home life—the neighborhood kids knew and commented in scornful tones similar to our next-door neighbors': "Your daddy's a drunk. I seen him stagger into the house cussing and yelling." Yes, he did yell, but never at Janet.

"The Last of the Mohicans," he would tease, patting her head. She couldn't be added to the brood of children in the same way as the rest of us because she escaped Dad's abuse. She was the baby. He didn't hold her; he never held any of us, as far as I know. But he never yelled at her and never hit her and—as much as was possible for him— loved her as madly as the rest of us did. We gave her our toys, our undivided attention and our hearts. When forced to leave home to attend school, we brought back tokens of our love: crayon drawings, crisp fall leaves, storybooks from the school library, marbles and bright yellow daffodils stolen from neighbors' yards. Even Dad came home from work bearing gifts: a child-sized wooden rocking chair and a used blue stroller with beads across the front.

A few days after Mrs. Lawrence signed us up for camp, Alice turned eighteen years old and married. She had been marking off the days leading to her eighteenth birthday on a March of Dimes calendar that came in the mail, recording in purple ink within the space of each day Dad's abusive behavior: *February 5, 1968—pulled my hair; March 20, 1968—slapped me—TWICE; April 3, 1968—threw out my only fishnet hose!!*

"I'm an adult now," she declared, blowing a cloud of smoke against the mirror as she painted her eyes with newly purchased blue eye shadow that matched the wedding dress Mother had made for her. "Besides, Silas won't let him hit me anymore." She had known Silas Pickett for only a few weeks. Nobody knew anything about him, but Alice believed that if he would hitchhike all the way from Kimberly, Alabama, sixty miles away, just to see her, he must really love her. Neither of them had a job or a car. They married at the Birmingham courthouse and spent the night in a hotel. Silas moved in with us the next day. Alice was needed at home to take care of Janet while Mother worked. But as soon as school was out for the summer and I was available to look after Janet, they moved to Kimberly to live with Silas's parents.

When Mrs. Lawrence arrived to pick us up for camp, Willie, Doris Ann and John giggled and scrambled for their things. I stood among them, arms crossed, still hoping there had been a mix-up and I would be going to camp, too. But when Mrs. Lawrence gathered them together to discuss camp protocol, Mother reached out and touched my shoulder, barely making contact—as if she were touching a hot iron—and said, "Barbara is needed at home." Mrs. Lawrence looked at me, then looked at Janet, who was asleep on the couch, and frowned. I tried to smile, but the shock was too great and I looked away.

I hadn't realized until the day before we were scheduled to leave that I wouldn't be going, and even then I didn't quite believe it. While the others packed their shorts and shirts in brown grocery bags, I went down to Village Creek and sat in the drainpipe, just inside the opening where I could see the reflection of trees on the water, and cried. And cried some more. And then some more. Dad had gotten us out of bed the night before and the lack of sleep had caught up with me. I fell asleep against the warm concrete, not waking until dusk. When I awoke, my face felt puffy and dry. I sat in the pipe, tossing pebbles into the black, oily water, until the swelling around my eyes subsided and the anger and self-pity were bound securely within my heart. Walking home in the dark, I thought surely something would change overnight and I would get to go. *I have to go. I have to see a dentist! I can't go back to school with this same face! I can't!*

"I understand," Mrs. Lawrence said, as she quickly gathered the kids under her arms and herded them out the door before Mother could change her mind about them, too. They climbed into a van with trees and a river painted on the side and waved out the open windows as they drove away.

With the younger kids at camp, Janet and I were alone all day. After Alice left, the band of shifty teenagers that hung around our house evaporated overnight, taking their motorcycles and radios with them. Stewart and David—also teenagers—weren't interested in hanging around without their friends. I looked forward to the afternoons, when they came home with cord-bound stacks of *The Birmingham Post Herald* to roll. I worked with Stewart, making a penny for each paper I rolled, while Janet sat in the middle of our work playing with the white balls of cord. Once they heaved the canvas bags onto their bicycles, I didn't see them again until suppertime.

I was afraid of being home alone. The quiet scared me. I sneaked through the house afraid to make noise. Janet and I spent our days walking up and down the sidewalk in front of our house. At 5 P.M. we walked the few blocks to Tenth Avenue to meet Mother's bus. Even Dad seemed unable to adjust to the quiet. He came in from work and left as soon as he had eaten, returning quietly during the night.

Then Mother lost her job. Her wages had been garnisheed for overdue debts. She worked as a secretary at an investment company and her boss—apprehensive that garnishment would blemish the company—let her go. Mother's paycheck had kept us afloat.

In spite of the repercussions, when she came home unexpectedly in the middle of the day, I was delighted to see her. For the next few days she and I cleaned house, cooked meals, drew paper dolls on scrap cardboard, helped the boys roll papers and played with Janet.

Two weeks after Mother lost her job the police came to our house, just as raindrops began to speckle the thirsty Birmingham sidewalk.

Mother was sitting on the couch feeding Janet tomato soup from a plastic bowl, and I was entertaining her, lining up soup crackers on the coffee table and sailing them into her mouth. The front door was wide open and a moist breeze flowed through the living room. The knock on the screen door rattled it against the frame. Mother went to the door and opened the screen, but before she said a word, one of the officers thrust a yellow paper into her hand and pushed past her into our house. I jumped when he entered, then immediately thought, *He's looking for Dad.* But he didn't walk through the house, as police officers had done before, opening closets and looking under the beds. Instead, he pulled several books from our bookshelf. Mother dropped the yellow paper onto the floor. I picked it up and read the bold black heading: *Eviction Notice.* The police officer dropped the books to the floor.

"Can I give the baby a bath?" Mother asked, standing between me and the officer.

"Our books!" I said, tossing the yellow paper in the air and picking up a red leather storybook. Mother took the book from me and put it on the coffee table.

"Shhh," she whispered.

"Make it quick," the officer said. "You've got till we get the furniture out of here, then you can't come back in the house." He dumped another armload of books to the floor, crossed the room and pulled the couch away from the wall. The other officer, older and rounder, had already gone into the next room. I heard him grunt as he pulled the mattress from the bed.

I picked up another red storybook and stared in astonishment, about to protest, when Mother lowered her brow. I closed my gaping mouth and put the book on the coffee table on top of the other one. Janet patted the book with both hands. Left alone for a minute, she had smeared tomato soup all over herself. She smiled and patted the spilled soup on the coffee table. Mother picked her up and walked toward the kitchen. I followed.

"Hey!" the officer shouted as he propped open the screen door and sailed Janet's little rocking chair out into the rain. "If there's anything personal you want to keep, you might better get it now. Once it's outside we can't keep anybody from stealing it."

Mother pretended she didn't hear him and walked on. She ran

warm water into the kitchen sink while I pulled the soggy shirt over Janet's head and unpinned her diaper. Mother lifted her into the sink.

"Put those dirty clothes in the hamper, Barbara," she said. I picked up the soiled clothes and dropped them into the laundry basket, but thought it was silly when they were going to toss the basket outside into the rain any minute.

"Find Janet's shoes for me, dear," she said, soaping the baby's belly. "And a pair of socks. Don't pay any attention to what they're doing," she added, looking over her shoulder at me. I walked into the living room as the two officers struggled to get the couch through the front door. I had watched Dad, Mom, Stewart and David bring it in, and knew it had to be turned sideways, with the couch's back facing the ceiling, to fit. I picked up Janet's shoes and watched them huff and puff, forcing it until it was stuck fast in the doorframe.

"Jesus Christ!" the younger officer yelled. "Push it back! It's not gonna make it! Jesus Christ!"

I smiled and went to look for socks. I heard the heavy material on the couch tear as they shoved it back into the living room.

While Mother dried Janet, the police officers walked away with the kitchen table. Before they had a chance to take Janet's clothes, I ran into the bedroom and grabbed a soft blue dress and ruffled rubber pants. When I returned with the clothes, Mother sent me to find a bottle and a blanket. I watched the officers stagger like drunks under the weight of Mother's carved oak wardrobe. It had belonged to her father, and Aunt Janet had given it to her when we moved into the duplex. I ran back to the kitchen, covering my ears and humming so I wouldn't hear it crash down the steps, but I entered the kitchen just in time to see Mother wince. She finished dressing Janet with exaggerated calmness, fastening each button and double-tying her shoes. She pulled a plastic comb from her dress pocket and combed Janet's fine hair into one tight little curl on the top of her head. Then she handed her to me as if she were a present: a clean, dry baby.

"Take her outside," she said. She pulled an umbrella from the kitchen closet and handed it to me. "I'll be there in a few minutes."

I carried Janet through the house, weaving through rooms scattered with toys, books, clothes and dresser drawers, maneuvering through the furniture lined up to be cast out. The officers disassembled Willie and John's bed as I passed by and I wondered about camp: Were they sleeping in beds or in sleeping bags? I sneaked out onto the porch. Our front yard looked like a junk heap. Janet pointed to our belongings and said, "Mine." The kitchen table sat on the other side of the sidewalk, heavy with rain-soaked clothes that sagged from hangers. A box spring and mattress leaned against one side of the table, forcing the legs on the other side into the mud. Another box spring and mattress leaned against the streetlight pole. A bed frame lay half in the mud and half on the sidewalk like a seesaw. I slipped between two chests of drawers, the torn couch and a sea of mismatched kitchen chairs, and sat on the blue-striped mattress from Mother's bed, damp and musty, that lay partially in the street. Just as I sat down, the red leather storybooks came flying out the front door one at a time, like stones skimming across water. The first three scraped the sidewalk and skidded into the gutter. The rest landed on the wet ground in a heap. I raised the umbrella and leaned it forward so I couldn't see anything except the ribs of the umbrella and the wet shimmering black cloth.

"Mine," Janet said, pointing to the mattress we sat on. "Mine."

The woman who lived across the street sneaked over, walking on her tiptoes, and handed me a platter of bacon and sliced cantaloupe. Before I could say anything, she dashed back across the street and into her house. The smell of bacon filled the air and my stomach rumbled. I sat cross-legged on the mattress, the platter of bacon and cantaloupe nestled in the cross of my bare feet, umbrella in one hand and baby in the other.

The officers escorted Mother out of the house, each cradling an elbow in their large hands. She stood straight and expressionless as they climbed into the police car, warning her that she would be arrested if she went back inside. She stood on the sidewalk in the rain until they were completely out of sight, then came and sat on the mattress, took the baby and held the umbrella higher.

I ate. Bacon and cantaloupe, sweet as honey in my mouth, from neighbors who had never spoken to me before. The rain rolled from the umbrella in waterfalls onto the blue-striped mattress, rivered down the sidewalk and soaked into the tired ground.

Kimberly, Alabama

Goddess of Beauty

We moved that night in the dark, shoving as much furniture as possible into an old Chevy pickup truck Alice's new husband, Silas, had borrowed from a friend. The pickup's doors were caved in and the crusty white paint peeled from the hood in paper-thin layers like a molting tattoo. Dad placed the furniture strategically: "The refrigerator's gotta butt against the cab." He stuffed our winter coats and blankets between dressers and headboards and tied them down, hoping nothing would shift or fall through the bed of the truck before we got where we were going. And we were going to Kimberly.

Silas had found us a house in Kimberly, just up the street from his parents, who lived in the holler at the edge of the woods. This house, Silas explained as he helped load the truck, was outside the holler, facing old Highway 31. Several weeks earlier, Stewart and David had visited Alice in Kimberly. As Silas described our new home, they made scowling faces and groaned.

While the boys helped Dad load furniture onto the truck, Alice and I helped Mother sort through the rubble for couch cushions, dresser drawers and headboards and footboards. The rain had stopped, but everything was wet. Alice cussed the Birmingham police as we gathered our damp, mud-splattered storybooks and Dad's encyclopedias.

Dad had ordered the set of encyclopedias from a door-to-door salesman who thought he had sold Dad with the idea that his children would do better in school if they had a set of encyclopedias in the house. But what had really caught Dad's eye was the free *Man o' War* poster that came with them. When the books arrived, he built a bookcase, stained it the same burnt sienna as *Man o' War,* and pinned the elegant racehorse on the wall above it—where he could see it from his favorite chair. Every time he looked at it he got a dreamy expression on his face. "Man o' War," he would say. "What a horse. Born the same year I was, 1917. Horse of the century; did a mile and an eighth in a minute and forty-nine. Won the Preakness and the Belmont in the same year. Great a fighter as Jack Dempsey."

The police officers had torn the *Man o' War* poster from the wall and thrown it into the yard. Alice picked it up and dried it with a washcloth, spreading it flat on the side of the stove, which had been toppled down the stairs.

Alice and I stacked Dad's encyclopedias, our red leather storybooks and Mom's novels on the back floorboard of the Cadillac. We wrapped dishes in kitchen towels and pried crusty silverware out of the hardened mud. When there was nothing left for us to do, we sat on the sidewalk while the men loaded the furniture onto the truck. Alice smoked and talked to Mother in a whisper, "How's he gonna get back and forth to work, Mom? That ol' Cadillac will never make it."

It was midnight by the time we drove away, leaving, once again, some of our possessions lining the sidewalk like the cast-off skin of a snake. We had left so much of ourselves so many times that I hoarded all of my things in a sturdy cardboard box. With my possessions safely packed away, I could say good-bye to a place without fear of leaving behind something dear to me. The box held my Betsy McCall doll (the only doll I had ever owned), her little handmade rocking chair, miniature Blue Willow china, a portfolio of drawings and a paperback book about drawing animals, a straw-stuffed black bear with a red collar, a cigar box of drawing pencils, a collection of pretty canceled stamps, foreign coins stolen from my cousin David Junior and a dozen cicada shells. Before Mother loaded the box into the Cadillac, I wrote my name on every side and checked the contents to make sure everything was in order.

Silas headed the pickup truck toward Kimberly. Alice rode in the cab next to him, hanging her cigarette out the passenger window like a flag of independence. Stewart and David rode in the back of the truck to make sure nothing worked loose and flew off. Dad followed in the Cadillac. He and Mother sat in the front separated by a stack of threadbare blankets and sheets, and I sat in the back on two pillows, my legs stretched across the books on the floorboard, shoulder pressed against a cardboard box filled with damp clothes hanging loosely on hangers. Janet made a game of climbing back and forth over the seat, from Mother's lap to mine. She sat on my lap and slapped the sides of the boxes until she was scratched by a clothes hanger; then, crying and angry, she crawled over the seat to Mother's lap and fell asleep.

We drove through mountains that had been sliced down the middle to let the highway pass through, sheer rock cliffs adorned with small pines, kudzu and dripping water. Then the landscape opened to sloping fields, bundled hay and pastures spotted with shadowy cows. We passed through small towns—Fultondale, Gardendale and Morris—where, every few miles, the cliffs along the highway flaunted hand-painted messages in huge red letters: GOD IS ALIVE, JESUS SAVES, JESUS IS LOVE, HE IS COMING SOON. As we drove toward Kimberly, the farms disappeared. There was nothing to see but waist-high weeds, stark pine trees and kudzu-covered electricity poles looming in the glare of streetlights. The rock cliff just before the Kimberly exit preached, BE PREPARED.

Kimberly couldn't really be called a town. It consisted of a dozen houses just off the old Highway 31 in northern Alabama, sixty miles and a hundred years from Birmingham. It had been built before the turn of the century to house coal-mining families, taking its name from the famous Kimberly diamond mines in Africa. The mine in Kimberly, Alabama, petered out and shut down in 1888. The miners and their families moved on to other coal-mining towns farther north in Tennessee and Kentucky. The wooden shacks they left behind, which lacked plumbing and paint, were rented out. Mostly alcoholics and their families lived in them. Off the Kimberly exit,down Dixie Fire Brick Road onto Lucas Street, was our new, sixty-five-dollar-a-month home, standing against the night like a shabby cuckoo clock perched on stilts. One house stood between our place and the Baptized Believers in Jesus Church to the east. Then the road turned off onto Patterson Drive and dropped into the holler, a sunken cavity that marked the edge of the woods, where another half-dozen rotting houses lined the narrow paved road.

We had two neighbors living directly behind us and another one on the west side across a dirt road. Behind the neighbor to the west, along the banks of Turkey Creek, was a brickyard that gave the street its name, Dixie Fire Brick. The brickyard claimed territory previously worked by the coal miners; bright-red brick dust covered thin layers of gray slate and black coal fragments unearthed by the previous occupants. The hazy purple-blue peaks of the Appalachian Mountains stood over the area, cradling clammy gray fog.

The house we moved into looked like a tree house built by children: five unpainted rooms of weathered gray wood twelve feet above the ground on poles. Brittle kindling awaiting a spark. Nineteen broken, rickety steps descended from the front porch. The back of the house was anchored into a red clay bank with another porch and three crooked short steps. A pencil-thin railing wrapped around the front and back porches.

Half of the windows had been broken out and, once we were inside, the night pressed through them, permeating the small rooms with a vulnerability that made Mother shiver. She unpacked boxes and moved from room to room replacing the broken panes with our paint-by-number paintings, fumbling in the bright spot of a flashlight to cut the paintings to fit.

"This is a wonderful way to display your art," she said, taping Alice's harlequins in the kitchen windows. She taped Stewart's clipper ships into the bedroom windows, one above the other. Da Vinci's *The Last Supper*, a long, narrow paint-by-number I had received for my twelfth birthday, was cut and the pieces taped side by side in the living room windows. Just as Mother was about to slice the thick cardboard, I asked her to put Jesus on the left side. Mother had once told me that most creative people were left-handed. She meant artists and writers, but I imagined, by the way Jesus held his left palm up and his right palm down in the painting, that he, too, was left-handed. I had searched the dime stores in Birmingham to find that paint-by-number. I wanted the same scene as Dad's light-up picture, so I could look at it anytime rather than just when he was showing it to some old drunk.

After the painting was cut in two, the pieces were still too big for the panes, so Mother sliced away two disciples on the left and one on the right.

"I hope one of them is Judas," she said and dropped the excised followers into a grocery bag of trash.

After finishing the windows, Mother dug through boxes until she found an adapter and screwed it into a socket that dangled from a black wire in the kitchen. She couldn't find the lightbulbs, but found the two-burner electric hot plate—the only cooking appliance we now owned; the electric stove in Birmingham had been destroyed when the policemen toppled it down the steps.

Mother was calmer once the windows had been covered. "Get us some water, Barbara." She plugged the hot plate into the adapter and rummaged through a box for the tea bowl. "I'll make some hot tea. Things won't look so bad in the morning."

Hot, sweet tea. Mother's cure-all. Other people had a teapot; we had a tea bowl—a large, round, dented aluminum bowl, stained to a dark walnut-brown on the inside from orange pekoe and sticky sugar. Hot tea: served with fried eggs and steaming grits for breakfast, bologna sandwiches for lunch, and meat loaf and mashed potatoes for supper. Served with any crisis. Mother believed that if you drank a cup of hot tea, the waiting—while you blew on the tea until it was cool enough to drink—provided time to figure out what to do next.

I cradled the bowl in my arms, walked through the house and circled back into the kitchen without finding a sink.

"There's no sink, Mom," I said.

Stewart walked in the back door with the slats from a bed. "There's a spigot about fifteen feet to the left of the back steps," he said. He carried the slats through the kitchen and dropped them onto the living room floor with a thud, raising a cloud of dust from the loose floorboards. "That's the only water in this place. There's an outhouse about thirty feet straight out the back door," he said, knocking the dust from his jeans. He pointed to a small fireplace that held a handful of cold gray ashes, "And that's the only heat." His expression was meant to divulge, just in case we hadn't noticed, that we had moved straight to hell. He shoved his hands into his pockets; a sulky sixteen-year-old. "How long did Dad say we'd have to live here?"

"Just a month," Mother said reassuringly. "Just long enough to find another place in the city."

I walked out to the back porch, looking for the spigot. There was a tone in Stewart's voice that lifted the hair on my arms. He was afraid. As long as Mother was with me, I hadn't thought to be afraid, but suddenly fear crawled over my skin like a spider. It was the middle of the night, bright with a million stars and a huge waxing moon. One of Kimberly's few streetlights stood at the end of our driveway. The spigot stuck out of the ground like a charmed snake and cast a shadow across the puddle of glistening water. I could hear every word spoken inside.

"What are we gonna do about the kids when it's time to pick them up from camp, Mom? Where are we gonna put 'em? They don't even know we've moved. That's an old joke, 'Send your kids to camp, then move . . .' " Stewart's voice trailed off.

"By that time, I'm sure we'll be back in Birmingham. It's just a month, Stewart. We're *visiting* here, really," Mother said in her most soothing voice, the voice she used when things were as bad as we suspected. They were silent for a long time.

I watched Dad walk around the pickup truck. His shadow grew long, then short, then long again. He shouted for David and Silas to help him lift the couch from the truck.

Inside the house, Stewart fretted, "It makes no sense."

"What doesn't make sense?" Mother asked.

"Them firing you. You didn't have enough money to pay the bills, so they fired you. Now you really don't have the money to pay the bills. It makes no sense." He stopped talking, but the floor creaked as he paced.

Dad, Silas and David slowly eased the couch off the truck, grunting and puffing as they worked. I stood motionless and watched. Stewart came outside and stood beside me. He watched the light blue couch as it floated through the darkness, the three male bodies visible only as legs, as if the couch were walking across the yard. I laughed and looked at Stewart, but he didn't laugh—he stared, hands still shoved into his pockets, shoulders hunched up around his ears. Mother came outside and stood behind him.

"You'd better help them, Stewart," she said softly.

"Have you seen the people that live in this place?" Stewart asked. "Some guy came over to see what we were doing. He drug a beat-up ol' shotgun around like it was a stick. His clothes were a mess; he looked like he hadn't had a bath in his life. Said his name was Fuzz and his shotgun's name was Beulah. He said Beulah meant heaven and she could pop the wings off an angel. He scared the hell out of me. How am I suppose to know if he can tell me from an angel?" He dropped his shoulders and sighed. "Claims he lives in the woods in a tree. Have you noticed there are no locks, or even doorknobs, on either door?" He whispered the last part so Dad, who was now approaching the back steps with the couch, couldn't hear him. He pulled his hands from his pockets and hurried down the steps, grabbing the end of the couch just as Dad called his name.

I backed up against the fragile railing as they struggled up the stairs and through the door with the couch, then I walked out into the backyard to fill the bowl with water. Fireflies blinked and the trees rustled sweetly. The large yard ran from the alley in front, alongside the house and touched the yard of our neighbor. Six mimosa trees and two chinaberry trees dripping with fruit lined the road. Stars twinkled through the pink fluffy blossoms on the mimosa trees, making them look like Christmas trees. Looking away from the house, it was the most beautiful place I'd ever seen. I breathed in the sweet fragrance of mimosa blossoms and kept my head turned away from the faint stink of the outhouse.

I walked to the back corner of the yard, where someone had planted a good-sized patch of okra. I snapped a peaked fuzzy pod. The sticky juice oozed onto my fingers, binding them together. I absentmindedly snapped them apart, touched them together, then apart, thinking about the man who had named his shotgun Beulah. *Maybe he wasn't that strange. After all, Dad occasionally called his car Golden Girl. Maybe he wasn't any stranger than that.* I looked up and caught the silhouette of a large man on the screened-in porch of the house across the dirt road. The neighbors were watching us. Even here, among the seedy, we were a curiosity. I dropped the pod and walked over to the spigot to rinse my hands. I filled the bowl, then stood and faced the silhouette, letting the water cascade into a muddy pool around my ankles. *There—something for you to look at.* I didn't go inside until he did.

Half an hour later we all sat on the ladderlike front steps balancing saucers on our knees and sipping hot tea. Stewart sat near Mother at the top of the stairs. Alice and Silas sat at the bottom, squeezed onto one step, and David and I sat near Dad in the middle.

"What a beautiful night," Mother said. I knew she was trying to make everything seem all right, so I said, "Yeah." Dad pointed toward the brightest star in the sky and said, "That's Venus." We all looked up.

"Named for the goddess of beauty," he said. "See it. That big one, there."

I followed Dad's fingertip into the night and stopped at the brightest twinkle in the sky. Venus: goddess of beauty, much-loved daughter of Zeus, stonecutters' muse—a star that encompassed everything I had been praying for. I closed my eyes and made a wish: *Change me into Zeus's daughter,* but the night was so bright and Dad's voice so sweet that I instantly took it back. I opened my eyes, looked at the star, and wished again. *Just a little bit of beauty.*

"See it, Stewart?" Dad asked.

"Yeah," Stewart answered, "you can see the goddess of beauty through the roof in the living room."

How Can a Distance
Be So Unendingly Near

*T*wice during our first week of living in the tree house, Dad, having located the only bar for miles, drove the Cadillac into the slender stilts holding up the front of the house, cracking the left corner one. Mother sent us to scout the neighborhood for large rocks to build a retaining wall in the driveway to prevent him from toppling the house.

Our house had already become the gathering place for the neighborhood kids. Silas's younger brother and sister, Henry and Donna Sue Pickett, were almost always there. They had brown eyes and dark brown hair. Henry was severely bow-legged, just like Silas, but refused to be insulted by our comments. "Couldn't stop a pig in a ditch," Stewart taunted. He mimicked John Wayne, hooked his thumbs in his belt loops and walked like a bow-legged cowboy.

Donna Sue was a year younger than me, but her small round breasts filled her T-shirt and her lips touched together to form a fat heart-shaped mouth. She had one flat brown mole in the middle of her left cheek that matched her hair and eyes. Occasionally she touched it with her index finger as if checking to make sure it was still there. Up close, the contrast between her and me was startling. I tried not to stand too close in the hopes that no one would notice, but I couldn't help but stare at her with admiration and jealousy. Donna Sue looked almost like a woman. A beautiful woman. And our first shared secret was that she had started her period. She *was* a woman. On the other hand, I looked like a skinny, bucktoothed boy, with no chin and wild, chicken-feather hair. I felt like the homeliest person in Kimberly, possibly the entire state of Alabama.

The Bells—Lydia, Lizzie, Robert Ray, Ernest and Birdie Bell— the kids who lived between us and the Baptized Believers in Jesus Church, gathered at our house, too.

Lydia and Lizzie, who were fourteen and fifteen, had shoulder-length curly blond hair, freckled pie-shaped faces and thick, stubby legs. They could both knock a home run just about every time they batted, so we put them on different teams when we played baseball or flies and skinners. Lizzie and Donna Sue immediately became my best friends. Donna Sue was secretly in love with Ernest, so we haunted the boys, following them everywhere: to the Bells' house, our house and the Picketts' house. We followed them through the woods to Turkey Creek and stood behind pine trees to watch them swim. They stripped down to their underwear and screamed like demons as they ran down the bank, jumped onto a fallen tree and cannonballed into the water. When they popped up in the dark water it was impossible to tell Robert Ray from Ernest.

Robert Ray and Ernest, who were twelve and thirteen, were often mistaken for twins. Their blunt-cut blond hair and smudged freckles matched perfectly. They both had blue eyes. But I didn't have any trouble telling them apart. Robert Ray's eyes were a darker blue and crossed so badly he often reached for things twice before he caught hold of them. (This endeared him to me because I thought he couldn't see my crooked teeth.) His hands hung with the knuckles straightforward like monkey hands, instead of to the side. But I never said that, not even to Donna Sue. His voice was higher and he was much quieter than his younger brother, Ernest. He let Ernest do most of the talking and sometimes let him finish his own sentences.

When Ernest wasn't talking, he whistled, twittering the music from Saturday morning cartoons or Hank Williams's love songs. He was the only person I had ever met who could whistle as well as my mother, smoothly changing the pitch from sharp sweet highs to thick, mournful lows. But his repertoire was much more limited. Occasionally he asked Mother to teach him something he had heard her whistle, like "Beautiful Dreamer," and they whistled back and forth until he got it, or at least thought he got it.

Another way to tell them apart was Ernest's hands. He had "Jesus" tattooed on his fingers. He had scratched the skin with a needle and rubbed ballpoint-pen ink into the cuts until they welted up into thick blue scars. He had scratched it there, not because he was a believer or went to church himself, but because he was in love with Gaynelle Hull, who played the tambourine at the Baptized Believers in Jesus Church, and he thought she would like it.

Birdie Bell was the youngest, six years old, but she still sucked on a bottle filled with water and sugar. She had dark hair and olive skin and didn't look or act like any of the others. Birdie Bell, always called Birdie Bell, as if Bell were her middle name, took the sugar bottle everywhere and snarled at everyone, flashing teeth decayed to the gums. She whined to get what she wanted from her brothers and sisters, making us thankful that she stayed glued to her mother most of the time.

The rest of the Bells were infatuated with *our* mother. They said, "It's nice to be around a mama that don't drink." They asked for her help with their homework and to look at their cuts and bruises, some from rough play, others inflicted by their parents.

It was only a few days after we moved to Kimberly that Robert Ray stumbled up the steep front steps squeezing his hand over a long wound on his arm as blood oozed between his fingers. He had been chopping wood and had propped the ax against a stump while he stacked the cut pieces. Not being able to see very well, he tripped over the ax and slashed his arm to the bone. His mother—usually intoxicated by mid-afternoon—had pulled the wound open and poured salt into it, to stop the bleeding. Just as Robert Ray reached our top step, he fainted. Mother revived him and washed the salt from the wound.

"It's a wonder you didn't go into shock," she muttered, painting the wound with Merthiolate and wrapping a piece of an old pillowcase around his arm.

So Mother became the community nurse, protector and tutor. To these kids, we were unique, special. Our mother didn't drink, she didn't run around, and she knew about art, music, poetry and plays; and because she knew, we knew. We could sing musical notes, recite poetry and make up plays. This made us preferred company, even me. They didn't tease me about my cracked dry mouth and protruding teeth and never mentioned my bony nose, or the fat dark moles scattered across my face. Nothing could dim their hunger and admiration for what we had. I was in. Accepted.

Henry, Donna Sue and the four older Bells volunteered to help us build the retaining wall to protect the house from drunk drivers. Shrugging off our embarrassment, they took us to the brickyard to steal seconds: broken red bricks and concrete blocks. Then they helped us stack them across the driveway fifteen feet in front of the fractured pole. While we worked, they told us stories of their parents' follies, to let us know there was no need for us to explain.

"One time our daddy got drunk, just fried," Robert Ray said. "Been drinking moonshine for days. Drove our car right into the Warrior River. We had to leave it there 'cause it cost too much to fish it out. He said it was Mama's fault and blacked her eyes."

Ernest stopped whistling and said, "Our mama got after our daddy with a butcher knife one time and nearly cut off his ear. Daddy tried to strangle her while she was in her slip getting ready to go out. Sometimes when she goes out we don't see her for days. Daddy drinks until she comes back home. Don't go to work down at the sock mill, or nothing. Just sits on the porch and drinks until she's back. The minute she walks in the door, they start up again."

"Last week," Donna Sue said, "Mama busted up Daddy's moonshine still out there by the mouth of the creek 'cause he's seeing that gal down at the Tavern."

As we stacked the bricks and listened to their stories, Stewart, David and I exchanged looks. We had never lived around people who were worse off than we were. Their stories made our snake of a father seem almost like a regular guy, and put our benumbed mother right up there with the Virgin Mary.

When the wall was finished, we sat on the warm bricks, thumping each other with chinaberries. Stewart asked about Fuzz, the guy who said he lived in the woods.

"His family lives right behind you," Ernest said, licking the corners of his mouth where whistling spit had collected. "Not the house up on the hill, that's Olla May Lowry. She's got eight kids. Man, she's gorgeous. She's *so* tall . . . She's got blond hair down to here and wears shorts up to here." The shorts and the hair fell to about the same level on Ernest's thigh. "She ain't never been married as far as I know. I think one of them kids belongs to Henry's oldest brother, Noel." Ernest shoved into Henry's shoulder with a short laugh. Henry pushed back.

"He ain't denying it's his kid," said Henry. "Heck, he wants everybody to know it's his."

"So Fuzz doesn't really live in the woods in a tree?" Stewart asked.

"Well, yeah, sometimes he does," Robert Ray said. "He's got a mama and two brothers living back there. But they're crazier than hell and everybody stays away from them. Even Fuzz. Hell, his mama talks to herself constantly, and I don't think them two boys can talk at all. If they can, they don't. They just been living there about six months."

Stewart began skinning a round chinaberry with his fingernail and flicking the wrinkled skin into the red dirt. I asked about our other neighbor, the large man I had seen watching us the night we moved in.

"Oh, that's Mr. Webb," Robert Ray said. Henry and Ernest went into a fit of snorting, wallowing their faces into each other's shirts. The girls laughed.

"He raises pigs," Robert Ray explained, whacking Henry and Ernest with chinaberries to shut them up. "He's probably worried about his okra patch planted in your backyard. You could keep all that okra if you wanted to . . .

"Both his boys disappeared 'bout five years ago. He's been looking for 'em ever since. They just up and disappeared; nobody knows what happened to 'em; not the police; nobody.

"Mrs. Webb's 'bout big as a house. She weighs four hundred pounds; can't get through the door no more. They busted out the doorframes on the front door so she can sit on the screened porch. She can go from the living room, where they got her bed, to the big chair on the front porch. That's all. But she can't do that by herself; she has to be toted."

"I think that's why 'em boys disappeared," said Donna Sue, shaking her long dark hair away from her face. "I think they got tired of toting that fat mama around and left. But most everybody thinks they was killed by somebody. They never found their car neither. An old Oldsmobile. I think they went off to California and joined a bunch a' hippies."

"They disappeared while that new highway was being built," Lydia added, "so the county dug up miles of new highway—Highway 65— thinking somebody killed 'em and buried 'em under the road. But they never found nothing."

That evening, we met Olla May Lowery and two of her eight children, a boy, almost four, and a girl, five. Jeb and Sissy sneaked into our kitchen, stole a quart of apple butter from the refrigerator, sat on our back steps and devoured the entire jar. Mother caught them. The boy's face was smeared with apple butter from trying to lick the inside of the jar. She washed their faces and we walked them home. Olla May came to the back door and unlocked the screen.

"I told y'all not to be runnin' off!" she yelled at the bandits. She twisted her long hair and tossed it behind her back. "They won't do it again. I promise."

But they did. We found Olla May's spoons in our jelly, apple butter and peanut butter jars. Sometimes they left the spoons in the refrigerator caked with sticky fingerprints, and sometimes they took the jar under the house and days later we'd find the jar and spoons coated with ants. Mother got tired of returning the spoons every day, so she stacked them by the dishpan and sent them back after we collected six or eight.

The day after we met Olla May Lowery, Mr. Webb ambled onto our back porch swinging an aluminum bucket. He was heavy and cumbersome, with thick weather-beaten skin and huge hands. He wore overalls and a blue shirt torn off to short sleeves. A dip of snuff dribbled from his stained lower lip. He nodded politely and took off his battered hat that covered a mop of gray hair. He bowed to Mother.

"Could I interest you in a bargain?" he asked, twitching the hat nervously. "I'll trade you a big slab of fatback come butchering time, if you'll save your table scraps for my pigs. I'll collect the bucket every other day so it won't be stinking up your house or nothing." He blinked twice. His small black eyes sat so far back into his face, it looked as if someone had pushed them there.

"That's a wonderful idea," Mother said, smiling at him. She took the bucket and placed it in the corner by the back door. Mr. Webb stood up a little straighter and held his hat in front of his belly with both hands, turning it clockwise by the brim.

"Would you like a cup of coffee?" Mother asked, smiling again.

Mr. Webb looked surprised. "Why, sure. I sure would like a cup of coffee." Mother lifted a small pan from the hot plate, poured hot water into a cup, stirred a spoon of instant coffee into it and handed it to him. He took the coffee, but continued to stand at the back door as if he might need to run. Mother made herself a cup of coffee, took a sip and said, "That's not bad for instant." Mr. Webb took a sip and nodded his huge head.

"How is your wife feeling today, Mr. Webb?" Mother asked.

"Call me Rufus," Mr. Webb said, blushing. Mother nodded, and he launched into his wife's health problems. When he finished that story, he went straight into the disappearance of his sons. Mother had heard it all before. I had told her when we came back from the brickyard. But she listened as if she had never heard it before, nodding and sighing "Oh my" at the right places. She expressed great concern about the missing boys—which made Mr. Webb's chest swell and his eyes dance—and even offered to visit Mrs. Webb, Alma, that afternoon. I listened and marveled. *Why would she make such a fuss over this old man when she couldn't put two sentences together for her old friend Betty?*

Before too long, even Fuzz had visited us several times, and each visit had made us less fearful. We began to look forward to his visits. He was strange, but entertaining. He brought colored bottles with cord wrapped around the necks and tied them in the chinaberry trees in our yard: green, brown and clear Coke bottles and cobalt-blue milk-of-magnesia bottles.

"'Em bottles'll scare off any evil spirits left around this house," Fuzz said as he tied the bottles onto the branches. "'Em last people lived here had lots of spirits, not none of 'em any good . . ." Fuzz also showed us his rifle, Beulah, the barrel decorated with scraps of cloth, colored rubber bands and copper wire. He pointed out a yellow plastic Cracker Jack ring tied to the barrel that supposedly held the power of accuracy in marksmanship: "A straight shot," he said. We didn't question the power of the Cracker Jack ring. Instead, we did our best to stay on the safer side of Beulah's barrel.

July and August came and went and we hadn't moved back to Birmingham. Stewart and David spent most of their time fishing with Alice's husband, Silas. Silas Pickett couldn't hold down a job, but he could fish and hunt tirelessly. He and Alice were expecting their first baby after the first of the year, and still lived with Silas's parents.

The Picketts' house sat in the deepest spot of the holler, so even the brightest sunny day was filtered to a dull, moist haze. Cicadas and tree frogs droned fiercely, interrupted only briefly by a loud noise or a car engine. The dense pines marched within three feet of the house, carpeting the entire area with pine needles four inches deep; snow-like drifts stood against trees and abandoned cars. The pines in the front yard had been cut, leaving stumps that stuck up like giant mushrooms; and like the blue caterpillar perched on the mushroom in *Alice's Adventures in Wonderland,* empty blue oil cans sat on the stumps. The house was squat, pressed into the ground, and covered with tattered red tar-paper shingles the color of Alabama dirt. The front porch *was* dirt, packed and swept to a glistening shine, lined with stolen Dixie Fire bricks. The rusty corrugated tin roof was propped on columns of two-by-fours.

The Picketts' furniture was about the same as at most Kimberly residences: a secondhand couch, table, chairs and beds. But Mr. Pickett worked as a carpenter and had built cabinets and a counter in their kitchen from scrap wood.

I went over with Donna Sue every day, but didn't often spend the night at their house because gopher rats walked arrogantly about like cats. They walked across the back of the couch while you were sitting on it, even in the middle of the day. One morning Mrs. Pickett swept flour from the floor into the dustpan, poured it into a bowl and made biscuits for breakfast. The flour had been ripped from the cotton bag by sharp rat claws, and white-powder paw prints spotted the floor and counter. After that, I wouldn't eat the fat biscuits she served with syrup in the mornings or the cornbread she served with butter beans at night.

Mrs. Pickett smoked a lipstick-stained cigarette between bites of cornbread and butter beans. She'd stare at me and shake her head as if confused. "You're the skinniest thing I've ever laid eyes on; you better eat up 'em butter beans, girl." But I wouldn't eat. As soon as it was dark, Mrs. Pickett would leave for the Tavern. "To shake a leg," she said. Sometimes with her husband, sometimes without. I didn't blame her for leaving. It was scary to be at their house when the sticky dampness of daylight was gone. Outside, the insects droned louder, and inside, the pink-tailed rats began to fight, twisting and snarling like alley cats—on the floor, on the counters and on the bed Donna Sue and I shared. I hid under the covers and kicked them to the floor. Donna Sue groaned and told me to leave them alone. "They won't bother ya." I hated the rats, their pointy faces, gleaming empty eyes and whip tails. I hated their fearless clawing and biting and the nerve to take whatever they wanted.

Henry talked us into waging war against them. We climbed onto the kitchen table and sat cross-legged. Donna Sue and I held flashlights and Henry steadied a BB gun against his shoulder, ready to fire. The rats ran helter-skelter in the dark until we flashed the light to reflect in their glowing yellow orbs and Henry shot out their eyes.

When it was time to pick up the younger kids from camp, Dad drove Mother into Birmingham, and Janet and I rode along. I was excited about having them home again. I wanted to tell them about moving, about the kids in Kimberly, the moonshine stills in the woods and, farther back, in the thickest part of the pines and cedars, the black skeletons of cars that had been stolen, stripped and burned.

Willie, Doris Ann and John ran from the Fresh Air Farm's brick building, across the parking lot and into the backseat of the Cadillac. They prattled like crows, running over one another's sentences as they described their summer. They carried their wares in decorated cardboard boxes and, before the car door was closed, began pulling them out to show them off. Willie, his dark hair cut so short he looked like an old man, held up a spaceship made of Popsicle sticks. "I painted it blue 'cause there wasn't any silver," he said. Janet stood on the front seat between Mother and Dad. Willie leaned forward and kissed her. "Hi, Boobay, did you miss me?"

"Yes," Janet said.

"Hey, Mom, she can talk!"

"Yes, I know," Mother said, taking the spaceship. "That's very nice, dear." She took the glued cone shape and quickly placed it in her lap as Doris Ann shoved a fist-sized coil pot in her face. "I made that for you," she said. "And this," she said, pulling a multicolored macaroni chain from the box and draping it over the seat. Her straight blond hair had also been cut short, making her blue eyes look as big as pie plates. "And this." She pulled out several drawings that had been stapled together and shoved them over the seat. But John had already captured Mom's attention with a spot on his arm where he had been given a shot. Doris Ann flipped the book into my lap. "You can look at it first." I thumbed through the pictures.

"That's Mom," she said, shoving her hand between the pages and opening the book wider. "And that's me, and that's Stewart, and that's our house." She pointed to a green crayon drawing of a duplex. I shook my head.

"That's not what our house looks like anymore," I whispered. "We moved."

"We moved?" Doris Ann whispered back, scooting closer to me. Willie, who had been showing Dad his fake tattoo, turned and looked at me.

"We moved to where?" he said out loud.

I socked him on the arm. John, who was still talking to Mother, stopped in mid-sentence.

"We moved?" he questioned.

"Just for a bit," Dad said, as he eased the car from the parking lot. "We'll be back to the city shortly."

They were quiet then, staring at me, their eyes pleading for information that I didn't dare give. I shrugged my shoulders and pulled Janet into the backseat. She captured their attention, hugged and kissed them. They began singing campfire songs as they passed her back and forth, kissing her round cheeks. Willie sang a line and Doris Ann and John repeated it: "Bill Grogan's goat; Bill Grogan's goat; Was doin' fine; Was doin' fine; Ate three red shirts; Ate three red shirts; Right off the line; Right off the line." After the songs, they performed hand-slapping chants: "Miss Mary Mac, Mac, Mac, all dressed in black, black, black. With silver buttons, buttons, buttons, down her back, back, back." They told stories of canoes, campfires, favorite counselors, visits to the doctor and visits to the dentist. My own teeth were in such pathetic shape that I was consumed with jealousy when Willie opened his mouth to show me the fillings in his molars.

After they wound down, I told them about Kimberly: the old spindly-legged water tower—an abandoned white cask overgrown with kudzu that hovered above the pines like a haint; the beaver dam at the mouth of the creek; the red-shouldered hawk's nest and the forest where he hunted. I told them about the time David and I almost stepped on a coiled rattlesnake and where to find water moccasins hiding from the sun. I saved the story of why we had moved for later, when we were out of earshot of Mom and Dad.

3 A.M.

Alice and Silas went back and forth from living at the Picketts' to living with us. Mrs. Pickett would throw them out, and they'd move in with us; Dad would throw them out, and they'd move back to the holler. One night while they were living with us, Dad came home drunk and threw them out. They gathered a few things and headed back to the Picketts' house. As soon as they were gone, Dad started on Mother again, cussing and stomping like an old bull as she fixed him something to eat. Us kids sat at the table, yawning, nodding off to sleep, bored with the familiar scene. David decided we could sneak back to our beds without being noticed, so we were all sneaking toward the kitchen door when Dad hit Mother. He slapped her so hard that she lost her balance and hit her head against the table, then slumped to the floor, unconscious. Janet, who had been clinging to her skirt, screamed as she fell, shrieking a high, pure note that the angels in heaven had to hear, an animal sound—filled with more terror than I had ever heard before. We froze, too stunned to speak. Dad stood over Mother, wobbled, then knocked over a kitchen chair and staggered out the back door. David and I dropped to our knees and crawled over to Mother. Panic filled the room—all of us moaning in unison. We crowded around as David gently lifted Mother's head and searched for the wound where she had hit the table. Mother blinked just as the car backfired in the yard. Dad spun the tires of the Cadillac and sped down the road. We listened, not moving until the sound of the beat-up muffler died away in the distance. Then we tried to help Mother. But she waved us away, pushed herself from the floor and slid onto a kitchen chair, clinging to the table for support. Then she slowly lifted Janet, who was crying hysterically, into her lap.

"What happened?" she asked, looking around the room. "Did I fall?" She ran her hands through her hair, stopping to explore the knot above her temple. She studied our pallid faces and trembling hands with a confused expression.

"Where is your father?" she asked, looking around the room again. She erratically sucked in air and stared at us as if seeing right through us. We shook our heads, unable to speak. She looked around the room again. "I can't remember what happened. I can't remember any-thing," she said. She wrapped her arms tightly around Janet and began to soothe her, gently bouncing her on her knees. She looked right into my eyes and asked, "What day is this?" and I could feel the threads in my brain unravel like a frayed rope. I shook my head—still unable to speak. Mother studied the room, forcing herself to focus. She looked at me, then David, then back to me. "What happened? What happened to me?" she asked, her lips quivering. I felt my mind leave, as if I were standing outside my body—unable to move, think or speak. But Mother brought me back.

"What happened to me?" she demanded. My mind snapped back into place and I answered her.

"Dad came home."

Welcome

One night between Thanksgiving and Christmas, Dad brought home a drunk from the bar he frequented. The smell of stale alcohol and body odor reached us before the stranger made it all the way up the front steps. He dodged the light from the doorway as if the dusk could conceal his flimsy body and dirty, dishwater hair. Mangy stray-dog whiskers grew in patches on his chin. As he slinked upward, he smoothed his wrinkled pants and stained, white-ruffled dress shirt; the linkless cuffs flapped over his hands like pancakes. His sockless feet slipped around in black wingtip shoes with no shoelaces.

"Eugene's gonna stay here for the night," Dad said, patting the skinny man on the back as they reached the top step. "Here, where he's welcome." He shoved away the rusty box spring that served as a gate to keep Janet from falling down the stairs, stepped onto the porch and slid the box spring back into place, moving carefully, trying to appear sober.

"This is Eugene," he said proudly, as if he made formal introductions to us all the time. Eugene brought his arm to his waist and bowed deeply. We stared. Mother nodded, but did not speak.

"Dorris, fix us up some eggs and toast," Dad said. "I know we've missed supper this late, but eggs'll be fine. Will that be okay with you, Eugene?" He patted Eugene on the back again.

"Oh, yeah, that's fine. Don't go to any trouble," Eugene said. He bowed again and licked his grimy top teeth, then his dry lips.

Supper had been elbow macaroni mixed with cut-up canned tomatoes. Dad knew it would have been something like that and, not wanting his new friend to know what we ate, pretended that the *real* supper had been missed and that they would have to *make do* with eggs and toast. He also knew that if they ate the eggs, there would not be enough to go around for breakfast in the morning. Mother counted and designated all the food; nothing was wasted. One chicken stretched into two suppers: baked chicken and mashed potatoes one night and chicken and rice soup the next. But eggs and bread slices couldn't be stretched. When someone not entitled ate them, someone else went without.

Mother brought kitchen chairs to the front porch for Dad and Eugene so they wouldn't come into the house, and then went back to the kitchen. She returned a few minutes later with plates of fried eggs, slid them onto their laps and went back inside without speaking to either of them.

Eugene nodded occasionally at Dad's conversation about cars—"Nobody makes a better engine than Cadillac"—while he sniffed the air like a hound and leered at us, instinctively knowing which kids to entice: the younger ones, Doris Ann and John. He gulped down the eggs and toast, then rolled up the cuffs of his shirt. He leaned toward Doris Ann, propped an elbow on his knee and smiled. She took two steps toward him and smiled back. He waved a hand over her head, pulled a nickel from her ear and placed it in her palm. She laughed delightedly.

"You can keep that, Princess," he said, slurring the word so it sounded like Prin-ccasss.

She crooned. I stayed on the other side of the porch, guessing the weight of the house-rattling semis and watching the cars zoom by on the highway a block away. I watched Eugene out of the corner of my eye, repulsed by his stench, his crusty rotting teeth and his friendliness toward Doris Ann. She laughed every time he did the coin trick, and every time he gave her the coin she ran between his spread knees and gave it back so he could do it again. He did the same trick for John, but John squeezed the nickel tightly in his fist, refusing to give it back, and moved out of reach. Eugene centered his attention on Doris Ann, calling her "Annie" and "Sweet Ann." He did the trick over and over and a gurgle rose from his throat. Each time he got a little friendlier, petting her like a puppy, long strokes that began at the top of her head and ended at her tailbone.

"How 'bout a hug for that there nickel," he said, flopping forward. A tattooed beauty appeared from under his right sleeve when he reached forward.

Doris Ann was just ten years old and dirt-covered from hard play, but she was also a beauty. She wore shorts and a long-sleeved shirt Mother had made from cotton skirts Aunt Lola had sent. She was barefoot, even in the November air, and her toenails were so blue they looked as if they had been painted. She brushed her straight blond hair away from her eyes with her fingertips, flicking it away like pestering dragonflies, and laughed gleefully at Eugene. She loved the attention and became more aggressive with her play. She swatted Eugene and jumped away when he tried to catch her. When she finally hugged him, I winced.

That night, Doris Ann and I lay awake watching ignited matches fly through the darkness into our bedroom. Eugene, who was bedded down on the couch in the living room, was thumping stick matches against the matchbox to make them strike and fly. We could hear him snicker every time we jumped from bed to blow out one that kept burning after it hit the floor. Eventually the matches stopped flying.

"He must be out of matches," Doris Ann whispered. We were propped up on our elbows, the cold night air seeping under the covers, and listened intently for sounds from the living room, but heard only the faint rumble of trucks on the new highway.

I shook my head and dropped flat onto the bed.

"He must have gone to sleep," I said, burrowing under the heavy quilt and breathing on the blankets to warm my face.

Hours later Doris Ann called me from outside my dream. Faintly. Flurried memories leaped and receded as I struggled to wake up. A wink of consciousness and the dream was gone. I tossed. The sobs grew clearer.

"Barbara," Doris Ann cried. I opened my eyes, closed them again. "Barbara, he's trying to kiss me." Doris Ann choked and sucked the air.

I jerked awake. Terror rose in my throat. Eugene was leaning over Doris Ann with his hand on her shorts. His chest was sunken in and dotted with purple nipples; his belt dangled loosely from unbuttoned pants. I propped myself up on one elbow just as he leaned forward to kiss her. He lost his balance and fell, catching himself with a bony hand between us. The nearness and stench of him made me gag and I rolled away. He pushed himself up and wobbled, clinging to the stretched waistband of Doris Ann's shorts. He reached back and touched the wall behind him to steady himself, tottered for a moment, then let go of the wall. He reached inside his own pants and adjusted himself, then leaned over Doris Ann and tried to kiss her again.

His eyes were droopy and he didn't notice that I was awake, or that I was even there. He struggled to concentrate on Doris Ann. I lay back down and pretended to be awakening, kicking at the blankets and tossing, calling for Mother. I rocked my head and tossed back and forth.

"Mom," I called. I didn't believe that she would hear me, but didn't know what else to do. "Mom, I have a stomachache. Mom! Mom!"

Doris Ann lay still, gently sobbing. I kicked the blankets off and rocked until my entire body was tossing violently. "Mom! My stomach hurts. Mom!"

I slowed down to look at Eugene, trembling, afraid he would grab me and make me stop. I reached out and touched Doris Ann's shoulder. She was shaking convulsively.

"Mom! My stomach hurts!" I kicked and rocked even harder.

Eugene finally realized I was there and that I was making a lot of noise. He jerked his hand from Doris Ann's pants and stood up, bumped the back of his head on the wall behind him and fell forward, catching himself between us again, lodging Doris Ann under his arms. He hauled himself upward, grabbed the headboard with one hand and slapped at the wall with the other, feeling his way in the dark, and tripped over his pants. He bumped into the wall and, like a wind-up toy, backed up and walked into it again, eventually stumbling through the doorway to the living room.

Doris Ann and I jumped out of bed, dragging the quilt with us, and ran into the boys' bedroom. The blanket swept the floor, collecting cold, black matchsticks. We shook in the darkness, choking back sobs; our teeth chattered. Doris Ann wiped her eyes and nose on the quilt and breathed a deep, jagged breath as she looked around the room. We were sure the boys would wake up; it seemed that we had been making a lot of noise—the pounding of my heart seemed enough to wake them. But they slept undisturbed. Stewart, David and Willie slept in army cots that lined the walls like a small train driven by soft rhythmic snores. John slept on a crib mattress in the middle of the floor that barely left enough room to step between the mattress and the cots.

We wrapped ourselves in the quilt and sat at the foot of the mattress, sucking the frigid air. We couldn't go back to our bed and there wasn't room to lie down in here. We had to move soon—our fingers and toes were growing numb and Eugene was too close. He would soon recover from his moment of fear and look for us. We blew on our fingers and stacked our feet one on top of the other in a futile attempt to keep warm. Finally I pulled Doris Ann from the mattress and over to the door of our parents' bedroom. We rarely went into our parents' bedroom, almost never when Dad was home.

"What are you gonna do?" she whispered, glancing over her shoulder to make sure Eugene wasn't behind us.

"Shhhh," I whispered, pushing the door open. "Follow me."

We slipped into the bedroom and stood between Janet's crib and our parents' bed.

"I'm gonna put Janet in with Mom and we're gonna get in the crib," I whispered, handing Doris Ann my part of the quilt.

"What is it?" Mother asked, sitting up in bed as she saw our figures huddled in the darkness.

We nearly jumped straight to heaven at the sound of her voice. My heart thumped so fiercely in my ears that I couldn't hear what she said next, but I knew for certain that if Dad woke up, he'd send us back to our own bed.

"Janet's gonna sleep with you," I whispered, lifting her from the crib. I carried her over and put her in bed with Mother. Mother was so astonished that she took Janet under the blankets without another word. Doris Ann and I climbed into the crib. We lay flat on our backs with our legs drawn up, knees pointed toward the ceiling. Our shoulders pressed against the bars of the crib, but we didn't care. We scooted our feet under the baby blankets—still toasty warm from Janet's slumber—and pulled the heavy quilt up over our heads. The length of the quilt gathered in a thick heap at our feet. We were safe. Doris Ann laughed, a short, hysterical laugh-cry. Dad mumbled and turned over. The springs of the bed screeched. We tensed and held our breath, but our shaking bodies rattled the crib.

"It's nothing, Stewart," Mother said softly. "Go back to sleep."

We listened for his snore: a deep, muffled growl followed by a long, soft whistle; at the same time, we listened for movement in the living room. But Eugene wouldn't come in here; he was too afraid of Dad, too afraid of Mom. We closed our eyes and breathed the warm air under the covers, letting our bodies melt into the firm crib mattress. We fell asleep, gently, very gently, rocking our heads back and forth, back and forth.

Dad jerked me from the crib by the collar of my shirt, carried me roughly through the house and tossed me out the back door. I grabbed the rim of the wringer washer as I fell forward. The cold porcelain bit my cheek as I struggled to breathe.

"The house is on fire!" He coughed spittle onto my face and ran back inside.

I gasped for air. Puffs of gray smoke swirled from the kitchen doorway, stinging my eyes. Streams of tears rolled down my cheeks and into the neck of my T-shirt. I closed my burning eyes, let go of the washer and leaned against it with my shoulder. I stretched the damp neck of the shirt over my nose and sucked in the soft, warm air next to my body. Goose bumps rippled my arms and thighs. Dad returned and tossed Doris Ann on top of me, knocking us both against the washer. Blue-black smoke rolled from the doorway, floated to the roof of the porch and curled back down into our faces. We sat up, waved the smoke away and coughed.

"Get 'em all together out by the outhouse, Barbara!" Dad shouted, waving toward the backyard. He tucked the front of his undershirt into his trousers and darted back inside.

I coughed and coughed, unable to move, unable to do anything but struggle for air. Stewart stumbled through the back door wrapped in a thick smoky vapor, hacking into his fist. He yelled at me between fits of coughing, but I shook my head, unable to understand him. I choked with every breath and bright specks danced in front of my eyes. A dull roar filled my ears. I tried to lie down, but Stewart clenched my hand into his, locked Doris Ann's wrist with his other hand and pulled us to our feet. He dragged us across the porch and down the back stairs; our knees buckled and our butts thumped on the stairs. He pulled harder, dragging us like stubborn mules out of the fumes.

He pushed us farther into the yard. "Stay here!" he yelled. "And watch for the others!" He raced back to the house, still shouting orders, his words whirled away by a sharp, dead-leaf gust of wind. We collapsed to the ground, coughing and hacking. The wind whipped at our shirts. We sat up, wrapped our arms against our chests and coughed into our fists. Doris Ann and I glanced at each other, but didn't say what was on our minds.

Mother rushed down the steps with Janet in her arms. As she tried to wrap a baby blanket around Janet's shoulders, she tripped on her own nightgown and hopped on one bare foot for several steps. I stood up and caught the baby just as Mother tossed her into my arms. She coughed into her fist, tried to say something but couldn't get it out, and raced back inside. Janet sneezed, hiccuped, coughed and burst into high shrill wails, reaching in the direction Mother had gone. I bounced her and tried to talk to her, but my voice was also broken and hoarse. Doris Ann walked her fingers up Janet's arm, wheezing the eensie-weensie-spider, but only convulsive coughing interrupted Janet's wails. Mother ran down the steps again, carrying the aluminum water bucket. She tossed the ladle to the ground, dropped the bucket under the spigot and turned on the water full force. She shouted for Stewart to bring a pan from the kitchen. David, coughing into his shirt, stumbled down the steps, and she ran to him with the filled bucket, splashing his feet.

She pointed to the back door. "Take it to your father!" she shouted. Stewart raced down the steps with the pan. Mother grabbed it and dashed back to the spigot. David stumbled up the steps with the bucket. Just then, Dad stumbled out of the back door with Willie tucked under one arm and John under the other. He slipped across the icy porch boards and stood them on the steps. He held the back of their shirts as they gulped the frigid air. The wind lifted dingy smoke from their bodies. Dad waited until they were steady and shoved them toward the slope.

"Go!" he shouted. "Move!" He grabbed the bucket from David and ran back inside, clipping it against the doorframe and soaking the length of his trousers and bare feet. David pushed Willie and John farther out into the yard, coughing onto the tops of their heads as they coughed into their fists. Doris Ann and I crept down the icy slope, dodging patches of ice-spiked brown grass, and called to them. We huddled together, coughed, rubbed swollen teary eyes, hopped on one numb foot, then the other, and inched closer and closer to the frantic processional: Mom standing at the spigot passed the water to David, David dashed it to Stewart, and Stewart sprinted it to Dad at the kitchen door.

The first bucket of water splashed and Dad's voice, higher than before, vibrated from inside. "What the Sam hell! The son of a bitch caught the couch on fire! The curtains are on fire! Stewart! Stewart, get in here! We've got to get this couch out of here!" Stewart ran inside. Recovered somewhat, Willie, Doris Ann, John and I dashed to the side of the house so we could see better. Even Janet stopped crying and stared up at the front porch. Moments later the couch, smoking profusely, crashed through the thin railing and toppled to the ground. It landed on end and folded in half like a jackknifed semi. Small flames jumped from the fold, flickered, then died to a smolder and sent up a line of black smoke. The soggy, smoldering curtains, thick drapes that Aunt Lola had sent, flopped through the air and landed by the couch. We heard Dad yelling inside and ran back down the length of the house.

Seconds later, Dad tossed Eugene off the back porch, flipping him over the fragile railing like a pole-vaulter into the frozen pond of dishwater below. His body cracked the ice like shattered glass. Dad stumbled forward and caught his knees to support a fierce bout of coughing.

"I'll beat you to death . . ." he wheezed, "you crazy little son of a bitch . . ."

Eugene sat up, squinting. He rubbed his head and coughed violently. He wiped blood from a gash on his forehead, smeared it down his gaunt bare chest and onto the open-fly pants wadded around his thighs. He tried to stand up, like a toddler, hands clutching the ice, butt in the air. He grabbed at his pants and toppled face first into the pool of fractured ice.

"What the hell have you been doing?" Dad yelled. He grabbed the railing with both hands and leaned over it to look down at Eugene. "You didn't drink that goddamned much!" He straightened, clenched his lower back and inhaled huge gulps of sooty smoke that rolled from the back door. He stooped again into a fit of coughing; his face turned purple. He squeezed his rib cage as if trying to push the smoke from his lungs. A moment later he straightened again, grabbed the water bucket from Stewart and ran back inside, coughing, cussing and coughing.

Wild Irish Rose

I heard the commotion and climbed from the bed to investigate. Mother stood in the living room, leaning over a large cardboard box sprinkling oatmeal into it, talking to Doris Ann and Willie at the same time. "Don't take them out of the box; don't hold them so tight. Put them back in the box. Get off of his head, for Pete's sake, and stop pecking him."

The sign on the box read: "Malcolm's Poultry Farm, 100 baby chickens." We hadn't had any chickens when I'd gone to bed several hours earlier. I yawned and looked around the room. *Dad must be home.* I reached into the box, picked up a yellow chick and held it to my cheek, while warming my backside against the hot coals in the fireplace. I wrapped the chick in my flannel shirt and followed the sound of voices out onto the high front porch. A half-moon and a million stars lit the night. It was the first week of March, still cool and gusty; the dew-wet porch boards chilled my bare feet. Thick green grass spiked from the red earth and mint-green leaves swelled on the branches of the mimosa trees. The remains of last summer's tree house dangled from a thick limb and tapped against the trunk in the breeze. Dad's, Stewart's and David's voices came from under the porch, directly below my feet. I peeked through the cracks between the boards and spotted David petting the two puppies Dad had brought home a month earlier. I scooted over a few boards and peeked again. Dad was marking with coal the area they would enclose for a chicken coop, planning out loud as he dropped the black lumps to the ground. Stewart followed behind him with his arms crossed over his chest.

*   *   *

The next morning was Saturday: Dad rose early, singing heartily in his deep gravelly Irish brogue, "My wild Irish Rose, the sweetest flower that grows, you may search everywhere, but none can compare to my wild Irish Rose."

Mother had expected this early rising and had already heated water on the hot plate, poured it into a bowl, and brought Dad's razor and shaving mug into the living room. He sat on the couch, as he did every morning, dressed in jeans and a white undershirt, his head propped on a folded towel, a steaming cloth draped over his face to soften his whiskers. Mother washed his hands and arms with a soapy washcloth, then splashed hot water into the soap-heavy mug and stirred the brush until foam climbed over the rim. She lifted the hot cloth from his face and painted the milky froth onto his steaming cheeks and down his grizzly neck. Just as he curled his upper lip like a horse nipping at a carrot, she quickly flicked the foam onto it. She guided the double-edged razor, sculpting his angular face from the white foam in short, velvet ribbons until the last of the foam floated in the pan of hot water, dissolving with a swish of the razor to tar-black nubs that drifted to the bottom. She then mopped his silky face with the washcloth. He lifted his head and she rubbed the wet cloth briskly through his hair until every strand gleamed like coal. Mother took a plastic comb from her dress pocket and drew a part on the left side, flipping a cowlick in the front, and combed the short sides behind his ears. Before Dad opened his eyes, she stood back and, with the discerning look of an artist at work, admired the handsome lean face, the wide shoulders and muscular chest. He opened his eyes and she looked away and handed him a starched long-sleeve blue shirt.

"Thank you, there, Gravel Gerty," he teased. He stood and slipped his arms into the sleeves, buttoned it and tucked it into his jeans, making demands with every crimp of the fabric. "Get me a piece of paper and a pencil; get me a hammer, a dropcord, wire-pliers." Doris Ann ran to the back porch and brought back the dropcord. "That's just the ticket, Slew Foot Lou."

David brought the wire-pliers and placed them in the palm of Dad's hand, handle first. "Just what I was looking for, there, Bonehead," he bullied. I contributed a sheet of typing paper and an HB drawing pencil. He glanced at the eraserless green pencil, shrugged and stuck it behind his ear. "Southpaw, you look like you traded butts with a jaybird and got cheated out of a pair of legs." He always teased me about my legs—sometimes positively, "legs like a gazelle," and sometimes not. But he *never* teased me about my misshapen face, crooked buckteeth, or the dark moles around my nose; and, consequently, neither did anyone else in the family. He stuck his hand out to shake, but I knew better and backed away, laughing. Willie dropped his hand into his palm and Dad squeezed his fingers, crunching the knuckles together. Willie buckled to his knees and spilled the bag of nails he held in his other hand. "Mom!"

When Dad was satisfied with the collection of accumulated tools, he sauntered down the front steps, singing again, and paused halfway down to burst into the chorus of "Wild Irish Rose," as if the rickety staircase were a theater stage. He took Stewart and David with him, "the boys," he called them (heedless of the fact that he had four boys), to Gardendale, the nearest town with a hardware store, to buy chicken wire and feeders.

While the chicken-coop builders were away, the rest of us entertained Janet with the baby chicks. We held the soft yellow balls in our open hands for her to pet. She sneaked up and touched them on top of the head, then jumped back and squealed like a cat with its tail caught under the rocker. Our hearty laughter encouraged her to squeal louder. We put the chicks on the floor and she marched around them, flapping her arms and grinning, showing off her sharp baby teeth. We laughed until we hurt. Our elation inspired her to greater antics and she let out piercing wails and throaty gurgles. We laughed even harder and searched for new ways to make her laugh. John and Doris Ann balanced chicks on their heads. I put one in the front pocket of my shirt; the tiny head bobbed up and down with the rhythm of my laughter. Willie lined up half a dozen peeping birds on the back of our newly purchased secondhand couch and put Janet on the cushions. The chicks ran from one end to the other and Janet did the same. She called the chicks, "Here, baby, baby," cheeped and cooed and collapsed into the cushions, snickering. We fell to the floor, holding our sides, and slapped one another on the back. Janet began staging falls where the cushions broke, crying "Down!" each time she fell, chuckling at her own joke and checking to make sure we got it. We shrieked and slapped the floor with our palms. "Mom, come here!" we cried. "Come watch!" Mother came into the living room. She chuckled at us as much as Janet, then gathered the frightened chicks and put them back in the box.

"Now simmer down," she said as she walked back to the kitchen. We started over, holding the chicks in the palm of our hands, giggling as we pointed out the beak, wings and toes. "Say beak, Janet. Say beak." Janet mimicked, "Beak, beak, beak," spitting the words out like peas. She pointed to the chicks and slapped her sides in mock hilarity. We crumpled to the floor again, hooting at her, never more delighted with anything in our lives. We sat on the floor, light-headed and fighting spasms of hiccups, until we heard the Cadillac turn off the highway onto Dixie Fire Brick Road.

Dad weaved the chicken wire in a rectangle around eight of the poles that held up the front porch. David held the wire taut while Dad nailed it securely. Stewart, with Dad's supervision and instructions, built a small wooden house with a front door and a hole in the roof. He cussed and muttered as he nailed the boards together.

"I'll be the one that has to get up early to feed them before school," he mumbled. "And I'll be the one that has to feed them again after I get off work—in the dark! And I'll be the one he raises hell with when a weasel sneaks away with a bird between his teeth. I hope the weasels get them tonight. All of them."

He finished the house and dragged it to the center of the wire coop, tossing the hammer into the dirt. He stomped up the front stairs and kicked a hole in one of the porch boards with the heel of his boot. He plugged a dropcord into the adapter in the living room ceiling and ran it through the hole in the porch down into the chicken coop, then screwed a heat lamp into the socket and positioned it over the little wooden house; heat to keep the chicks toasty-warm.

While David and Dad strung the chicken wire, and Stewart built the little wooden house, Doris Ann and I played with Janet in the coal pile. Janet examined the dusty black lumps, dropped them into a bucket and then poured them out again. I lingered on the fringe of the coop project hoping to talk to Stewart. *Was I the only one thinking about what it would be like to live above chickens in the heat of June, July and August?* But he was in such a foul mood, I didn't mention it to him. I did mention to Doris Ann that "Stewart was in a foul mood, get it? *Fowl* mood?" We chuckled over our joke and passed it on to Willie, but we never talked about the chicken coop. It was one of those things that everyone knew was a bad idea, but no one was brave enough to say it out loud to Dad. When Stewart turned on the heat lamp above the little house I walked over to see it.

"Hey, it works," I said.

"Shut up," he scoffed.

Mother brought a filled water jug and placed it in the coop, then a feeder, two more feeders and another water jug. She went back inside the coop several times to adjust the position of the feeders, as if arranging furniture.

Blackie and Brownie, the two shepherd pups that lived under the porch, had been moved and were tied under the steps a few feet from the chicken coop. They scratched at the red dirt and wagged their tails, eyes focused on the chicks. Saliva dripped from their pink tongues, and they whined.

Mother walked over and stood beside Stewart. She put her hands on her hips and said, "Well, if you really want to get rid of the chicks, I guess you can toss them into the air, one at a time like dog biscuits, and Blackie and Brownie can eat them."

Stewart didn't feed the chicks to the dogs, nor did the weasel eat them. They thrived in their porch-shaded captivity, traded their yellow fuzz for scraggly white feathers, grew lanky and exuded a smell rivaled only by the outhouse.

Six weeks later, the colored bottles Fuzz had tied onto the limbs of the chinaberry tree began tapping together like wind chimes. Suddenly there was a change in the air, a stillness, and the room darkened as if someone had turned off the lights; but it was midday. Mother closed the book she had been reading and listened: the bottles started clanging violently together and there was now a hum that almost drowned them out. Her brow wrinkled and she cocked her head to the side. We listened too. She jumped up, dropping her book to the floor, picked up Janet and walked outside. Willie, Doris Ann, John

and I had been playing cards with Ernest and Lizzie Bell. We tossed
the cards into a pile and followed Mother out onto the front porch.
The wind almost knocked us down. Stewart and David were leaning
against the corner pole staring at the sky. I looked out and gasped. It
was coming toward us, humming intensely.

"It's a tornado!" Stewart shouted, clutching the pole tightly.

"Uh-huh," Mother said. She shifted Janet's weight higher onto her
hip and the skirt of her dress billowed like an umbrella, lifting to
mid-thigh.

"Shouldn't we go somewhere?" David asked, turning away from
the funnel cloud to look at Mother.

"Where would we go?" she asked, nodding. But it was too late to
run, too late to do anything but stare; the tornado was already on us,
sucking at our bodies like a giant vacuum cleaner.

Ernest pulled himself along the rail toward Stewart and David
until he was sandwiched between them, and gripped the corner pole.
Janet covered her eyes and rolled into a ball in Mother's arms; Mother
locked both arms around her and buried Janet's face in her neck.
Willie, Doris Ann, Lizzie and I inched closer to Mother, moving our
feet in small steps, afraid that if we picked them up we'd be sucked
away. Panic rose in my chest as I stared at the sky. A black thin funnel
with swirling clouds and streaks of rain bounced toward us with
incredible speed, moaning as it came. The dogs howled in unison with
the tornado. I thought to untie them, but couldn't move, certain that
if I moved even an inch I'd fly off the porch into the air. I stood with
the others, transfixed, our eyes glued to the dancing black spiral.

Lizzie covered her ears and I did likewise; the sound changed to a
deep rumble like a freight train. An empty gasoline can smashed
through the front window and rolled onto the floor inside with a
heavy thud. Mimosa-tree limbs snapped like string beans. The number 8 tub used to rinse clothes slithered across the yard, scraping
against rocks; the metal handles clattered a fast rhythmic beat as it
lifted, still upright, into the air.

Willie sat down and laced his fingers into the porch boards as if he
were riding a sled, his dark curls pulled by the draw. He lifted his face
to the wind, closed his eyes and smiled. I realized I was smiling too;
the initial fear of the tornado had been replaced by a gleeful fascina-

tion. We were charmed. The twister danced and swayed enchant-
ingly, holding us immobilized. But we, as a group, seemed to have our
own power and we stood counterbalanced, offsetting the force of the
wind. A flush warmed my body and tingled into my fingers, cheeks
and scalp. I closed my eyes and huddled closer to Mother. Doris Ann
and I dropped our heads into the curve of her back. We laughed out
loud, but the mighty roar drowned it out. Our shirttails snapped like
whips and tiny bits of dirt and debris lashed at our arms and legs,
stinging like bees. We clung to one another, bobbing our heads and
peeking at the tornado as if we were playing a game. The fierce suction distorted our faces each time we lifted our heads over Mother's
shoulder. Stewart, David and Ernest began shouting. I opened my
eyes, cupping my hands around them to keep my hair from snapping
them out, and shifted so I could see.

The chickens, now fluffy-white with new mature plumage, were
being sucked from under the porch in a feathery cloud and whirled
into the air. They fought against the pull, flapping violently as they
tumbled in rhythmic circles. Their shrill squawking joined the drum
of the tornado like a choir. Yellow beaks and legs flashed like
sparklers against the blue-black sky. A rooster, his red comb flopping
in the wind, lurched forward, pumping all of his strength to propel
himself out of the cloud. He crowed and pecked at the gauzy demon,
only to be sucked back into a dark, wavy undertow and disappear into
a fold of black cloud. The silvery chicken-coop wire snapped from
the porch poles and rolled back into its original tube shape. It tumbled along in the red dirt, gathering a clump of weeds and small
branches in its mesh, then was lifted on end and whipped into the air
like a tossed baton. The tornado danced and twisted in front of us
without moving forward or fading; yet we held to the porch as if
magnetized. Tattered feathers sailed around our heads and fluttered
around our feet.

Then, as quickly as it came, the twister was gone—and the chickens too, as fast as the cars that zoomed down the highway. Swept
away. The wind subsided and a strange pervasive light glowed around
us. One crack of lightning pierced the dark sky and needle-like rain
pelted down. The spell was broken. We laughed, brushing wet hair
from our faces. Stewart cheered the parade onward, waving his arms

and slapping his legs. He straightened and burst into a chorus of "Wild Irish Rose," imitating Dad's lilt. Mother walked to the edge of the porch, leaned over the rail and watched the black funnel spin away. We followed on her heels, giddy, squeezing the water from our shirttails, and watched the last fat hen helplessly flapping its wings as it somersaulted into the spooky sky.

The chickens dropped like rain about the holler, tucked into pine trees and scattered in clucking swarms over yards and on rooftops, confused and rumpled, but unharmed. Everyone knew they were Dad's chickens, but none was returned.

In the crisp of October, David, Willie, Doris Ann and I walked down the steep bank into the holler. Old man Butterworth was sitting on his front porch, leaning against the wall in a wobbly cane-bottom chair. A pint jar of homebrew sat on a concrete block by his side. He was eating sliced tomatoes from an aluminum pan that was propped on the back of a puppy that slept on his lap. He watched us until we were right in front of his house. Then he chuckled and snorted, "Hey, why don't y'all come on over for Sunday supper. We're serving up S.K.'s chickens."

Learning to Behave

We could hear the Cadillac long before Dad made it to the house; the exhaust pipe had been repaired with beer cans and heater-hose clamps and the noise could be heard for half a mile. Mother usually went out to meet him and surrendered. We knew she would be devoured, like a Christian being offered to the lions. But this time she wasn't home. Aunt Janet had given David Junior's old '53 Plymouth to Stewart and he had gotten a summer job in Birmingham. Mother had also gotten a job in Birmingham, catching a ride every morning with Stewart. Without Mother to soothe Dad, we were caught—trapped in a mesh of loyalty, stupidity and fear as strong as chicken wire holding captive a flock of birds.

"Run!" David shouted. He jumped up and turned the small wooden lock on the front door. "Dad's home!"

David, Willie, Doris Ann and I had been playing Canasta and eating Cheerios from the box. John, who was too little to play Canasta, had been building a house of cards with the Rook deck. We ran, knocking over the box of Cheerios and dropping a trail of playing cards behind us. David and Willie ran into their bedroom. John jumped behind the couch. Doris Ann ran into the kitchen. I could hear her moving the pots and pans and climbing onto the bottom shelf of the cabinet. I picked up Janet and hurried into Mom and Dad's bedroom.

The car poked along, coughed into the driveway and crunched into the retaining wall. The front bumper scraped on the red bricks, making a high screech like a wounded owl. I shoved Janet under the bed and crouched at the window to watch Dad's progress. I knew that

I wasn't completely safe, but I was safer than the others. I was Janet's caretaker, and he never harmed her. But really his reasons for not hitting me went beyond my guardianship.

The winter before, the Bells had gone to stay with their aunt. Their mother had cut their father with a knife, actually drawing blood this time. With the absence of the Bells, we didn't have enough players for volleyball. We asked Fuzz's brothers, Frank and Cory, to play. They didn't talk, but they were good volleyball players; especially Frank. I played right beside him, as close as I could get without causing him to move away. I wanted to see him smile. When he slammed the ball to a place impossible for the other team to return, he smiled, twisting his mouth into a barbwire bow that transformed not just his somber face, but his entire being into crackling electricity. He ran his hands through his straight black hair and dusted the bottoms of his cold bare feet before every play. I wanted him to talk. I wanted to know more about his older brother, Fuzz, and his mother. I wanted to ask him why he didn't wear shoes and why he didn't talk or go to school. I plotted ways to make him talk instead of paying attention to the game and missed easy setups. David accused me of being for the other team. I tried to focus on the game, but kept slipping back into fantasies of heroism. *I would make him talk; and he would be smart, even though he had never attended school.*

After the game we stood on the front steps, panting. The team I was on had not won a single game. I was confronted by my teammates, pushed and threatened.

"Benedict Arnold," David spat.

"Yeah, Benedict Arnold," Doris Ann said.

"Doris Ann, you're on the winning team!" I whined defensively. Eventually they settled down and we sat on the front steps. We were hot and thirsty and took off our coats and hats, letting the winter breeze chill our bodies. Willie brought the water bucket down the long flight of stairs; we passed it around and sucked the water into our dry mouths straight from the ladle. Frank took the ladle and drank, wincing as he swallowed. He patted his throat and opened his mouth for us to take a look. We stared into his throat and made sympathetic cries at the sight of his raw, red throat and white-spotted tonsils. He took another drink of water from the ladle and flinched with pain. He died ten days later. The Red Cross volunteer who came to inform the family said he died of strep throat that had developed into rheumatic fever.

Within a few days of Frank's death, I was sick. Very sick. High fever. Thick, spotted, purple tonsils. The thought of food nauseated me, and everything I attempted to eat came back up. I lay for days, half-conscious. My knees and elbows became inflamed and my heart pounded in my chest as if it would burst—especially when I tried to sleep. When I was awake, it skipped beats or beat so slowly it seemed as if it was struggling to beat at all. I was already thin, but grew thinner. Knees and elbows jutted sharply beneath ghostly pale skin.

Late one night when Mother thought I was asleep, I heard her beg Dad to take me to the doctor. "She's going to die, Stewart," she cried.

"I'll take her to the doctor, Dorris. Don't you worry about it," Dad slurred as he staggered out the door. But he didn't. He didn't come back home for three days and when he did, he avoided looking at me.

I was scared; I didn't want to die. The fever eventually subsided, but my heartbeat grew more erratic; I had to suck in a sharp breath every few minutes, as if someone had poured ice water over me, just to keep the slow irregular heartbeat from jumping to hyperspeed and pounding against my rib cage. My joints were also getting worse, especially my knees: swollen, stiff hard knots, hot to the touch, as if fire burned in my bones.

Mother made me chicken soup and put me in her bed during the day. Sometimes she read to me from the poem book as she had done when we were little, "Whose woods these are I think I know."

Other mornings she sat next to me reading a novel, while Janet slept. She talked to me during the afternoon while she ironed clothes or sewed. She made quilts from old coats, cutting squares from areas that weren't worn through. I recognized squares cut from a jacket that David and I had both worn, squares from Mother's Marine Corps jacket that had, years before, been altered to fit Stewart and squares from Aunt Janet's plaid coat. I mentioned Aunt Janet's coat, struggled to get the words out, bringing up her name in hopes that Mother would call her and ask her to take me to the doctor. But if she thought of it, she never acted upon it. As soon as my fever stopped climbing so high, she—as if in conspiracy with Dad—went blindly through the days, pretending I wasn't sick. She became irritated if I vomited or collapsed dizzily into a chair. Both of them looked through me as if I weren't there at all.

For a few minutes, Dad sat in the car with the door open calling for Mother.

"Dorris! Dorris! Dorris!" When she didn't appear, he staggered from the car, almost fell over the brick retaining wall, and leaned against the hood of the car. He kicked at the bricks.

"Son-of-a-bitchin' rocks!" he shouted. "I'll clean this whole goddamned block off!" He flailed about, waved his arms jerkily, and kicked at the black-eyed Susans growing around the retaining wall. He steadied himself against the car, then staggered through the uncut grass toward the steps, calling for Mother again. "Dorris!!"

"Please, God," I whispered, "let him break his leg right now. You don't have to kill him, just make it so he can't get up the steps." I prayed to the God of the Baptized Believers in Jesus Church. I'd seen Gaynelle Hull sprawled on the floor for hours, unconscious, possessed by the Holy Ghost. *If he could knock her to the floor, a perfectly normal girl most of the time, then he should be able to knock Dad to the ground.* I watched as he climbed the stairs and hoped he'd fall. But he pulled himself along, clutching the thin handrail and giant-stepping over the broken step as if playing "Simon Says."

He stopped halfway up and jerked at a honeysuckle vine that climbed the rail, ripped it into pieces and tossed it into the air like confetti. He rocked back and forth from the effort and I was sure he would tumble over the rail. But he rocked a moment longer, then continued up the steps. He had wet his pants and a dark stain circled down to his knees. The stain ended just above a patch of dried blood that looked like it could have come from his thick blood-crusted lower lip. He had been fighting again; and his pain usually meant our pain. This would not be one of the days that he wanted to play poker, blackjack or twenty-one, dividing the change in his pocket among the players, praising a good hand and a well-maintained poker face. This was a day to hide. There had been more and more days to hide since Dad lost his job two months earlier. The Cadillac had broken down and he'd been hitchhiking from Kimberly to Birmingham to work. Most days, he was late. They fired him before he could fix the car.

I grabbed Mother's blue sweater, dropped to the floor and slid under the bed next to Janet. We rolled onto our bellies, propped on our elbows and waited. The box spring at the top of the stairs slammed aside. I handed the sweater to Janet and she scooted into a ball and buried her head in it.

"Just make it so he can't find anyone," I prayed again, annoyed that, according to Gaynelle Hull, it took time and patience for God to hear prayers. I didn't go to church anymore; mostly because the one time Lizzie had convinced me to go with her to the Baptized Believers in Jesus Church, it scared the bejesus out of me. Gaynelle passed out on the floor, sprawled out with several other members of the faith. Her miniskirt barely covered her rear and she drooled onto the carpet. The rest of the congregation shouted "Amen" and "Praise God," jumped on the pews and pounded on various hand drums and tambourines. Between the moment Gaynelle fell to the floor, dropping her tambourine into the aisle, and the moment I ran out the door—kicking her tambourine so hard it ricocheted off a pew and hit the back wall—two old men began talking in tongues, shouting God's secret language into each other's face like a cuss-fight. They looked as if they were going to whack each other any minute. Nobody understood a word they were saying except for old man Butterworth—who shouted that God wanted the church to build a restaurant.

I ran home on shaky legs and told Mother. But she just rolled her eyes and kept ironing. I was used to the Methodist Church in Birmingham, the one Aunt Janet belonged to, where we sang in the choir, Mother too, soft, sweet music that made the congregation smile and whisper to one another. I missed our soft-spoken preacher and tranquil service. I missed Birmingham, missed Aunt Janet and, right now, missed Mother most of all.

I let out a weary sigh and lifted my head into the cobwebs that clung to the two-by-four slats overhead. The silvery threads stuck to my hair and eyelashes and made me shiver. I picked a coal-dusty strand from my lips and looked around at the webs, checking for spiders. But the webs had been long abandoned, the edges tattered like torn cheesecloth. Once, when I was about eleven years old, while we still lived in Birmingham, I had tried to make a cross out of similarly dusty, cobweb-covered two-by-fours.

It was June 1964. The omnibus civil rights act, banning discrimination in voting, jobs and public places, had just been passed. Birmingham was abuzz with the news. The mailman stood on the porch talking to Mother for ten minutes. She wasn't paying much attention to him, and neither was I, until he mentioned the Ku Klux Klan. Dad had been in several fights with Klan members, at the Jet, a small bar four blocks from our house. He had, on several occasions, staggered home with a busted mouth and scraped knuckles, bragging about the teeth he had knocked from the mouth of a "sheet-wearing bastard." He eventually wasn't allowed into the Jet at all; the owner forbade it, saying he couldn't afford to replace broken barstools and glasses anymore.

"It's too bad the Klan has gone so wrong," the mailman said. "You know, their original intentions were good. They originally gathered to make sure people behaved, that families were taken care of. If a man wasn't taking care of his family, they'd burn a cross in his yard as a warning to straighten up. Then they lost that whole idea and started torturing the colored people . . ."

That was all I heard of the conversation, all I needed to hear. I told Mother I was going over to a friend's house and walked down the sidewalk. *What we need is for the Ku Klux Klan to burn a cross in our yard so Dad will take care of us, so he'll stop drinking and hitting everybody.* I imagined Dad coming home with a briefcase and a kitten tucked under his arm as I'd seen on the TV show "Father Knows Best." The Ku Klux Klan obviously didn't know about Dad or they would have burned a cross in our yard long ago. Somebody needed to tell them. I walked down to the Jet to do just that. But the Jet had been closed. Boards covered the windows and a yellow "Condemned" sign hung on the front door.

I walked back home and decided to make a cross and burn it in the yard myself. Everybody would *think* the Ku Klux Klan had done it. I planned it carefully in my mind, saw the flames leap from the cross and the frightened and remorseful look on Dad's face. I imagined that same man, sober and in good humor, standing at the head of the table, carving a golden-brown roasted chicken.

I searched inside the house, looking in corners and closets, annoyed that with all the junk I found—two broken lamps, a battered hat, an empty birdcage, rusted car parts and an array of broken toys—there were no long pieces of wood. I scrounged through the trash and the burning pile in the backyard, but still couldn't find anything big enough. Finally, I climbed under the house by the back steps and found two dusty two-by-fours, one slightly longer than the other, neither over three feet long. I couldn't find any nails long enough to go through the wood, so I tied them together with a red-striped rope that I found in the boys' bedroom. When I stood up the cross, it sagged into an X, but I envisioned it jumping to attention and looming overhead when the time came to torch it. I leaned it against the house and planned the letter. The letter would have to be typed. Dad might not recognize my handwriting any longer, but Mother certainly would; and she'd be mad. I decided to use Aunt Janet's portable typewriter, the one Mother had used to practice her typing skills so she could get a job.

I sauntered down the block working out the fine points of my plan and walked into Aunt Janet's without knocking; we never knocked. Katie, the Negro woman who took care of Sweetpea while Aunt Janet worked for the phone company, was sitting on the couch, folding clothes and watching soaps on TV. She shook out a towel and the flesh jiggled under her large arms. I said, "Hello," and went straight to the hall closet, pushed aside stacks of old Bible-study magazines, folded paint rags and vacuum-cleaner parts. I found an open package of typing paper, folded two pieces and tucked them under my shirt.

"Whachew doin' in that closet?" Katie asked. Her brow twisted into a V-shape.

"I'm looking for something," I answered, knocking over a can of paintbrushes.

"I see dat," Katie said, snapping another towel into the air. "Whachew lookin' far?"

I picked up the brushes and put them back on the shelf and pretended not to hear her. If Katie knew I had the typewriter, she'd tell Aunt Janet, Aunt Janet would tell Mother, and Mother would know I typed the letter—not the Ku Klux Klan. The typewriter was not in the closet. I closed the door and studied the living room. It wasn't sitting out on the table or on the desk in the corner. I decided it must be in Aunt Janet's bedroom. Katie was still giving me the eye; her lips grew fuller. I walked from the hallway into Aunt Janet's bedroom and shut the door. About the time I lifted the bedspread to check underneath. Katie grabbed me by the shoulders and escorted me out, shuffling her bedroom slippers as she walked.

"Get on outta yhar. You ain't gonna do nothin' but cause yo'self grief," she said, pushing me all the way out the front door. She stood on the porch with her huge hands on her hips, shaking her head as I walked back up Thirteenth Avenue toward home.

I twisted my brow back at her, but I couldn't stay mad. She had been good to us when we lived there, never complaining about the extra work, never hitting us with the hickory switch she carried. And after we moved down the street, she had taken care of me one day when I was suffering from the measles. Stewart and David had stayed out of school to take care of me that day, but mostly they played with the Erector set Stewart had gotten for Christmas. They built a crane and put it on top of the refrigerator to hoist our dead grandpa's mustache cup from the floor, turning the crank slowly so the cargo wouldn't fall from the small hook. I fell asleep in the rocking chair, watching the TV screen flip faster and faster. I woke up seeing big blue spiders and flying cats and cried for Mother. We didn't have a phone, so David ran down to Aunt Janet's to call Mother at work. Mother asked Katie to take care of it. And Katie did. She picked me up from the rocking chair and plopped me right in Alice's bed. She rubbed me with alcohol and talked to me in a sweet voice, "Here, baby, drink some a' this juice; it'll make you feel better."

I walked back home, determined to write the letter to the Ku Klux Klan in an unrecognizable, mysterious, style.

I hid in the boys' bathroom and stuck the eraser end of the pencil into the sink filled with crayfish, turtles and tadpoles, while I thought of what to say. I wanted to ask for bicycles, dark blue tennis shoes and dresses for Mother, but decided to keep it simple:

S.K. MOSS,
YOU BETTER STOP DRINKING
AND TAKE CARE OF YOUR FAMILY.

KKK

I wanted to put "Ku Klux Klan" but had no idea how to spell it. After wasting one of the typing paper sheets practicing, I scratched the initials in large stick shapes across the bottom of the page. I held the letter up. It looked just fine; even I couldn't recognize my handwriting. Now, all I needed was gasoline from the lawn mower to burn the cross.

I'd seen Stewart siphon gas before: stick a small hose in the gas tank, then suck on it till the gas comes splashing out. It didn't look hard. I got a jelly jar from the kitchen to siphon the gas into. I would hide the jar under the steps until dark. As soon as it was dark enough, I planned to sneak out the back door, plant the letter on the front door and the cross in the front yard, douse it with gas, light it, then run around the house and in the back door. But when I pulled the tattered, dusty lawn mower from under the house, the gas tank was empty. I sat down on the back steps to think.

David came out the back door, sucking on an ice cube, and whacked me in the back with the screen. "Hey, that's my rope!" he shouted. "What are you doing with my rope?" He threw down the ice cube, dragged the X-shaped cross away from the house and dropped it into the dirt.

I jumped up, trying to save what was left of my plan. "I found that rope!" I cried, pushing David. "I'm making something."

"Not with my rope, you're not," he shouted and pushed me into the dirt. He untied the knot and pulled the rope from the boards. They tumbled apart. He kicked a puff of red dirt onto my legs and walked back inside with his rope. I sat in the dirt, frustrated and angry—my plan ruined. Inside, the refrigerator door opened and the ice cube tray rattled from the shelf. I stared at the toppled cross, the layers of dust tracked with my fingerprints, the bits of cobweb clinging to the ends.

I kicked the two-by-fours with my tennis shoe, pulled my knees up and dropped my head against them. Then I vowed to seek out a Klansman who would burn a cross in our yard and make my father take care of us.

Dad kicked the front door open, knocking the nail that held the wooden lock out of the doorframe and rattling the thread-spool doorknob. My parents' bedroom had two doors, one that led into the boys' bedroom and one that led into the living room. Both were opened and I could see from under the bed into the living room. Dad stumbled inside and the stench of smoke, beer and urine entered with him. He reeled back and forth and cleared his throat as if to speak. He cleared his throat again and stood still, listening for movement, honing in on a target. He touched his raw lip, cocked his head to the side, then reached into his shirt pocket and pulled out a pack of cigarettes. He tapped the opened pack against his wrist and dropped several cigarettes to the floor before he caught one and adjusted it in the corner of his mouth, rolling it away from the crusty sore. He patted his pockets for matches and cleared his throat again. He pushed his hand into his pants pocket, but couldn't find any matches.

"Son of a bitch!" he shouted and kicked the Cheerios box, slamming it against the wall. John bobbed his head from behind the couch to see what was happening just as Dad turned in his direction. Caught! Dad dropped the pack of cigarettes and darted to the couch. He jerked John from his hiding place and tossed him into the air like a rag doll, bumping his head against the low ceiling. He let go and John crashed to the floor, screaming and calling for Mother, kicking his bare feet toward Dad. But Dad clenched his hand around his thin ankle and wrenched it, rolling him over and over on the splintery wooden floor. He clenched the cigarette in his teeth and muttered, "You'll learn to behave, by God, or I'll kill ya." He released John's ankle and jerked him to his feet. Shook him hard. John's head flopped back and forth and he screamed, "Help me! Somebody help me!" Dad swung him around and began spanking him, beating his back, bottom and bare legs. "You'll learn to behave, by God!" His hands raked across the impetigo on John's legs. The blotchy sores burst open and spilled blood and puss down John's thin legs in milky red streaks.

He ran in a circle, screaming shrilly. He wet his pants and the urine, mixed with blood, puddled onto the floor, splattering the white cigarettes Dad had dropped earlier. John screamed one long continuous scream, until Dad dropped him to the floor and stumbled into the kitchen, coughing and panting. John jumped up and ran into the boys' bedroom, leaving a trail of urine and blood.

I buried my face in the sleeve of Mother's sweater. My heart raced. As bad as I felt for John, I was glad I had not been the one caught. Janet pressed against my side and I dropped an arm over her back. I could hear the refrigerator door open and the clatter of glass as Dad searched for a jar of the homebrew that he and Mr. Pickett had recently made. He stumbled back into the living room and I lifted my head to listen. Fear climbed into my throat. He was coming my way. I couldn't see him, but I could hear him gulping the homebrew, hear the liquid splashing inside the jar. He made that "Aahhhh" sound and then there was silence. The silence continued. Janet lifted her head slightly and peeked from beneath the sweater. I shook my head for her to be still, cover up. She snuggled closer and covered her eyes again. I listened, waiting expectantly. I could hear whispering in the boys' bedroom, slight shuffling—*David soothing John*. The dogs tied under the steps outside whined softly, unnerved by the earlier cries. I could hear the faint tick of the clock and the distant chatter of birds and tree frogs. I turned my head, straining to hear movement in the living room. The silence stretched the minutes endlessly.

Then he fell—toppled to the floor like a tree felled by a crack of lightning. The Mason jar hit the floor and rolled into the doorway, spinning like a top, slinging drops of homebrew in a circle. Janet and I jumped as if he had fallen on our heads. We grabbed each other and Janet cried out a muffled "Mom!" into the sweater. I wrapped my arm tightly around her. Dad grunted, as if exhaling all of the life from his body. It was over. He wouldn't get up for hours and Mother would be home by then. I dropped my forehead onto my fist. Janet pulled the sweater from her head and rested her chin on her fist.

"He's down," she said. Her small body relaxed under my arm and she wiggled. I could already hear the others coming out of their hiding places, whispering to one another. David comforted John as he began to cry again.

"But I didn't do anything," John sobbed.

I lifted my head and propped my chin on my fist, too. Janet looked up at me and smiled a very weak smile.

"How do you learn to behave?" she asked.

Reverence

FREE—One Pair of Shoes—Compliments of the Shriners, Zamora Temple, Birmingham, Alabama—Nov. 10 & 11, 1969. A letter, addressed to Dorris Robinette Moss, came with the certificate explaining that she must present her school-aged children, along with their birth certificates, to the Zamora Temple in Birmingham to receive the shoes.

I was elated. My shoes were ragged and falling apart at the seams. They were too small and smelled like spoiled milk. I couldn't wait to throw them away and pick out a new pair. Fantasies clouded my head: shelves and shelves of shoes, dozens of styles and colors to choose from. *I'll pick a heel, just a small heel, an inch, with buckles on the sides, black—no, brown. No, no. Saddle oxfords. I've always wanted saddle oxfords. The two-tone kind, black and white, lace-up. No, wedges.* I imagined myself dressing for school, tying white leather wedges, the wedge covered in cork as I'd seen in magazines, folding lace-trimmed socks neatly against my ankles. Then I switched back to saddle oxfords and imagined myself lacing them up, pulling the strings into a neat bow. *Yes. That was it. I'd get black-and-white saddle oxfords.*

But a trip to Birmingham for free shoes would be difficult. Dad forbade acceptance of charity. "I can take care of my family, by God!" he would shout when a church tried to give us a food basket at Christmas. Any kind of help, whether it was money from Aunt Janet, boxes of clothes from Aunt Lola or a chicken and canned vegetables from the church, had to come when Dad wasn't home or we couldn't accept it.

In order to get the shoes, we'd have to sneak away to the Zamora Temple while Dad was at the bar Saturday afternoon. Chance being caught. He would never notice the shoes once they were on our feet. He had a peculiar blindness, seeing only what he wanted to see, a self-absorption that seldom extended beyond his own desires. But the trip itself, if he found out about it, would be an excuse to pitch a fit, the heaviest blows, as always, falling on Mother. She worried about it all week, weighing the need for shoes against the possible destruction the trip could cause. After a final look at our shoes— smelly, holes in the soles, missing shoestrings, the boys' sneakers lying open-toed like a string of wide-mouthed bass—she decided the need outweighed the consequences of being caught.

We spent Saturday morning taking baths. Mother heated water on the hot plate and poured it into the number 8 tub that sat close to the fireplace. One at a time, we knelt on folded towels to wash our hair, then climbed into the tub, giggling and splashing, while Mother ironed our clothes in the kitchen. The clean kids danced around in damp towels while the dirty kids shouted "Hurry up!" through the door to whoever was in the tub. We dressed in our best clothes, cotton print dresses and shirts that Mother had made. Except for Stewart, who wore a navy pullover and jeans purchased over the summer when he'd worked at Grayson's Ice Cream Parlor in Warrior, Alabama.

The old Plymouth had finally died and Stewart was now driving a copper 1960 Rambler convertible, purchased from his boss for seventy-five dollars. The payments for the car were deducted from his weekly paycheck. And the Rambler, with bare tires and an engine that resisted cranking, would be our transportation to the Zamora Temple in Birmingham. We piled in, packed shoulder to shoulder, Janet on Mother's lap and John on mine. We all knew how hard it had been for Mother to decide to go and we're grateful—tried not to fight with each other, no poking or tattling. In fact, the excitement of getting new shoes made us downright joyful. We smiled at one another like teammates, the squeeze of our shoulders playful rather than annoying. Driving toward Birmingham, we passed through Morris, Gardendale and Fultondale, playing license-plate games, seeing who could spot the car from farthest away.

When we finally arrived in Birmingham, Stewart passed the

Zamora Temple parking lot and parked on a sloping street, just in case we needed to coast downhill to crank the car when it was time to leave. We walked the two blocks to the Zamora Temple with the sun bright in our faces, comforted by the smell of exhaust fumes and the familiar noise of the city. Stewart told stories of when we lived in Birmingham as if it were a lifetime ago. Mother stopped at the front door of the Zamora Temple and checked our clothes, straightened Willie's collar, licked her fingers and rubbed a spot of dirt from John's cheek. She looked down at her own shoes: tattered blue canvas slippers with threadbare toes. She shrugged and opened the heavy wooden door, holding it until we were all inside.

We stood blinded in the huge hallway waiting for our eyes to adjust to the darkness, seeing only vague shapes. The musty odor of an old cellar assaulted us, but also the pungent smell of new leather. I felt a rush of exhilaration, a tingling across my scalp and down my spine. The walls of the temple hallway were dark mahogany, and burgundy carpet, soft as a pillow, covered the floor, flowing forth like the Red Sea, past doors that led into various rooms.

An old man greeted us. He wore black slacks, a white shirt, a navy tie and a tasseled, bucket-shaped hat with a glittery knife, crescent moon and a star on the front. He stood inside the door like the person that hands out bulletins in church, but we didn't see him when we came in. When he spoke, we jumped as if we were in the spook house on Halloween. We laughed nervously, staring at him until the round sun-shape in our eyes faded and his face became visible. He held his hand out to Mother, bowing slightly. The burgundy tassel on the hat swung like a silent bell.

"Good afternoon," he said. He had on a gold ring that matched the design on his hat. The men I knew didn't wear jewelry, even wedding rings, and it looked out of place on his wrinkled, splotchy hand. But even more out of place were the perfectly shaped nails that glistened with clear polish. *A man wearing fingernail polish.* I felt embarrassed for having stared at his hands, blushed and looked for something to appear interested in. From the hallway, I could see into the next room, where two Shriners were measuring a small girl's foot with a wooden board. The men looked just like the one speaking to Mother. There were two dozen more Shriners in the room, dressed identically, wearing Shriner hats and rings, differing only in height, weight and the shape of their glasses.

We were ushered into an adjacent room, cozy with the strong smell of coffee. Long wooden tables covered with white tablecloths sat in the middle of the room. In the center of each table stood a short row of white candles in round crystal candleholders, surrounded by gold spray-painted pine cones and holly leaves. The room was dim. The thick velvet drapes blocked all but a thin strip of sunlight where the curtains met, but the candles weren't burning. We sat down at the table, gathering on either side of Mother. An old, stoop-shouldered gentleman with tufts of white hair jabbing from under his hat brought Mother a cup of coffee. His arthritically warped hands rattled the cup and saucer as he placed it in front of her. He wore his Shriner's ring on his little finger between the first two gnarled knuckles, and he adjusted it as he shuffled back to the coffee station as if it were painful. Two other gentlemen, also older than the men fitting shoes, served us hot chocolate in styrofoam cups and chocolate-chip cookies on burgundy napkins. They whispered, "You're welcome," when we said, "Thank you." They walked back to the table set up for cocoa and stood in front of it, their arms leaving their sides only long enough to check the water level in the pot or push their glasses back up on their noses. Other than the men serving coffee and cocoa, we were alone.

We squirmed in our seats, excitedly. Mother sipped her coffee, nodding politely to the gentleman who had served it. At first we didn't talk, intent on cooling our cocoa and eating our cookies, but then we began to entertain Mother again—to show our appreciation. After we reminisced about living in Birmingham for a little longer, Stewart told a story about his after-school job serving ice cream at Grayson's. A little boy ordered a strawberry ice cream cone and licked the ball of ice cream into the floor three times. We laughed. David told two "little Johnny" jokes and each received a round of giggles. Willie asked an absurd question we all knew the answer to, "Where does a two-hundred-pound gorilla sleep?" We all answered at once, "Anywhere he wants to!" and, once again, we laughed out loud. We were delighted with the sound of Mother's soft laughter and continued our celebration with more stories. I told about a ride through the woods on Robert Ray's bicycle: I was on the handlebars when Robert Ray hit a limb that sent me flying into the air like an acrobat and planted me on my feet three yards behind the bike. Everyone laughed. Doris Ann—trying to be heard over the laughter—gave her version of how I looked in the air. "Ernest and I were right behind them! We could have caught her on the handlebars of our bike!" We were having a wonderful time, thoroughly enjoying ourselves, when David noticed that the Shriners were watching us. Their gray identical heads bobbed in and out of the doorway, their mouths twisted into puzzled frowns.

His mouth full of cookie, David asked, "Why are they watching us?" and stuffed another piece of cookie in his mouth as soon as he swallowed.

"I don't think we're suppose to be having fun," Mother whispered. "They're helping the poor and the poor aren't being reverent enough."

I was startled. "Wouldn't they *want* us to have a good time?" I asked. My eyes darted to the doorway just as one of the Shriners from the other room entered. He stopped briefly and looked at the men guarding the refreshments, then walked briskly, like the principal at our high school, to the table where we sat.

"We're ready for you now," he said sternly, as if we'd been caught stealing cookies. He stepped back to let Mother slide from her chair, and waited impatiently, a frown still curling his lip, while we dusted cookie crumbs from our fingers and took another swallow of hot chocolate. He escorted us into a long room where shelves stacked with white shoeboxes filled the upper portion of the room. I skipped with excitement. The aroma of new leather grew stronger as we neared the boxes. My heart fluttered like a captured bird. The man with the stern voice took us to a wooden bench and we sat, sliding on the smooth surface an arm's length apart, still giddy and smiling broadly. We kicked off our shoes and pushed them under the bench as far from sight as possible, hoping they wouldn't be noticed or mentioned. Mother stood Janet at the end of the crowded bench so she could watch, then backed away and leaned against the wall. One of the Shriners brought a chair made of thick dark wood and placed it at the end of the bench. He held his arm out toward Mother. "The wallpaper is flocked," he explained. "The chair will be more comfortable."

"Oh, I'm sorry," Mother said, looking at the elegant silver-flocked wings and examining the area where her back and hands had touched the wall.

"That's perfectly all right," he said, bowing slightly as she sat in the chair. He smiled and patted her shoulder. "You see, it's very old and we're trying to preserve it as long as possible."

"Well, it's very beautiful," Mother said. She settled into the chair. Janet climbed into her lap and Mother looked grateful. She smiled and ran her long fingers through the curls on the top of Janet's head. Several Shriners gathered in front of the bench to assist, because there were so many of us. We giggled, twisting and turning on the bench as they knelt on one knee. They measured our feet with the wooden boards and jotted down the sizes in small spiral notebooks from their shirt pockets.

Only then, after they stood and walked into the aisles to pull our sizes, did I realize that I wasn't going to pick out my shoes. Not only was I not going to pick them, they were all the same shoe: burgundy penny loafers, boys' and girls', differing only in sizes. I looked at the stunned faces of my brothers and sisters and realized that they too had been fantasizing about their new shoes. We fell silent, dropped our heads and avoided eye contact with the Shriners, with one another and with Mother.

On Monday morning everyone at Kimberly Elementary would be wearing burgundy penny loafers. At Kimberly Elementary it would be so unanimous it wouldn't matter much. But I was in the eighth grade, David in the ninth and Stewart in the tenth—and we went to Mortimer Jordan High School, where it would matter. It would matter a lot! On Monday, all the poor students would be wearing identical burgundy penny loafers. We might as well wear sandwich boards that read, "I'm Poor." The shoes would say out loud what had been just touched on before, separating us as if we had lice. Now they would have no doubt about their superiority, would point to the loafers and snicker, call them "Po' shoes."

I bit my lower lip and tried to smile at the gentleman who knelt at my feet, concentrating on the glittery spangles on his hat. I started chewing my fingernails, forcing back tears that swelled in my chest. I refused to look at the burgundy loafers that the Shriner placed at my feet. He smiled and lifted my foot in his hand.

"You're cold," he said, rubbing my toes briskly between his palms. "I've got a granddaughter just about your size." I nodded and dropped my hands into my lap. He reached behind him into a basket and pulled out a plastic bag of crew socks, bit it open with his teeth and dropped the plastic back in the basket. He rolled a sock into a tight ball and slid it onto my foot, gently pulling and tugging it into a perfect fit. He rubbed more warmth into the soft cotton, then did the same to the other foot, dropping it into a slight swing while he fished for the aromatic penny loafers. He snapped them from the box and tossed one of them into the air so it faced the right way. He put the shoes on the carpet just below my feet and pulled a silver shoehorn from his back pocket, ducking his head a little to catch my eyes.

"You ready," he said. He misread the tears in my eyes and patted my shoulder. I nodded again. I wanted him to stop patting me before Mother noticed. I glanced down the pew at my brothers and sisters and knew we were all thinking the same thing: hide the disappointment from Mother.

The Shriner cocked the shoehorn behind my heel and lightly twisted, easing the right shoe onto my foot, then did the same with the left.

"Now stand up," he commanded. I jumped to the floor and stood up straight, glancing at the shelves of white shoeboxes in front of me. It hurt to know the color and shape of every single shoe. The Shriner pushed his thumb onto the toe, then squeezed the sides with his large hand.

"Perfect." He stood and clapped softly. "Ideal.

"Now walk up and down the lane," he said. I walked forward, coaxing the stiff leather to flex, showing off the fit, falling in line with Willie, Doris Ann and John, who were also instructed to walk. I glanced at them, noticed the glisten of tears in their eyes, and looked away. We walked faster to catch up with the boys, who were ahead of us, and walked with them the full length of the long room. We slowed, walking past the heavily burdened shelves and past the last burning fluorescent light, into the dark. We gathered together in a circular huddle and composed ourselves, wiped away tears and caught our breath.

Finally, Stewart cleared his throat and said, "Let's go." A thin, forced smile stretched across his face and he turned back toward the Shriners. The rest of us followed, mimicking his posture and smile. At the far end of the room the Shriners, standing in a cluster, hands on their hips or in their pockets, smiled back. Broad, toothy smiles. For, suddenly, we were as reverent as they thought we should be.

Leave It in the Wings

After a long night of blocking Dad's drunken blows, Stewart joined the U.S. Marine Corps. He had graduated from high school a month before and had been working full time, along with Alice's husband Silas, for Asplundh Tree Service, trimming the trees away from power lines and cleaning up after storms in the Kimberly and Warrior area. But Dad started picking fights with him almost every day, sometimes forcing him into a fistfight. It was no surprise when Stewart joined the military.

The day before he was to leave for Camp Lejeune, he drove his convertible Rambler down into the holler to Ralph Yates's place to see if he wanted to buy it. Dad rode along to help him bargain. I took the shortcut through the woods and got there just as Stewart wheeled the Rambler into the red dirt yard, scattering children and chickens and dogs. I hopped onto the rickety front porch and sat on a concrete block, slid my pink flip-flops off and pulled my left foot onto my lap to search for a splinter, just as Ralph lumbered out the front door and slammed the screen on a mangy yellow dog that was trying to slip inside. He stood on the porch, his huge frame filling the space: massive shoulders almost touched the support poles on either side and thin red hair brushed the corrugated tin roof above. He shifted his weight from one foot to the other and the porch boards buckled and groaned. He stepped off the porch and they snapped back into place, just as the Rambler engine died and the red dust began to drift back to the haggard ground.

Ralph flipped a pack of Marlboro cigarettes from his shirt pocket and offered one to Dad. Dad reached out and took a cigarette from the pack. Ralph offered Stewart one, but he declined and Ralph took it for himself.

"How you doing, Stewart?" Ralph asked. He wrapped his lips around the cigarette and dug in his pants pocket for matches. "S.K.?" he said, nodding toward Dad.

Stewart nodded and Dad said, "Oh, can't kick," as he climbed from the car, leaving the door wide open, and leaned into the burning match between Ralph's thick fingers. He puffed on the cigarette and blew smoke into the air.

Stewart got out and closed his door. He walked around, leaned against the hood of the car and surveyed the yard. "I leave for Parris Island tomorrow," he said. He crossed his arms in front of his chest, propped a steel-toed work boot on the front bumper and looked at Ralph.

Parris Island didn't register with Ralph. He stuck out his tongue, nipped a shred of tobacco from the tip with his thumb and middle finger, and looked at Stewart suspiciously, as if he were speaking a foreign language.

"The Marines," Stewart explained, pridefully straightening his shoulders. "I joined the Marines and need to sell this car before I go."

"Oh," Ralph said. He flicked the ashes from his cigarette, took a step backward—rubbing his arm as if trying to clear away the thick layer of freckles that coated it like a smeared tattoo—and ran his eyes over the car for the first time. "Damn," he said, shaking his head as he stuffed a hand into his dirty blue jeans, "the Marines. What in the world did ya do that for?" Before Stewart could answer, several children ran from the porch and swarmed over the car, climbing onto the hood and into the open door.

"Hey! Hey! Hey!" Ralph yelled, swatting a small redheaded boy from the hood into the dirt. "Get away from that car. That ain't ours!" Two small skinny girls pretended not to hear, climbed onto the front seat and began blowing the horn in short rapid bleeps. Ralph walked over and pulled them from the car, cussing between puffs on the cigarette clamped between his lips.

Ralph's wife, tall and skinny with limp blond hair, came to the door wiping her hands on a dishrag. She looked out, smiled at me and went back to the kitchen.

"Hell, I ain't got no money, Stewart," Ralph said. He smacked the girls on top of the head and pushed them toward the house. They turned around to come back and he yelled, "Get on out of here!" They puffed out their lower lips and jumped onto the porch, pulled their sour-smelling dresses up to their bellies and watched me pick at the splinter in my foot.

"I'd love to have it, you know. I always wanted a convertible." He paused and rubbed the faded black canvas top with the palm of his huge hand. "Does that top come down, Stewart?"

"Oh, yeah," Stewart said, "everything works. It's a little hard to start sometimes. Needs a tune-up, I think, but it runs just fine." He walked around and climbed back inside, pumped the gas several times and turned the key. It cranked the first try and the lines on Stewart's forehead eased.

Some mornings, it took time and patience to get the Rambler cranked. Stewart would cuss so loudly it could be heard two blocks away at the Baptized Believers in Jesus Church. The cussing would be accompanied with occasional door slamming and fender kicking. Once while working on the Rambler carburetor, down on his knees on the high front porch, Stewart lost his temper, picked up the carburetor and slammed it back to the porch, smashing it right through the rotten floor and into the chicken coop below, surprising himself and everyone watching—not to mention the hundred yellow chicks in the coop. Willie and I burst out laughing and Stewart chased us halfway to the holler.

Stewart unsnapped the hooks that held the canvas in place and hit the switch to drop the top on the Rambler. It bounced into thick, crackling folds just behind the backseat. Ralph Yates's mouth eased into a long straight grin and his eyes widened. "Man, oh man," he said. "I always wanted a convertible." He threw his cigarette to the ground and walked around the car, leaned onto the trunk and pushed down with both hands, bouncing the entire car like a basketball. He kicked the tires on the driver's side and touched spots on the fender where the copper paint had rusted away. Eventually he settled back into his original spot near the passenger-side door and made a sour face. "Damn, I just ain't got no money, S.K." He looked from the car to Dad, who stood just out of the way, silently smoking.

"Well," Dad said, "we better get on then. We got to sell this thing today." He threw down his cigarette butt, stepped on it so none of the kids would burn their feet and climbed back in the car. I shouted to Stewart, asking if he'd give me a ride back to the house. He nodded and I climbed into the backseat as Stewart pulled the car into reverse. We backed into the road.

Ralph took two steps forward and waved one of his giant freckled hands. "Hold up, S.K. Hold up." He put both hands on the door and leaned forward, glanced quickly toward the house, then looked back to Dad and whispered, "I got seventy-five dollars in food stamps stuck in my pocket right here." He tapped three times on the pocket of his washed-out shirt. "I'll trade you them food stamps for the Rambler, even-steven." He looked down and spit between his grimy work boots, waiting for an answer. We had never received food stamps; Dad was too proud to accept any government help, even when he was out of work, and he had a low opinion of those who did. From the backseat I could see his body stiffen, feel the scorn creep into his posture. Stewart looked away, dropped his arm out the open window and snapped his fingers and clicked his tongue, feigning interest in the spotted dog at his fingertips.

I held my breath. Seventy-five dollars' worth of food was more food than we'd had in the house at one time since we moved to Kimberly; the thought of it made my mouth fill with saliva.

Dad considered Ralph's proposition for a moment, then said flatly, "Just don't believe I could do it." He shook his head. "I don't know a thing about food stamps and don't want ta be seen in no grocery store with 'em." Ralph and I exhaled at the same time and he glanced up, catching my eye. I blushed and looked away. Ralph shook his head to let Dad know he understood and hunched his shoulders as he pushed himself away from the car. He spit again and kicked red dirt over it. But before Stewart began to move, Ralph lurched forward and grabbed the door again.

"I could buy the groceries!" he said excitedly. "We could all go! You could pick out the food and I could pay for it. Nobody would have to see you at all! You could head on out the door before I get up to the register."

Dad and Stewart looked at each other skeptically, their eyes locking for a moment. They shrugged their shoulders at the same time. Dad looked at his hands, squirmed and then looked up at Ralph. "We'll have ta go out ta the supermarket in Gardendale. I'm not gonna chance being seen over at Sandlin's store . . ."

Ralph held up his hands like a hostage in a cowboy movie and blushed so pink the splatter of pale freckles on his cheeks faded. "Fine, fine," he said. He put his huge rump on the side of the car and threw his legs over, just missing Dad's head with his feet, and dropped onto the backseat with a thud. Dad shouted and ran his hand over his head to make sure his skull was intact and shot a hostile look over his shoulder at Ralph.

"Sorry 'bout that, S.K." Ralph said, smiling, ignoring Dad's shaking head, which was meant as a further rebuke. He ran his hand along the tarnished and crinkled seat, taking in every inch of it, a smile growing into a long thin rope across his face. We drove away, the wind whipping at our clothes. I stared at Ralph as he caressed the car and realized that he wasn't much older than Stewart. He was huge, his cotton shirt and jeans were ragged; he was married with four children, but there were no lines in his face, in a town where lines showed up early, marking faces like deep scars.

Stewart wheeled the Rambler up the steep hill out of the holler and headed toward the highway without dropping me off at home. I could hardly believe my luck. I sat like a stone and held my long hair away from my face as it flapped in the breeze. I was thankful that the wind made it hard to talk, hard to hear, and hoped Ralph wouldn't speak to me until we had driven far enough so it would be too much trouble to double back and take me home. I glanced at Ralph again and realized I didn't need to worry. He was preoccupied, still running his hands along the seat and door handle. As he explored the interior of the car, he grinned and turned his head back and forth so the wind tossed his scraggly hair from one side to the other and back again. We were halfway to Gardendale before Stewart shouted over the roar that he had forgotten to drop me off. Dad shouted back to forget it. My grin matched Ralph's. I relaxed and began to enjoy the whip of the wind, the warmth of the sun, and my thoughts wandered back to the weekend before.

🌿

We had all driven out to Anniston to visit Uncle Jake. Even Mother went, not to see Uncle Jake, but to look at a house that was on the other side of the soybean farm he lived on. Like the one Uncle Jake rented, this house also belonged to Edson Tucker, but hadn't been in good-enough condition to be lived in for years. Edson had been using it to throw poker parties. There were beer bottles and pizza boxes scattered throughout every tattered room. It was an old two-story plantation house with four large rooms and a hall downstairs and three bedrooms upstairs. The hot-water heater didn't work, but at least the cold water ran freely and there was an inside toilet. Termites swarmed around a crusty patch in the living room floor, some of the windows were broken, and dried blood crusted the floors from countless drunken brawls—but it was still in better condition than the spindle-legged Kimberly house. What's more, the porch of the plantation house was just two feet off the ground and made of poured concrete. There was a huge yard surrounded by soybean fields, a pasture and a small pond.

Before we drove home that day, Dad had given Edson Tucker fifty dollars. We would be moving again in a few days. The month we were supposed to live in Kimberly had stretched into two years, and instead of nine people living in a five-room house, there were thirteen.

Alice had had her baby. A boy. But when rats from the holler had chewed through the baby's bassinet and then chewed the nipple from his bottle, Alice, Silas and the baby had moved in with us. A year later, Alice had another baby boy. That brought the total population of our household to thirteen. We needed so much that it was hard to calculate what was most important, but a bigger house was certainly high on the list. And this house, sitting on the edge of Edson Tucker's soybean farm, was big. Stewart hadn't liked the house. He said it was too far from civilization. The closest neighbor was about a quarter of a mile away and it was fifteen miles to the city of Anniston. He said he wouldn't live in that house if he were a ghost. But I thought it was glorious compared to the Kimberly house. Dad, of course, called it "an immaculate mansion," and Mother said nothing at all.

❧

Stewart parked the Rambler well away from the supermarket door, as if distancing himself from this lowly business of food stamps. Ralph didn't notice; he fairly floated into the store with the straight grin still on his face. Dad let Ralph get a shopping cart while we waited in the produce area, then he picked up a ten-pound bag of russet potatoes and asked me if that was the right kind. Suddenly I realized there had been a reason Stewart had not dropped me off at home. He and Dad could guess at some of the food we needed: milk, eggs, cereal, oats. But they didn't know the ingredients needed for beef stew, or chicken soup, or any of the things Mother cooked regularly. When we lived in Birmingham, Willie and I had met Mother every evening when she got off the city bus from work. The bus stopped right in front of the Tenth Avenue Winn Dixie. Every Friday Mother would cash her paycheck at the front courtesy counter and buy groceries, with us tagging along trying to talk her into sweetened cereals. She selected the groceries. Willie and I chose only the lunch meat and dessert for our school lunches, but I knew exactly what she bought every week.

I felt important as I studied the shelves and searched for the products that Mother used. At first I would tell Dad what item to get from the shelf and tell him what it was used for—cornstarch for gravies, Crisco for biscuits—but pretty soon I took over, not bothering to explain each selection. Eventually Dad and Ralph began talking about the Rambler again, so Dad was distracted when I slipped two boxes of diabetic cookies, vanilla and chocolate chip, into the cart.

Every now and then, when Mother bought groceries, she'd buy diabetic cookies for our neighbor, Mrs. Webb. She'd take the cookies and some Luzianne tea bags over to the Webbs', make a pot of tea, arrange the cookies on a clear glass plate and sit on the porch with Mrs. Webb, sipping hot tea and discussing Mrs. Webb's health problems. I loved to go to these tea parties. Mrs. Webb always gave an update on the missing Webb boys: "Ain't nobody seen hide nor hair of 'em. I do believe somebody done kilt my boys." But eventually she'd start talking about her spongy cells. She said she weighed three hundred and eighty pounds because she had inherited spongy cells and big bones. She would go into long detail about how spongy cells work against the person who inherited them, and that it was no use cutting back on the amount of food you ate because spongy cells would fatten up without any food at all.

Mrs. Webb also believed she was diabetic, so Mother brought diabetic cookies. I didn't like them very much, they weren't very sweet; the vanilla cookies sort of tasted like the tea cakes Mother used to make for church gatherings, but not nearly as good. But I went along to visit Mrs. Webb anyway. It was like watching a play, and I didn't want to miss a single performance. Mother talked to Mrs. Webb the same way she talked to Mr. Webb when he collected our food scraps for his pigs, acting amazed and interested, agreeing completely with whatever they said, even if it was as ridiculous as spongy cells. Occasionally she added information that went along with Mrs. Webb's theory that she knew perfectly well wasn't true—like the time she told Mrs. Webb that she had heard a doctor's report that exercise wasn't good for some people. I had to look away when she told that one. When we walked back home, I questioned Mother about why she would say such a thing. She said, "That old woman feels bad enough about her situation. She'll never be able to leave those two rooms as long as she lives. If a little white lie makes her feel better, then I don't mind telling it."

Stewart came over to the cart and smiled when he saw the two boxes of diabetic cookies. He whispered, "Planning a tea party?" and pulled three loaves of white bread from the shelf and placed them on top of the boxes. I smiled and nodded, filled with love for him. He chuckled. We were well away from the register, so he took over the job of pushing the cart. He whistled a tune as we moved through the aisle.

The year before, while I was recovering from rheumatic fever, I had complained to Stewart that I was bored and wanted to go to the store. He gave me a dollar and sent me to the store for a loaf of bread and an RC. Sandlin's was just across the highway, two blocks away. But somehow, I lost the bill. I had folded it into the palm of my hand, but when I got to the register, it was gone. I searched the store aisles and searched the ditches along the road as I walked back home, but couldn't find the dollar. I felt disoriented and at one point forgot what I was looking for. When I climbed the front steps at home, Stewart was sitting on the porch scraping mud from his work boots with a putty knife. I told him what had happened and started to cry.

"Don't worry about it," he said. "There will always be more dollars."

He pushed the cart now, absently whistling a Beatles tune, "Hey,

Jude." It had been the number-one hit while I was sick. It was a long song and it played so often on the radio that I would fall asleep to "Hey-ey Jude, Jude, Judy! Judy! Judy! Judy! Judy!" and awaken to the same music, not knowing if I had been asleep for a minute or an hour.

Stewart stopped the cart in front of the dry goods and I put flour, pancake mix and grits in it. We went around the corner and Stewart pulled a flat of eggs from the cooler and slid them onto the lower shelf of the cart. There were thirty-six eggs in the flat, but that would only last for a few days at our house. On previous shopping trips, I had heard Mother say, "Eggs are delicious, good for you and cheap." I pulled another flat from the shelf and stacked it on top of the first; that would make seventy-two eggs, five apiece, with seven left over for making pancakes and cornbread. We turned into another aisle and ran into a cardboard display of Little Debbie cakes. I decided to take my chances and chose two boxes of my favorites, the kind I used to pick for our school lunches: devil's food with white creamy icing in the middle, coated on the outside with a hard shell of chocolate.

I used to get an extra cake for making the school lunches every morning. Mother got me up early, before anybody else was awake. She thought I didn't mind because of the extra Little Debbie cake. But I really liked it because I had my mother all to myself for forty-five minutes every day. We were both working in the kitchen; she was cooking breakfast and I was making lunches. Sometimes we talked. One morning, while I was smearing mayonnaise on twelve slices of white bread, I told her I wanted to be a model. She had heard me say I wanted to be an artist before, but she had never heard that I also wanted to model. I was eleven or twelve and tiny, the smallest in my class. Mother was standing at the stove frying eggs and reading a book at the same time. She looked up from her book and stared at me a moment. She didn't say I was ugly—as the kids at school did—she said, "You're too little; too short. Models have to be tall and I don't think you'll be over five feet two inches." She went back to her book, then looked back at me again, pointed the spatula in her hand at the Little Debbie box sitting on the table and said, "Maybe you could be a Little Debbie model," and went back to her book.

Four months earlier, when I turned fifteen, I had shot straight up, growing four inches taller than my mother, to five feet eight inches, almost as tall my dad. I had grown tall enough to be a model, but my face had grown tall too, long and thin; the upper portion growing so long it reduced my lower jaw to a bump of a chin. My puffy, red upper gum-line showed, and my upper teeth protruded so badly that I couldn't touch my lips together. When I brushed my teeth, my mouth filled with blood.

I dropped the Little Debbie cakes into the shopping cart and remembered that my health book at school mentioned a vitamin deficiency as the cause for bleeding gums. I studied the food in the cart: eggs, butter, milk, sausage, rice. It was all nutritious food, but it wouldn't last. I tried to think of something that had lots of vitamins. Raisins. Raisins were supposed to have everything, especially iron. I was looking for raisins when Dad tapped me on the shoulder and motioned toward the door, where Stewart was already exiting. He crooked his finger for me to follow him. I abandoned the cart. He walked casually to the register, purchased a pack of Raleigh cigarettes and a piece of Bazooka bubble gum. He put the cigarettes into his shirt pocket and slid the gum down the counter to me. I dropped the gum into the pocket of my blue-jean shorts so it would be soft later when I was ready to chew it, and followed him through the door and across the parking lot to the car. Stewart already had the trunk open and was busy moving jumper cables and empty oil cans around to make room for the groceries.

"Well, that was practically painless," Dad said. "But it still made me edgy."

"Yeah," Stewart said, "I don't know how he can do it. It'd be embarrassing to have to pay for everything with food stamps." I felt embarrassed for Ralph too, but I also wondered how Ralph got the food stamps, exactly *where* he went to apply for them and if there was any chance to get them for us. But I knew Mother and Dad would certainly never apply, regardless of how bad things might get.

On the ride home I opened a box of Little Debbie cakes and gave one to Stewart, Dad and Ralph, and bit the cellophane off one for myself. Stewart had put the top up for the ride home, making it possible to talk, so Ralph talked, and talked some more, describing the fine points of the Rambler as if we hadn't been looking at it for two years. He couldn't wait to show it to his brother.

"He's gonna be so jealous!" Ralph exclaimed as he popped the entire Little Debbie cake into his mouth and swallowed it.

"Let's take Ralph home first," Dad said to Stewart as we exited the highway onto Dixie Fire Brick Road. "We'll unload the groceries and drive the Rambler back to you in half an hour, Ralph," Dad said over his shoulder. "That way Stewart'll have time to find the title."

I started to say that the title was in the glove compartment, but Stewart cut off my words. "Hand me another one of those cakes, Barbara." I could tell by his tone that something was amiss. I handed out cakes again and kept my mouth shut, waiting to see why they didn't want Ralph to know the title was in the glove compartment. We drove into Ralph's yard and the kids ran to meet us, jumping to look in the open windows. Ralph climbed out of the backseat and handed his cake to the little boy, as much to move him out of the way as anything. Stewart tossed his to one of the girls and Dad tossed his to the other. I handed mine out the window to Ralph and told him to give it to the baby, and dug into the box for another one for his wife. I knew she was going to be mad, and could only hope they had enough food to make it till next month's food stamps arrived.

Stewart pulled out of Ralph's yard and headed for home. As soon as we were out of earshot Dad said, "Now let's keep this food stamp thing amongst ourselves. There's no need to tell your mother. I'd just as soon she thought we got cash money. Don't mention it to her and don't mention it to the others. Let's leave it in the wings."

His words crushed my illusions of being needed. The real reason I had been allowed to go was so I could be told to keep the food stamps a secret. I would just file it with all the other secrets; I had so many secrets already that I couldn't always remember what I was keeping from whom. There were secrets to be kept from Mother. Secrets to be kept from Dad. Many, many secrets to be kept from everyone at school. On our school records, Stewart, David and I made up addresses so no one would know where we really lived, or we'd scribble so it couldn't be read. Last year the school gave everyone a flu shot. After the shot, I got sick and fainted into my math teacher's arms. When I woke up I was in the principal's office wrapped in a blanket with a space heater at my feet. The principal asked where I lived so he could take me home. He had looked on my file card in the office, but the address wasn't legible. I pretended not to understand what he wanted, closed my eyes and rolled my head back. At that time Mother was working in Birmingham and Dad was out of a job, home alone. The thought of being home with him, just him and me, sent chills down my spine. I didn't understand it, but I was more afraid of Dad than of whatever was making me dizzy; and certainly more afraid of Dad than of anyone seeing where we lived—which was why the card was written illegibly in the first place.

My math teacher sent for David, but David, after deciding I wasn't going to die, wouldn't tell them either. He shuffled around, pretending he couldn't remember the address or exactly how to get there. Finally, exasperated, the principal sent David back to class, staring at him as he walked away as if he were a complete moron. He paced the floor mumbling to himself for a while, then brought the girls' gym teacher in to sit with me until time to catch the bus home. She sat down beside me and placed a glass of orange juice and a straw on the principal's desk. "Keeping secrets?" she asked, smiling. I buried my face in the blanket and closed my eyes.

But at least the food stamps wasn't a bad secret and wouldn't be nearly as hard to keep as others, such as Dad getting thrown in jail—which was always printed in the newspaper, read and announced by some yahoo at school. Or like the big continuing secret of our lives—pretending normalcy, pretending that we had not been up all night cleaning house, dodging bruises, listening to endless lectures that made no sense, or hiding in the dark. This was a good secret. The groceries would make Mother happy. Dad and Stewart would both win points for the groceries and she would never know they had no choice but to buy them: food stamps can't be redeemed for cash and can't be used for alcohol and cigarettes. And since neither one of them would touch the food stamps—they had jumped back when Ralph pulled them from his pocket as if they were fresh poison-oak leaves—they couldn't take them and sell them for cash later. If Stewart had sold the car for cash, he probably would have split the money with Dad and used his half for travel money to Camp Lejeune. Dad would have taken his share straight to the Tavern, bought a round for the house and slowly drunk until the last dollar slipped into the barmaid's pocket.

The Gift

While Stewart packed his bag to leave for Camp Lejeune, I sat in a rickety chair on the high front porch and ate food-stamp-purchased french fries and watched the traffic flash by on the highway. I didn't want Stewart to leave, but I didn't want Dad to fight with him anymore either. I dunked a fry in ketchup and wondered whether Dad would go back to torturing Alice, or would he go down the line in birth order to David, then me. I was figuring up how much time it would be before Dad got to me, when Fuzz climbed the front steps. He dragged his shotgun by the barrel, bumping the stock against the steps as he walked. He called to Stewart before he got halfway up the steps, and Stewart met him just as he reached the top.

"I brung Beulah for you to take to war," Fuzz said. "She's a sureshot and you won't miss your target."

"I'm not going to war, Fuzz," Stewart said. "I'm just going to Camp Lejeune and they'll give me a rifle when I get there." Fuzz looked disappointed, so Stewart added, "Besides, Beulah's too good for the military. She needs to stay here with you, Fuzz." Fuzz smiled, exposing a mouthful of rotting, broken teeth, and lifted his hand to cover his mouth.

I dropped the plate of french fries onto my lap and stared at Fuzz. I did the same thing—covered my mouth with my hand, especially when I smiled! It had never occurred to me that Fuzz was conscious of his appearance, or that anyone else was, for that matter. Until that moment, I thought the struggle was mine alone. I felt a rush of empathy for Fuzz and my hand automatically covered my mouth. Fuzz kept his hand over his mouth until the smile was gone, then he socked Stewart on the arm and turned to go back down the steps.

"Wait a minute, Fuzz, I've got something for you," Stewart said. He charged back inside and came back a minute later with the burgundy penny loafers the Shriners had given him. They were still brand-new; he had never worn them. He put the shoes on the step next to Fuzz's boots to see if they would fit, but it was hard to tell since the boots Fuzz wore were too big for him. Fuzz didn't make a move to take off his boots, so Stewart picked up the shoes and handed them to him. "I think they'll fit you just fine," Stewart said. "They won't let me wear penny loafers at Camp Lejeune, so you might as well have them." Fuzz nodded his head, socked Stewart on the arm again and walked back down the stairs. He shouted over his shoulder as he walked, "Take some spirit bottles with you, Stewart. There's bad spirits up north; real bad spirits."

Anniston, Alabama

Crazy Is as Crazy Does

*B*ut for us, the bad spirit of the North had already moved south. From the moment we moved into the two-story house near Anniston, Dad was glued to Uncle Jake. And because Uncle Jake was fascinated with guns, overnight Dad became fascinated with them. They talked about guns, bought guns and traded guns: pistols, rifles and shotguns. And they spent an enormous amount of time loading and unloading them, spilling the cartridges onto the floor. Uncle Jake was certain that somebody was out to kill him—the goons, he called them—so he carried a pistol all the time, day and night, drunk or sober. He also convinced Dad that they might be after him, too, just because he was his brother. When Dad was home, he kept a devoted watch for the goons.

One Saturday afternoon he sat on the porch in a wooden rocking chair, cradling an old Remington Eight-Seventy twelve-gauge pump shotgun with a missing stock. Uncle Jake had given him the shotgun after whacking it against a tree because it wouldn't fire. Dad brought the defective gun home and laughingly showed us the reason it wouldn't fire: the safety had been on. Ragged steel and a nut protruded from the point where the stock had been, making the shotgun particularly short, so Dad named it Shorty.

"Shorty kicks like a mule," he proclaimed as he sat on the front porch slapping mosquitoes and staring into the soybean fields with the shotgun across his lap. A glass of Kentucky Tavern sat by the rocker and when the whiskey was half gone, he forgot his vigil and began reciting poetry.

"He'll be squattin' on the coals, Givin' drinks to pore damned souls, An' I'll get a swig in hell from Gunga Din! Din! Din! Din! You Lazarushian-leather Gunga Din! Tho' I've belted you an' flayed you, By the livin' Gawd that made you, You're a better man than I am, Gunga Din!"

After reciting his favorite lines of "Gunga Din," he jumped to his favorite lines of "The Village Blacksmith."

"His hair is crisp, and black, and long. His face is like the tan. His brow is wet with honest sweat, he earns whate'er he can. And looks the whole world in the face, for he owes not any man." He recited the same verse three times, then recited the last verse of "Invictus": "It matters not how strait the gate, how charged with punishment the scroll, I am the master of my fate: I am the captain of my soul."

Us kids lazed on the porch behind him, catching fireflies and talking. David rode a homemade skateboard around and around in a figure eight, chattering about a girl he had seen when we took Mother for groceries that afternoon.

"Maybe she'll go to our school," he said. "She was beautiful."

"Beautiful," I scoffed. "Her hair was dyed blond and she wore two tons of purple eye shadow."

"I thought she was beautiful," John said.

"You're only ten years old. What do you know?" Doris Ann said. "She looked like she'd been in a fight and got both her eyes blacked." David rode by and swatted Doris Ann on the head. I jumped out of the way.

"Well, pretty then," he said. "She was pretty." Willie howled into the night like a dog. Mother walked out onto the porch and looked over at Dad—checking on him to make sure he wasn't into any mischief.

"Mom, wasn't that girl we saw at the grocery store pretty?" David asked.

"Pretty is as pretty does," Mother said and walked back inside.

Dad started reciting Edgar Allan Poe's "The Raven."

"Once upon a midnight dreary, while I pondered, weak and weary. Over many a quaint and . . . Over many a quaint and . . .

"What's the rest of it, Southpaw?" he yelled.

David stopped the skateboard and yelled, "Over many a quaint and curious volume of forgotten lore." He rolled his eyes and pushed off on the skateboard. We all smiled, knowing any second that Dad would ask for the next line. He never could remember past the first one.

"Over many a quaint and curious volume of forgotten lore," Dad repeated. He paused and gently rocked his chair.

"What's next?" he yelled. David pointed to me as he sped by on the skateboard.

"While I nodded, nearly napping, suddenly there came a tapping," I recited. Dad rocked for a minute, mumbled the first two lines again, then gave up and burst into song.

"My wild Irish Rose!" he sang. "Sweetest flower that grows!" He stopped rocking and shouted over his shoulder, "I'm singin' this for your mother." He continued rocking and sang out: "You can look everywhere, but none can compare to my wild Irish Rose!" He paused again. "'Cause she's got that fiery-red hair."

I loved to hear Dad sing. It was terrible. Especially compared to Mom's. He jumped keys and half the time he sang flat. He was completely tone-deaf. But he put so much gusto into it, emphasizing certain words like *wild* in "Wild Irish Rose," that it was great fun to listen to. I hummed along with him, swiped another firefly from the air and waited for it to light up in my cupped palm before releasing it. "Will you sing 'The Ballad of Barbara Allan' next?" I asked.

"I'll do it," Dad answered. "Your mother named you after that ballad, you know?"

"I know," I said.

"How the rose got its thorns!" Dad bellowed. "The thornbush twisted around the rose, and the rose grew thorns."

David stopped the skateboard again and said, "Yeah, but she's just twisted thorns." He pushed off on the board again.

"Hey," Dad reprimanded over his shoulder, "don't be mean to her. She's your *sister*."

That was one of the things I liked best about Dad. Everybody else in the world could be mean to us, but he wouldn't let us be mean to each other. He didn't mind if we argued about school or chores, as long as we didn't pick on the things that bothered us about ourselves. And he had a real sense for what those things were and how certain types of kidding could be linked to it—like my face and the twisted thorns.

I stuck out my tongue to David and he tried to run over me with the skateboard. I jumped onto the steps and stuck out my tongue again.

We fell back into the conversation about the girl at the grocery store as Dad began to sing again. He finished "Wild Irish Rose," then sang "The Ballad of Barbara Allan." He was singing "When I Was Single"—"Oh, when I was single, oh then, oh then, when I was single, oh then/When I was single my pockets did jin-gle, I wish I was sin-gle a-gain"—when suddenly he stopped short. David dropped one foot to the ground and stilled the skateboard. We stopped talking and listened, thinking that maybe he had actually heard something. I could hear the distant clatter of dishes in the kitchen and the low mooing of the cows in the pasture; I could hear the scrape of loose tin on the roof and the buzz of summer bugs, but nothing that sounded unusual. Without turning his head in our direction, Dad announced, "I think it's time y'all learned to fire Shorty."

We ran, tossing our fireflies into the air. We had heard and seen enough of Shorty's kick to know we didn't want to fire that shotgun. John was standing beside Dad when the announcement was made and Dad caught him by the sleeve of his shirt before he could escape.

The rest of us dashed up the stairs, kicked off our shoes and climbed out the window onto the front-porch roof, our favorite hiding place. The porch roof didn't have much of a slant, so you wouldn't roll off; you could watch the stars at night; and Dad had never thought to look for us up there. We tiptoed onto the tin roof and lay on our bellies, quietly slithering down a few feet behind Dad's chair so we could hang our heads over the edge and see what was happening.

John stood frozen beside the rocking chair, shaking his head.

"By God, shoot this gun!" Dad demanded. John tried to pull away but Dad held him tight.

"By God, shoot it!"

"I can't shoot it," John trembled, "it doesn't have a stock!"

"By God, shoot it!" Dad yelled. John shook his head again.

"Boy, don't make me get out of this chair; shoot it and shoot it *now!*" He lifted the shotgun into the air with one hand on the barrel, balancing it for John to take. John took a deep breath and stepped forward. But he didn't embrace the shotgun, he didn't butt the steel against his shoulder and he didn't check the sights; he just reached out, locked two fingers around the trigger and pulled. The shotgun exploded like a bottle rocket and the jagged steel hit Dad squarely in the forehead. He flipped backward in the rocking chair and rolled right off the porch into the yard. The shotgun twirled in the air, nicked the edge of the porch and landed on the ground at his feet.

John let out a cry and ran for Mother. We all gasped. David, who was lying on the roof next to me, shouted, "Holy shit!" Mother came running out of the front door and bumped into John.

"What's going on out here?" she cried. John pointed at Dad, who was prostrate on the ground, and yelled, "He's gonna kill me! He's gonna kill me!" Dad moaned and lifted his hand to his bleeding forehead and John jumped behind Mother, emitting a guttural sound: "Yaaaaaaah!" Mother walked down the front steps with John clutching her arm.

"I don't think he's going to kill anyone in that condition," she said.

By the time we crawled off the roof and got downstairs, Mother had a pillow under Dad's head and was wiping the blood from his forehead with a wet washcloth. She shook her head and had that disgusted look on her face. We crowded around and watched the bloody knot rise on Dad's forehead, shooting disapproving looks at John as if he had intentionally tried to kill our father.

But Dad raised his hand toward John, patted the air as if petting a kitten, and in a very sober voice whispered, "It's all right. It's all right. I told you to shoot it. I guess I didn't make myself very clear."

Glad

*D*ad and Uncle Jake decided to go into business together, a brand-new "get-rich-quick," "impossible-to-lose" moneymaker that wouldn't require hiring outside help. They would simply pay David, Willie, Doris Ann, John and me a dollar an hour to do the work, keeping all the money in the family. They mail-ordered forty thousand multicolored gladiola bulbs, rented two acres of Edson Tucker's soybean fields—the two acres closest to Uncle Jake's house—and had Edson disc under the stubble from last year's soybeans.

When the bulbs arrived, Dad and Uncle Jake walked into the tilled damp field and showed us how to plant them: push the trowel into the ground and pull up a plug of dirt, put the bulb into the hole—one bulb every six inches—and cover it with dirt.

"Make the rows twelve inches apart so yas can slip between them later and weed," Dad instructed, handing the trowels to me, David and Willie. Doris Ann and John were to drop the bulbs into the holes and cover them with dirt. Dad and Uncle Jake retired to the kitchen to drink Southern Comfort and talk of profits while we did the planting.

On the first day of planting we carried plastic mesh bags of bulbs into the field with dollar signs guiding our steps, each of us calculating how many hours of work it would take to purchase our dreams.

"I'm buying a motorcycle jacket," David said as he pushed the trowel into the ground and pulled up a cylindrical section of red earth. Doris Ann walked behind him, stopping at each hole to drop in a bulb and cover it with dirt. "I'm buying a bike," she said as she patted the mound of clay until it was firm.

"You're not gonna have enough money to buy a bike," David said sarcastically.

"I can buy a bike. If you can buy a motorcycle jacket, I can buy a bike."

"How you gonna buy a bike?"

"There's a twenty-inch at Mason's for thirty-four dollars; add tax, that's just thirty-six dollars. In thirty-six hours, I'll have enough. We've been out here an hour already and we haven't reached the end of the first row. We've got a jillion more rows to go. I could buy two bikes."

"You're not gonna be able to buy two bicycles," Willie said, but there was a hopeful look on his face as he pushed the trowel into the ground.

"I'm gonna buy a bike," Doris Ann said again.

Dad had bought Doris Ann a bicycle for Christmas while we were living in Kimberly. A red twenty-inch with butterfly handlebars. He and Mother had put Christmas on layaway at the Top Dollar Store that year and paid it off the week before Christmas. But on Christmas Eve Dad took the most expensive present—the bicycle—back to the store, exchanged it for cash and went to the bar. Doris Ann paced back and forth in the living room, too afraid to cry, as he ripped the snowflake Christmas paper from the large cardboard box. Mother tried to reason with him, but he was already half drunk. He lugged the box down the stairs, mumbling that he would buy her another one as soon as he got paid. Doris Ann sat on the steps in the cold the rest of the afternoon. Mother stayed up late Christmas Eve making Doris Ann a shirt out of a poodle skirt Aunt Lola had sent so she would have a present to open on Christmas morning. She even clipped the poodle off and sewed it on the back.

I got a Spirograph that year. I didn't usually share my things with Doris Ann; for one thing, she was interested in sports and I was interested in drawing. But we spent Christmas Day making pictures with the Spirograph. She sat beside me wearing her new blue shirt, spinning the clear plastic wheels around and around until the pen tore through the paper. The bike was never mentioned.

I pushed my trowel into the ground and dropped the plug of red dirt beside the hole as I calculated how much money I needed for what I wanted. We had changed schools when we moved to Anniston and I was now attending Oxford High School. But school was still school and I was already being tormented about my face again. Oxford High School wasn't any different from the last school I attended. In fact, it was worse. As my face grew more unsightly, the teasing worsened. And the kids mocked without remorse, as if my ugliness justified their behavior. They took my face apart and ridiculed it in pieces: lips, teeth, jaw. "Bucktooth Beaver. Bucktooth Beaver." I told myself it didn't bother me, that it made me strong. And maybe it did make me strong. I could pretend I didn't hear the heckling, I could pretend I didn't hear at all. I could put on my mother's vacant stare and not react to anything said to me—on the outside. But inside, I could hear my heart weeping. I didn't want to be strong. I didn't want to pretend. I wanted to be liked.

Some of the boys, mostly the school athletes, tortured me at every opportunity during the day. I had looked forward to attending high school, the excitement of changing classes. But changing classes was a nightmare. I cringed every time the bell rang. The heckling began before I made it to the door of one class and continued until I entered another. They pointed out each of my flaws as if I'd never looked in the mirror, starting with the most obvious one—my teeth—and on to the least offensive—the moles on my face. I didn't have acne, but that's what they called the moles; that, or worse.

"Hey, Pimpleface!" Bob shouted, pushing through several people to catch up with me in the hall. Several boys who weren't on the football team or basketball team but wanted to be part of the "in" crowd followed him. I was enraged by how willingly they went along, like sheep—too stupid to think for themselves. Even away from the school athletes, on the bus in the afternoons, they felt they could continue the harassment by proxy. In the past, they had emptied the contents of my purse out of the bus window and torn pages from my history book. They wanted to see me cry like Charlene, another girl they tortured.

Charlene wasn't particularly unattractive. She was poor. But it was a different kind of poor from mine. She had moved to Alabama from the hills of Kentucky. She spoke in a hillbilly dialect and barely passed her classes. She wore a puff-sleeved dress with overalls pulled over it, as if she couldn't make up her mind what to wear; and occasionally, she chewed tobacco. She was teased everywhere she went, even by students who didn't tease me. I felt sorry for her. I wanted to tell her they were thoughtless jerks. Tell her my theory that half of them would be looking through steel bars in ten years. I wanted to tell her not to let them make her cry. Never, never cry. But whenever I approached her, she fled. I didn't know if she was afraid of me, or if she thought being seen with me would make things worse for her.

When Bob called out to me, I straightened my shoulders and walked on, miming my mother's unaffected stare.

"Hey, Scarecrow!" Bob shouted, bumping against my shoulder. "Where'd you get those giant warts?" I ignored him and walked on. "Wait a minute, she's such a dog, those are probably ticks!" The boys laughed and slapped each other. "Hey, Bucky, can you eat popcorn through a fence with those teeth?" Bob asked, doubling over at his own joke. The others laughed and imitated, "Hey, Bucky Beaver." "Where you headed, Dogface?" "A face like yours could stop time." One of them reached out to slap the top of my books, but I moved them and he swatted the air. I turned into my English class, sat at my desk and once again made a list on notebook paper of the improvements I planned to make on myself.

1. Remove moles on face
2. Get braces on teeth
3. Fix face
4. Exercise to build legs and chest
5. Go to modeling school
6. Go to art school
7. Learn to play the piano
8. Learn to fly a plane

❧

I sat on my knees in the plowed field planting gladiolas and tried to calculate in my head. If I saved the money I earned each week, I would be able to get the moles removed from my face. My English teacher had had a mole removed from her arm. After class I questioned her about it. She told me the doctor had removed it in his office, and gave me his name. I used the phone in the school library to call Dr. Reynolds's office and ask how much it would cost to have several moles removed. "Eighteen dollars a mole," the receptionist had answered. Less than a bicycle for one mole, but twice as much as a bicycle for all the thick dark moles on my face.

I looked at the expanse of field we still had to plant. Doris Ann was right. We should be able to work every weekend until school got out just planting and watering, and then pull weeds and pick flowers all summer. I should be able to get all of the moles removed and maybe have enough left to talk to a dentist about my teeth. I didn't have much hope of making enough to afford the dentist anytime soon, so I started with what I could afford, the first item on my list: Remove moles.

We worked the gladiolas every evening after school and every weekend, without receiving a dollar in pay. "Yas have to wait till the flowers bloom to get paid," Dad said. "We got to bring in some money before we can shell any out." We were still hopeful and kept track of every hour worked. After school, we carried buckets of water from row to row, watering each lumpy mound until the glads shot up like javelins pointing skyward from the crusty red earth, smelling like fresh-cut lemongrass, renewing our spirits as we shuffled among them.

Summer came and much more of our time was invested in the money-making green daggers. Water and weed. Water and weed. The hot red earth stained the seats of our shorts, knees of our jeans and even our fingers a bright copper. Our noses and shoulders peeled from constant sun exposure and our hands felt like old leather. After weeks of work, the incessant heat and lack of pay took its toll; we began to argue.

"You've been sitting in that same spot for fifteen minutes, Doris Ann!" I fumed.

"I have not!"

"Yes, you have," David scowled.

"Well, Willie hasn't moved in an hour; and John's not weeding, he's just playing with ants!"

"I've weeded more than you have!" Willie cried.

"How am I supposed to weed this area if I don't get rid of the fire ants! You tell me that, Miss Priss!"

"You don't have to move every goddamned ant—just step on 'em!" David shouted.

"You step on 'em! They spread like crazy," John cried, "and they sting like wasps!"

"Well, I'm not weeding another weed until they've done as much as I have!" I whined, dropping on my rump into the dirt and folding my arms across my chest.

"You get over here and kill the ants then!" John cried.

"I'm not killing the ants! Make Doris Ann kill the ants! She's not doing anything!"

"I quit!" Doris Ann yelled. She stood up and threw her burlap weed sack on the ground. "We're never gonna get paid anyway!"

"We'd better get paid!" Willie yelled. He jumped up and rushed toward Doris Ann as if she were responsible for our lack of pay just because she said out loud what we had all been thinking.

"You're not quitting!" David bawled. He tossed a clod of dirt at Doris Ann that smacked her on top of the head. She tossed a clump back at him. "Nobody's quitting!" he barked, dodging the dirt bomb. "Now get back to work! And shut up! None of us are gonna get paid if these damned flowers die!"

But the flowers didn't die. At dusk, after the slender stalks had soaked up energy from the sun all day, we could hear them grow, jubilantly crackling as they pushed toward the stars. Solar furnaces. Cosmic rockets. The dark green spikes climbed toward heaven with spear-shaped leaves clinging to either side; cocoon-shaped florets clustered on the stems like pop-beads, opening into frilly, radiant colors that took our breath away. We stood in awe and sniffed the faintly lemon-scented air as they grew around us. We walked quietly between the rows as if the flowers were delicate visitors from outer space, identifying them by the colored pictures that were on their bulb bags: Plum

Tart, Bright Eyes, Rapid Red, White Cloud, Candy Cane, Littlest Angel, True Love, Scarlet Ruffles, Bread & Butter, Irish Lass, Blue Bonnet and First Kiss. Blue Sky, a large violet-blue flower with a heavy white throat, waved above the others, stretching to join the blue sky of its name; Bread & Butter sailed sharply against the sky in tones of yellow; and Rapid Red burned like stalks of fire, fading the terra-cotta earth from which it sprang.

The day the glads began to open, bursting to trumpet the sun, was the day Dad and Uncle Jake made their first inquiry to the local florists about when to cut the blooms. They had called originally to find out if there was a *demand* for gladiolas, but they had neglected to ask *when* the flowers should be cut. With the second call, they found out that the florists didn't want fully bloomed gladiolas; they wanted them when the florets were tightly wrapped cocoons, the bright flower tips just peeking from the green buds.

David cussed when he heard the news; we all did. *How could they have left the most important detail to guesswork?*

The next day we stalked the rows slashing the glads at the base of their stems with kitchen knives. We skipped the fully bloomed flowers and cut the ones that were still buds, sliced the crunchy green stems at an angle and wrapped them in newspapers for delivery to the florists. But three-fourths of the field stood fully blooming, a sight so glorious that motorists pulled to the side of the road and walked to the edge of the field, smiling as if they were seeing a mirage.

Once the florists had taken as many as they wanted, we cut the fully bloomed flowers, tied them in bundles, loaded them into Alice and Silas's hatchback Opal Cadette and—with Alice as our driver—peddled the flowers door to door in town. A dollar a dozen. The hope of payday evaporated in the Alabama sun. Our spirits were lifted only by the exclamations of joy the flowers brought from those who saw them. And almost everyone who saw them bought them: old ladies, old men, young couples, young women and young men, even two little girls who emptied their piggy banks to buy a bouquet that stood almost as tall as they did as a surprise for their mother. Gleeful with excitement, they shook eighty-seven cents from their pink plastic pig into my palm. Then walked away leaving the door wide open, hugging the gladiolas between them.

Alice was sympathetic toward us in our predicament. As she drove slowly down the city streets so we could knock on every door, she smoked and declared what morons Dad and Uncle Jake were. On the second day as our driver, she took dollar bills from our cigar-box cash drawer and bought us all ice cream cones—and a pack of cigarettes for herself. That same day she told us to keep a dollar for ourselves occasionally rather than rely on Dad or Uncle Jake to pay us later. "You'll probably never see a dime of it," she said. And she was right. At the end of the summer, I had twenty-one dollars, and most of that was from baby-sitting for Edson Tucker's children.

When school started in August, I used the phone in the library and called Dr. Reynolds's office again. Since I only had twenty-one dollars and the nurse had quoted me a price of eighteen dollars for the removal of one mole, I made an appointment for the removal of one mole. I didn't have a way into the city, so I rode the school bus to Oxford High School, sneaked down to the mall a block away from school and caught a city bus into Anniston.

Dr. Reynolds put both hands on my jaw and ran his thumbs over the dark thick moles around my nose. "You just want this biggest one removed?" he asked, moving his chair closer to mine.

"Yes, sir," I said.

He sat back, rolled his chair back a foot and looked at me. "Hey, didn't I buy some flowers from you Sunday afternoon? Some gladiolas?"

"Yes, sir," I said, "probably."

"My wife loved those things." He scooted the chair forward and ran his fingers across my face again. "You sure you just want the biggest one removed?"

"Yes, sir."

"Okay," he said, sounding a little perplexed.

"I'm gonna get the others off later," I explained. "As soon as I can."

"Oh," Dr. Reynolds said. He put a topical ointment over the area and sat back to wait until it began to tingle. "This might leave a little scar. Not much; just a little one." I shrugged my shoulders.

"So you're going to have them removed one at a time?"

"Yeah."

"It'd be a lot easier to get them all at once," he said, lifting a hypodermic needle from the tray.

"Yeah," I said, shrugging again.

Dr. Reynolds pushed the needle into my cheek and involuntary tears rolled down my face. He gave me several injections, dabbed the tears with a gauze square, then sat back to wait again.

"So you want *all* of them removed eventually?" he asked.

"Yes, sir," I answered. "I'm gonna make another appointment as soon as I save up enough money."

"I see," he said. He leaned back in the chair and crossed his arms over his chest.

"So, what grade are you in?"

"Ninth."

"Oxford High School?"

"Yeah."

"Got any brothers and sisters?"

I held up seven fingers.

"Good Lord," he said.

Dr. Reynolds burned off the mole, talking to me as he worked. "I know this hurts; it'll be over soon; just hold still." When he completed the task, he put a dot of ointment on the area, wiped the tears from my cheeks again and sat back.

"How 'bout I take them *all* off today. For the price of one. How would that be?" he asked. My heart leaped in my chest. I wasn't sure I had heard him correctly, but I nodded. All I could think of was clear, smooth skin.

Dr. Reynolds burned off six moles, wrote me an excuse for missing my morning classes, and had his receptionist take me back to school in his dark blue Cadillac.

She drove into the school parking lot, and I gathered up the extra bandages, ointment and doctor's excuse.

"Thank you," I said and opened the car door.

"You're more than welcome," she said, reaching out and touching my bandaged face. "I bet you're glad that's over."

"Very glad," I said, smiling and sliding from the soft leather seat.

Car Wash Blues

On perfect cue with Jim Croce's hit song "Workin' at the Car Wash Blues," we got jobs at an automatic car wash. A middle-aged couple, Cheryl and Gaylord Hood, who thought people would make a connection between their last name, Hood, and clean cars, owned it. So they named it Hood's Car Wash. As owners, they wanted to handle the money but not the nasty business of dissatisfied customers, delinquent employees or plumbing leaks, so they hired Dad for that. David, Willie, Doris Ann, John and I came with the package—five dependable employees to vacuum, scrub and deodorize the interior of the cars, buff the cars dry after they came through the wash, apply top coat to vinyl roofs and keep the towels washed and dried—all for the amazing price of a dollar an hour per child, paid under the table, of course. We worked every Saturday and Sunday for nine hours straight, no breaks.

On our first day at work, Duck and P.J., two black teenagers who ran the vacuum, called us to the back of the car wash and taught us how to walk and dance at the same time so we wouldn't be bored.

"If you ain't got something for your mind, you'll lose it," Duck said, sticking a fist-shaped black plastic comb into his Afro. He had been walking on the heel of his tattered white sneakers so they fit like bedroom slippers, but when he dropped his feet to the ground and twirled around, they moved like fancy dance shoes. He did a short jump and twirled again. He held his hands out for us to follow. We fumbled around, attempting the steps. He raised an exasperated eyebrow.

"Like this," he said, moving slowly, as if he were teaching a kinder-garten class. He repeated the steps a little faster and stepped aside. We tried again, bumping into each other as we twirled.

"Loosen up!" Duck instructed. He watched as we practiced the steps and spun around.

"Damn, you so white. You'll be exhausted by the end of the day! Loosen up; loosen up!" We practiced a few more minutes, imitating the lilt he gave the middle step, and actually twirled without knock-ing one another down. P.J. had been leaning against the vacuum, his baseball cap pulled over his eyes, chewing on a twig. We thought he couldn't see us, but once we had the steps down, he spit out the twig, shook his butt and said, "Now throw in a little hind end." We stopped and stared as he walked over. "You know, a little hind end," he repeated, shaking his butt again.

"A *little* hind end is all I have to throw in," I said, rotating my hips.

Duck shook his head in disapproval. "Y'all gonna be dead tired by the end of the day."

The cars came in droves, lining up bumper to bumper all the way out into Quintard Avenue. Duck sent the car owners inside to pay and wait, and as soon as they were out of sight, he changed the car radio station to WDNG, turning it up loud, blasting music from the speak-ers. Jim Croce's "Workin' at the Car Wash Blues" played every five minutes. We knew the words by heart and sang along with the radio: "Now I got them steadily depressin', low-down mind-messin' workin' at the car wash blues."

Duck checked the floorboards for change and pocketed the stray quarters and dimes—which he called "one hundred percent profit"—while P.J. vacuumed the seats. When the car was clean of debris and money, Duck sprayed a mist of cleaner on the inside of the windows and sent the car through the brushes. We waited on the other side, popping each other with damp towels whenever Mrs. Hood wasn't watching through the large windows. We sashayed behind the cars as they moved away from the twirling brushes, singing to the radio and daydreaming about what we were going to do with our money.

Occasionally Dad walked through the car-wash tunnel, checking pipes and water pressure—saw us dancing and yelled, "Stop flailing around and get to work!" We waited until he disappeared into the tunnel of mist and went right back to the shimmy step, quietly spending our fortunes in our heads.

At the end of each day, Mrs. Hood hand-delivered our fortunes to us in ocher coin envelopes: nine folded one-dollar bills. She furtively slipped them into our palms as we waited for Dad to lock up the building and turn on the alarm system. She had warned us never to tell anyone we worked at the car wash. If questioned, we were supposed to say we were just "hanging out." She said she was doing us a favor— that if anyone found out, she'd have to start taking taxes out of our pay.

I made eighteen dollars a weekend, seventy-two dollars a month— tax-free. Enough to at least *talk* to a dentist about my teeth. Mother agreed that something needed to be done; and on one of their few trips to town together, she convinced Dad by pointing out a middle-aged waitress with a weak lower jaw, protruding, rotten teeth and blistered lips.

"That's what Barbara's going to look like when she's thirty if we don't do something about her teeth."

The woman must have looked horrible because that night—for the first time—Dad mentioned sending me to the dentist.

Dr. Weaver was the orthodontist most of the "braces" kids at school used, so I made a consultation appointment, taking the first one available. David took me to my appointment in the 1959 Oldsmobile Dad had helped him buy. The floorboard was rusted out, and I watched the street flash by under my feet as we drove to Dr. Weaver's office. I prayed all the way to town that the car wouldn't stall, blow a tire, or fall to pieces until after I had seen the dentist.

Dr. Weaver rubbed his chin, shook his head and exclaimed, "This is by far the worst case I have ever seen!"

Peg, his assistant, agreed. She sat on one side of the dental chair and Dr. Weaver leaned over me from the other. Occasionally she took my hand, squeezed it and smiled at me.

"Look at this," Dr. Weaver said. He lifted my upper lip so she could see. "I've never seen a more severe protrusion." He tapped my tooth with the mirror. "Open up, honey." I opened and the assistant lost her smile.

"Pyorrhea," Dr. Weaver explained. "Gum disease at fifteen. Can you believe that? And this jawline! I've never seen anything like this in all my years of practice!"

After thoroughly examining my mouth, he called his wife, Phyllis, who was the receptionist, into the room to take a look. He stretched my cheeks with a dental mirror so she could see better. "Why, I don't know how she chews!" he exclaimed.

"It'll certainly be a challenge," Phyllis said, winking at me. I smiled and blushed.

"The upper portion of her face has grown too long," he said, running his finger along my cheekbones and chin. He shook his head. "I can't imagine what caused such a thing." He studied my face contemplatively and spoke as if I weren't in the room. "Malnutrition, maybe? She's thin as a rail. God knows, some parents just don't take care of their children." Dr. Weaver looked up, saw that I was embarrassed and cleared his throat. When he spoke again, he addressed me and used a softer, well-practiced tone.

"I can fix your bite; I don't know if it will ever be perfect, but it will be a world of change from what you have now." He touched my upper lip. "You have a short upper lip, which exposes a lot of gum line." He paused and then sighed deeply. "Well, right now, let's just work on getting you a decent bite so you can chew." He and Phyllis left the room. He came back a few minutes later with a dental plan and explained what I needed: six-year molars removed, two amalgam fillings, a cleaning and full braces for at least four years, maybe five. The cost: five hundred down and thirty-five dollars a month until the $2,300 balance was paid. I felt my jaw drop and the blood drain from my face. Mother had promised to help me with the dental bill, but the price sounded like a million dollars. And five hundred dollars up front was completely impossible. We never had that kind of money. Even the cars Dad bought were purchased by trade and weekly cash installments. I thought I was going to be sick and sat up in the chair. For a moment I was too astonished to say anything. *I'll look like this forever!* Finally, trying to climb from the chair, I said, "Well, thank you for seeing me, but I don't think I'll be able to get braces right now."

"Wait a minute," Dr. Weaver said, gently pushing me back into the chair. He sat down a moment and studied the bill, then went out to the receptionist's desk to talk to Phyllis. He returned a few minutes later with Phyllis and a new plan for payment. Phyllis explained the figures. "The five-hundred-dollar down payment has been added to the full cost of the braces and divided into thirty-five-dollar-a-month payments," she said, running the pencil along the sheet. "How's that?" She smiled and handed me the paper. I swallowed. It was an enormous amount of money, but if I looked only at the amount due each month—thirty-five dollars—it seemed possible. I nodded and smiled.

Mother was standing at the stove stirring a pot of beef stew when I got back from the dentist. When I handed her the bill, her jaw dropped—not as much as mine had when I saw it—but a definite drop. She stared at it for a long time, then touched the corner of the paper to the eye of the stove and burned it. She dropped the charred sheet into the trash. "Let's not tell your father how much this is going to cost. If he saw that bill he'd have a fit and call the whole thing off. If he asks, just tell him thirty-five dollars a month. He knows you're making that much."

For a year, I wore headgear: a metal bow that fit into the bands on my back molars and wrapped around my cheeks like a butterfly. The butterfly was hooked onto an elastic strap that fit snugly around my neck. I was supposed to wear it at night, but Dr. Weaver said the more I wore it, the faster it would pull my teeth back, so I wore it all day and all night. I wanted my teeth pushed back as soon as possible and I wanted the kids at school to *see* that my teeth were being fixed.

I continued to work with Dad at the car wash that year, every weekend like clockwork. So did the others. Mom and I paid the dentist. I handled most of the bill alone until Dad got fired from the car wash for drinking on the job. A few months later he got a civil service job repairing military weapons for the Anniston Army Depot. It was a much better job—more money and benefits—and Dad really seemed to be interested in *keeping* this job. But for us kids—it ended our income. The only money I had coming in was from baby-sitting Edson Tucker's kids on Saturday nights and that wasn't nearly enough. Mother made up the rest of the dental payment with grocery money. She never said anything about it.

I felt guilty about taking the money, but the guilt wasn't nearly as strong as the fear that the grocery money wouldn't be there, that I wouldn't be able to make the payments at all. *If I didn't have the money, would Dr. Weaver take off the braces? Would the tight metal bands rust on my teeth? Would my teeth move back to the crooked mess they were before?* Occasionally, when Dad was in a good mood or feeling proud that I had braces, Mother would hit him up for a payment, but as a rule he had already handed his money over to the bartender at the American Legion—his favorite haunt since moving to Anniston.

I was so afraid the braces would be taken back, repossessed—like one of Dad's cars, or the electricity—that I often slipped the elastic strap to a tighter notch than had been set by the orthodontist, hurrying the process. The added pressure tensed every muscle in my body, causing my hands to tremble. I felt like a jack-in-the-box wound to the point of snapping right out of my skin.

Out of the Night That Covers Me

*A*n old woman and what appeared to be her grown daughter came to our door just after dark. The cicadas screamed and in the wet, plowed fields, mud frogs sang maddeningly, as if trying to drown them out. Mother stood with one hand on the door, the other on the doorframe, blocking the entrance into our house, listening to the old woman's request. David stood in the corner behind the door with a loaded rifle. I, along with everyone else in the house, hid just out of sight, but close enough to see the two women. When Alice and I realized there were no men with them, we crept up behind Mother. The women were bathed in the light from the hallway and Mother's shadow fell across the face of the old woman who had just spoken.

"No," Mother said quietly. "They've taken twenty years off my husband's life. He won't be dropping the charges. Not now, not ever." She stepped back and closed the door, leaving the women in the dark.

A week earlier, Roscoe Mansfield and his mother had found Dad, severely beaten, lying on their porch in the middle of the night. They brought him home. "Mrs. Moss!" they shouted. "Mrs. Moss!" Doris Ann and I jumped from our bed, pulled on jeans over our nightshirts and ran down the stairs right behind Alice, Silas and David. Willie and John followed sleepily behind us. When we reached the hall, Roscoe and Mrs. Mansfield were carrying Dad into the living room; his arms were draped over their shoulders and their arms were wrapped around his chest. His bloody head hung to his bloody chest and a stream of blood ran from his boots where they scraped the floor.

For a moment Mother held her hand over her mouth, but then

helped carry him into the living room. After they laid him on the couch, Mrs. Mansfield began sobbing into a kitchen towel. "The dogs woke us up," she said. "They was barking somethin' terrible. He's beat so bad I wouldn't've knowed it was S.K., but he was conscious then, calling for you, Dorris." She paused while Mother shooed us back into the hall, allowing only Alice and Silas to enter the living room. Alice looked at Dad and also put her hand over her mouth. We crowded into the doorway, trying to get a better look, trembling with fear.

"He said it was them two boys that works for Jake: Henry Page and Lester Boswell," Mrs. Mansfield continued. "He said they thought he was dead and throwed him in a dry septic tank in Jake's backyard." Mrs. Mansfield wiped her nose on the kitchen towel and took a deep, staggered breath.

The septic-tank business was Uncle Jake's latest moneymaking adventure. After Dad had been fired from Hood's Car Wash and before he took the civil service job, he'd invested in Uncle Jake's new business and worked the summer pouring cement into iron septic-tank forms. Uncle Jake talked as if he and Dad were partners. But if they were partners, it wasn't equal partners. Uncle Jake drummed up business and took care of the books and Dad handled most of the physical labor. The small crew that Uncle Jake had hired didn't always show up for work, so Dad often had to take Stewart and David along with him to get the job done. Occasionally, Willie, Doris Ann and I had also been hired to set up the metal forms. But—due to the heavy machinery and Uncle Jake's drinking habits—Mother didn't think it was safe and wouldn't let us go unless it was absolutely necessary.

That evening Uncle Jake had insisted that Dad come over to talk business. David had been promised the use of the Cadillac for his prom that night, so, not wanting to let the car out of his sight, he had driven Dad over to Uncle Jake's and waited for him. When it started to get dark and Dad wouldn't leave, David got upset. Uncle Jake told David to go on to the prom; he said he would drive Dad home later.

Mother put her arm around Mrs. Mansfield and quickly escorted her to the front door. Roscoe followed. "I'll send one of the boys over later to let you know how he is," she said. "Thank you for bringing him home, Roscoe." She gave him a nudge toward the door, then ran to the kitchen, yelling for Alice to keep us out of the living room. She returned with a pan of hot water, a washcloth, a blanket and a pillow. She sat on the edge of the couch and began washing blood from Dad's face. She insisted that we stay in the hall, so we paced the floor—peeking into the room as we passed the doorway—listening to the water repeatedly being squeezed from a washcloth into the pan. The blood puddle on the floor terrified me. I rubbed my arms and tried not to look at it, but it drew my attention as if the deep red had a pulse of its own. I was afraid I would scream and Mother would slap me. I closed my eyes, rocked gently and began typing against my forearm: *All good men should come to the aid of their country. All good men should come to the aid of their country.* I opened my eyes. David stooped and touched the blood with his index finger. He stood up and examined the red dot. *All good men should come to the aid of their country.*

"I shouldn't have left him there," he said, wiping the blood onto his jeans.

"You couldn't have known," I said, pacing again. "Uncle Jake was supposed to bring him home. He said he would. It should've been just fine." I shuddered, rubbed my arms harder and started to type again. Shaking violently, I stumbled over my own feet and bumped into the broken apartment-size refrigerator that sat in the hall. David and Willie caught my arms before I fell; I could feel them trembling as they steadied me. The water trickled into the pan in the living room.

We crowded in the doorway to watch Mother work. The lamp at the end of the couch filled the room with a soft glow and she looked as if she were caring for a child with a fever. But we could see a little of Dad's battered head as she moved her arm. Only her composure kept me from screaming hysterically. *Mom won't let him die.* She looked over her shoulder at us and we moved back to our pacing.

"Do you think Uncle Jake is beat up, too?" I whispered.

"Maybe," David answered. "But who would beat them up?"

"Lots of people probably want to beat up Uncle Jake," I said. "He cheats people all the time." I stopped pacing and looked at David. "If Uncle Jake's not beat up, where is he?" David hunched his shoulders.

"How would somebody get Dad out of Uncle Jake's house if Uncle Jake's not beat up?" David mumbled.

"Maybe Uncle Jake wouldn't take Dad home and he was walking

home and somebody beat him up," Willie offered. Doris Ann had been holding her hands over her ears. She lifted her hands slightly away from her head and said, "Beat him up for what?"

"Maybe 'cause they wanted his billfold and all his money," John whispered.

"You don't have to beat a man to death to steal his billfold," David said crossly. He stopped pacing and looked at John. John's lips were blue and he shook violently. David pulled off his faded sweatshirt and tossed it to him. John caught it and climbed inside, letting his teeth chatter as he stuffed his arms into the sleeves. It wasn't really cold, but I wanted a sweatshirt too, or a blanket, something to wrap up in, but I was too afraid to go get it.

Mother shouted from the living room, "Barbara, mop up that blood in the hall!" She paused a moment and then added, "David, throw water on the porch and front steps and get that up, too!"

Mop up the blood! I can do it; I can mop it up without looking at it. I went to the bathroom, soaked the mop in the tub, dripped water all the way through the hall and dropped it onto the stream of blood. I pushed it back and forth, typing in my head. I ran back to the bathroom, rinsed out the mop and returned to the remaining puddles. This time I mopped slower, more deliberately, gaining control with the jabbing motion. I switched from typing the sentence from my typing book to typing poetry, accentuating each letter with the thrust of the mop: *Out of the night that covers me, black as the Pit from pole to pole, I thank whatever gods may be, for my unconquerable soul.*

Mother came out with the pan of red water and Dad's blood-soaked clothes. She went to the kitchen, threw the clothes into the trash and returned with clean water. By the time she returned, I had mopped up the blood, rinsed out the mop and was about to go over the floor again.

"Bring the mop," she said. "I want you to mop up the blood in the living room." I started to follow her. She stopped just inside the room and said, "But I don't want you to look at your father." I nodded and followed her into the living room, concentrating on Roscoe's boot prints, a mixture of red mud and red blood tracked across the linoleum.

"Is he going to die?" I asked in a whisper. I wasn't sure Mother had heard me. I pushed the mop over the largest puddle of blood, fighting the urge to look directly at my father.

A moment later she answered. "I don't know." She paused and then, wiping his face gently with the wet cloth, said it again. "I don't know." I mopped, teeth chattering, typing in my head poems I had heard Dad recite: *It matters not how strait the gate, how charged with punishments the scroll, I am the master of my fate: I am the captain of my soul.*

After David and I finished cleaning up the blood, Mother came out into the hall and told us all to go back to bed. Alice had been standing in the living room whispering to Silas all this time. She walked over to the couch, looked at Dad again, then came out into the hall.

"Silas and I are going to Pinson to get Stewart," she said. Stewart was home on leave from the Marines. He had just gotten married and was staying with his bride's parents in Pinson, Alabama—a two-hour drive from Anniston. Mother nodded and Alice and Silas rushed to the front door as if they'd been held after school and just let go.

"Watch the kids, Barbara!" Alice yelled as she dashed down the front steps toward the car.

Mother checked on Janet, who was asleep in Mom and Dad's bedroom across the hall, turned off the hall light and went back into the living room. There was nothing to do but go back upstairs. We hadn't turned on any lights when we came down and now we had to go back up the enclosed staircase in the dark. Clinging to one another, we climbed the stairs in order of birth: David, me, Willie, Doris Ann and John. David moved to the middle of the room, waved his arm overhead, found the string attached to the light and clicked it on. There were three rooms upstairs. Doris Ann and I shared one, Alice and Silas had the middle room and David, Willie and John shared the other. Alice and Silas slept on a mattress on the floor and the boys slept on army cots; Doris Ann and I shared a king-sized bed. We had found the big bed leaning against a tree by Edson Tucker's trash cans and carried it home a piece at a time: box spring, stained mattress, metal frame, and a slightly warped black crushed-velvet, cardboard-backed headboard. The bed was big enough and firm enough to sit on and play cards.

We lifted Alice's babies from the mattress on the floor and put them in the middle of our king-sized bed. Then all of us climbed in around them, sitting crossed-legged in a circle, our shoulders touching. It was quiet except for the cry of the cicadas in the fields and the gentle snore of the babies at our feet. David climbed off the bed and, after turning on every light as he went through the rooms, retrieved from his room the pink plastic tape player Stewart had brought him from overseas. He came back, turning off the lights, and plugged it in next to the bed. Stewart had also given him two eight-track tapes: Aretha Franklin and Neil Diamond. We sat in the dark playing Aretha Franklin's "Respect," and Neil Diamond's "Red Red Wine," speculating on what had happened. We went through all the possibilities over and over again, but the conversation always ended with David saying, "I shouldn't have left him." Eventually we sat trance-like, too tired to speak and too scared to sleep.

Daylight began to filter into the room, but no one moved except to rewind the tapes. Mother didn't call up the stairs for us to get ready for school. She didn't call us for breakfast either. The school bus came and left without us. Eventually we crept down the stairs, afraid Dad had died during the night. Mother was still sitting on the edge of the couch looking down at Dad. She looked very pale and very tired. She saw us peering into the living room and came out into the hall.

"He hasn't regained consciousness," she said, avoiding our eyes. She peeked into her bedroom to make sure Janet was still sleeping and walked toward the kitchen. "Let's make some breakfast. You'll feel better after a cup of hot tea."

Mother made hot, sweet tea, grits and fried eggs, gently mandating our morning chores as she cooked. "David, would you feed the dogs, please. Barbara, make everyone some toast. Doris Ann, can you put these pots and pans in the cabinet so I've got some room over here." We followed her orders, moving groggily as if hypnotized, then sat at the kitchen table miserably silent, glancing over our shoulders toward the living room as if a ghost might walk through the door at any moment. Mother put our plates in front of us and said, "I want every one of you to eat your breakfast this morning," a command she had never had to make before. Even after one of Dad's all-night sessions we were always starved. As a rule, Mother prepared individual plates for us so we couldn't take more than our fair share of food. Only Dad was allowed special treatment. He could have as much as he wanted and occasionally she made dishes just for him: oyster stew, pickled pig's feet, a medium-rare T-bone. The babies received the smallest allotment of food and sometimes part of that was eaten by a sneaky caretaker.

I picked at my breakfast. I no longer felt the need to scream. In fact, my mind had shut down. I couldn't think at all and wondered if I had gone crazy during the long night. Sounds seemed far away and indistinguishable. Mother's commands came as if from a deep well.

Janet wandered into the kitchen rubbing her sleepy eyes. Mother kissed her on the cheek, sat her in a chair beside me and put her breakfast in front of her. "Barbara stayed home from school today just to play with you," she said. She poured herself a cup of tea and went back to the living room. Janet climbed into my lap and I snuggled against her warmth. It felt good to be needed.

After breakfast, David corralled the others back upstairs and I took Janet out on the porch. I leaned against the ornate cast-iron post and stared down the long road, tracing it to the point where it slipped over a hill and was gone. A ubiquitous ringing, like the screaming cicadas, droned in my ears. I tried to think of what could have happened to Dad, put the puzzle pieces together, but couldn't focus; my mind drifted from *how* it all happened, to simply *that* it had happened. And I wondered what we would do now. Several times a year Dad would leave Mother. Or at least he made a pretense of leaving her; he always came back within a few hours. I had often wondered if we could get along without him. I knew families who received federal aid—food stamps and ADC—and had mentioned it to Mother, but she had said she was afraid Social Services would take her children away, divide them up and put them into foster homes. Maybe that's why we were all so careful to hide our situation—fear we'd be taken away. *Anything* was better than living without Mother.

Janet and I sat on the edge of the porch counting the cows in the distant pasture when Edson Tucker's pickup truck came barreling over the hill and down the road. He turned into our long driveway, sending a red dust cloud into the air, drove right between the two huge cedar trees that stood guard fifteen feet from the porch, and skidded to a stop at the front steps. Edson, dressed in his deputy-sheriff uniform, hopped out of the truck and slammed the door.

"Did S.K. get beat up last night?" he asked as he charged up the front steps two at a time. I nodded.

"Dad got beat up?" Janet asked. She tried to stand; I picked her up and followed Edson through the open front door. "Roscoe came to the house a while ago and said S.K. got beat near to death last night; but you can't half believe anything Roscoe says." I stopped in the doorway—the imaginary barrier Mother was enforcing—while Edson walked across the room to where she leaned over Dad's body. I backed up so Janet couldn't see. Mother sat up straight and Edson saw him. "Good God Almighty!" he cried. "Is he breathing?"

"Yes," Mother said.

"He been this way since Roscoe brought him home?"

"Yes."

"I'm getting an ambulance," he said. He turned to leave, paused for a second and turned back to Mother, handing her a ring of keys coated with dried blood. "I found those on my front porch. They S.K.'s?" Mother nodded and flipped through the keys with her fingers.

"He must have tried to wake me up. When he couldn't, he crawled all the way over to the Mansfields'." He walked swiftly out of the room, brushing past me in the doorway. He nodded and said, "I'll be right back," and dashed down the steps toward his pickup.

Janet's face clouded. I carried her back to the front porch, soothing her:

"It's all right. Dad's fine. He just fell."

"Is he in there with Mom?" Janet asked, pointing toward the living room.

"Yep. He's asleep on the couch," I coaxed. Janet tried to wiggle out of my arms. "No, we can't go see him. He's asleep. Let's get the checkers and play out here on the porch." I dashed inside and got the checkers game, returning to catch Janet just before she made it to the front door.

We played several rounds of checkers before the ambulance broke the horizon—silent, but with flashing red lights.

"They're here!" I shouted. Mother came outside and watched as they sped down the road toward us.

"Take Janet upstairs, Barbara. And make sure they all stay upstairs," she said, turning back to the living room. I carried Janet upstairs and put her on the bed with Darrell and Chris, Alice's children, who were just waking up. From the window I watched the ambulance speed into the yard.

"I'm going down," David said. He had been leaning into the window frame, watching the road all morning, just as I had been doing on the porch.

"Mom said not to," I said. He went anyway. Willie and John followed him. A minute later Doris Ann helped me guide Darrell, Chris and Janet down the stairs. We huddled in the hall, watching as they carried Dad out the front door and put him in the back of the ambulance. Mother climbed in beside him. David ran after the paramedics. "Is he going to live?" he shouted. The paramedics shut the back doors and quickly climbed into the cab.

"We don't know," the driver answered. "He's pretty bad. Call up to the emergency room and they'll let you know something as soon as possible."

"We don't have a phone!" David shouted as the paramedic slammed the ambulance door. They sped away, lights flashing and siren shrieking, trailing a cloud of thick red dust.

We moved from the hall to the porch to watch the ambulance as it flashed down the road and out of sight. David held Alice's oldest son, Darrell, and I held Chris, the younger one. Janet wrapped her arms around my legs so I couldn't move. We were still standing there, staring, when Alice's car raced down the road. Silas lurched into the driveway and Stewart opened the car door before it had fully stopped. He jumped out and ran up the steps. David stopped him. "Edson came. They took him to the hospital in an ambulance."

"She's with him," I said, answering Stewart's next question before he got it out of his mouth. He ran back down the steps. Silas had cranked the car and was backing up by the time Stewart jumped into the backseat. Alice leaned out the front window and shouted, "Watch the babies!" as they sped away.

Darrell started to cry.

"Is Dad going to die?" Janet asked, tearing.

"Oh, no," I said, soothing the babies. "He just needs to see the doctor for some medicine." I walked to the edge of the porch and stared into the soybean fields. I felt vulnerable, like an easy target for a shotgun. Maybe Henry Page and Lester Boswell *were* hiding out there, waiting for a chance to kill us. David walked over beside me and glanced into the fields.

"There's no telling what's going on, or what might happen," he whispered. "Let's get everybody inside, at least out of shooting range." We herded everyone back inside, even the dogs. We gathered the tape player, the skateboard, some toys and the checkerboard into the living room and set up camp. I played checkers with Janet while Doris Ann read to Darrell and Chris. Willie and John took turns riding around and around the room on the skateboard, stopping occasionally to look out the window for the goons.

David loaded Dad's rifle and stood in the hall, just out of sight, keeping watch through the small square windows of the front door. Janet hadn't been separated from Mother since we moved to the two-story house and she was anxious, turning this way and that, listening to our whispers and asking for Mother in a worried voice. Darrell and Chris did the same. Even though Alice was their mother, their grandmother was the one who took care of them all day.

Just before dark, Alice, Silas and Stewart returned. I picked up Janet and, with the other kids crowding behind me, opened the front door for them. Stewart climbed from the car, stumbled toward the porch and collapsed on the top step, trembling. He dropped his pale face into his hands. We thought Dad had died and all of us began to wail, "Is Dad dead?" All three babies burst into tears. Alice climbed the steps waving her arms.

"Hush, now! They think he's going to live," she said. I caught my breath and tried to calm my pounding heartbeat and soothe the babies at the same time.

"Everything's all right. Hush," she said, taking Chris from Doris Ann. "I've got a headache the size of Texas." The babies quieted. "Mother's going to stay up there tonight but she'll be home tomorrow." She looked at David, who was standing in the doorway holding the rifle. "Get that thing away from the kids, David," she stormed. David took the rifle into Mother's bedroom and Alice went inside, motioning for us to go back in and leave Stewart alone. I glanced over my shoulder at him as I followed her through the door.

"The police came to the hospital," she continued. "They waited until Dad regained consciousness and questioned him. They've got a warrant for Henry Page's and Lester Boswell's arrest. Dad could just barely get out who did it. He didn't mention Uncle Jake. Of course, he wouldn't. He's always been blind where Uncle Jake is concerned." She paused for a moment, her thoughts drifting. Then she looked up and said, "I've never seen anything like that in my life! I don't know how he's alive . . . except he's too damn mean to die." She walked toward the kitchen and stopped. "You kids stay in here and leave Stewart alone!" She nodded for me to follow her. Doris Ann took Janet and hovered in the doorway with Willie and John, staring out at Stewart. David broke through the crowd, walked across the porch and sat beside him. I followed Alice to the kitchen. She pulled a box of macaroni from the cabinet and turned on the stove. She leaned close to me, covered Chris's ears and whispered, "Stewart got hysterical when he saw Dad." Chris pushed her hands away and wiggled to get down. She eased him to the floor and reached for a pan. "I thought they were gonna have to lock him up."

Dad stayed in the hospital for three weeks. He had a concussion from being hit over the head with a metal pipe, five broken ribs and a fractured clavicle. His body was covered with severe contusions from being punched, kicked and hit. His eyes and mouth were split in the corners as if cut with a sharp knife. As horrible as he looked on the outside, the doctors were more concerned about the internal injuries to the stomach, pancreas, spleen and liver. They told Mother the best they could do was watch and wait.

We took turns staying with Dad so that he was never left alone in his hospital room. The first time I stayed with him, I didn't look at him at all. I flipped through a magazine or watched TV. The second time, I glanced at him twice with my eyes squinted, catching only a glimpse of him. Finally I mustered up the courage to look right at him. It wasn't nearly as difficult as I thought it would be because he was completely unrecognizable; it somehow made it bearable—as if it weren't really him. I sat in the chair next to his bed and studied the purple face, the swollen cheeks, eyes, nose, mouth and ears, searching for traces of my father. Even his hands were unrecognizable, raisin-black balloons.

Two days after Dad was hospitalized, Henry Page and Lester Boswell were arrested. Two other men had been beaten that same night; both had died. Dad was the only witness, the only one who connected Henry and Lester to the murders. The marks on Dad's body matched the marks on the dead men—and Dad was alive. He was alive but he was terrified, certain Henry and Lester, even from jail, would have him killed. When he recovered enough to speak, he spoke of dropping the charges.

"We will *not* drop the charges!" Mother cried. I wasn't sure if her courage came from his weakened state, or because he was what mattered most to her, but she was adamant and would not be moved.

Edson Tucker tried to prove Uncle Jake was an accomplice to Dad's beating. He had been hit on the head while sitting at Uncle Jake's table and had been dragged into the backyard where the beating occurred. Uncle Jake had turned a deaf ear. And, after Henry and Lester had thrown Dad into the dry septic tank, Aunt Nina had mopped up the blood from the floor. But not very well. The police found it caked between the boards of the kitchen, the back porch, and soaked into the concrete steps.

Edson Tucker was convinced that Uncle Jake had paid Henry and Lester to beat Dad, but Dad refused to bring charges against his brother. He told the police that Henry and Lester had acted on their own. Still, that did not explain why Uncle Jake had not tried to stop them, had not called the police and had Aunt Nina clean up the blood.

For the next few weeks I felt as if I were walking in a thick fog with someone following behind, about to grab me. I looked over my shoulder constantly, even at school, where it felt safer. In class, I fell asleep because I was too afraid to sleep at home. Nobody slept. Alice and Silas argued in the middle of the night. The boys got up and looked out the window every time the dogs barked or car headlights beamed on the walls. We shared nightmares of being chased, stabbed or lost, and compared our horrors as we waited for the school bus in the morning. I dreamed the same dream three nights in a row: A man was chasing me with a kitchen knife. I came to a steep rock cliff and jumped down to a small pine tree wedged in the rock ten feet below. The man who had been chasing me reached the cliff. He stood and looked out over the valley. If I didn't make any noise, he wouldn't find me; but if he didn't find me, I had no way to get back up.

Willie dreamed of being a stigmatic. (We were baptized in the Methodist Church.) In the dream he was standing on the porch roof and blood dripped from his palms onto the corrugated tin. He squatted and examined the blood spots; there were bullet holes in the middle of each spot.

We didn't share these nightmares with Mother, but she knew we were afraid.

"Why are you looking out that window?" she asked, glancing at me, then at David, who was peeking out the other window. Willie, Doris Ann and John stopped what they were doing and fixed their eyes on Mother.

"The dogs are barking," I said, dropping the curtain.

"The dogs are always barking," Mother said, putting her hands on her hips and glancing at each one of us. "Now I want this nonsense to stop. Every time the dogs bark or a car goes down the road, you panic. There's nothing for you to be afraid of. Henry and Lester are in jail."

I stared at the floor and said, "They could get some of their brothers or cousins to kill us."

"That's ridiculous," Mother said. "Henry and Lester aren't the least bit interested in harming you."

To prove we had nothing to fear, she sat in front of the windows, worked in the garden without looking up when a car drove by and stood on the porch in the dark. But the fear held. We startled each other when we opened doors, walked into a room unexpectedly or dropped schoolbooks on the floor. We jumped every time the wind blew and every time the dogs barked. And every time the cicadas held their breath, we did, too.

Dad came home from the hospital and we were even more disquieted. His face was black and swollen; sickly looking bruises covered most of his body. Mother put him back on the couch in the living room, but every half hour he got up, gasping for air, to stare into the fields. He was so frightened that he had David move his army cot downstairs and sleep next to him. When Dad woke during the night, which was often, he'd wake David and send him out into the dark with a rifle to patrol around the house.

The morning after the two women came to our door and spoke with Mother, Dad, once again, decided to drop the charges. He said that we would move far enough away that we couldn't be found. He sat at the kitchen table while Mother cooked breakfast and went over and over the night he was beaten, trying to make sense of it.

"Jake and I were arguing," he explained, "almost coming to blows. But you know Jake would never really hurt me. Henry and Lester— they were working for Jake, you know—they thought they were doing the right thing. They thought they were doing what Jake would've wanted 'em to do. They didn't know no better." He lit a cigarette and coughed into his fist, holding his ribs with his left hand. "Maybe I should quit smoking," he muttered, crushing the cigarette into a saucer. He coughed again and wheezed air into his lungs. "They thought they were doing right, Dorris," he said. Mother stood at the kitchen sink peeling potatoes with a kitchen knife. She listened but would not budge. "We are *not* dropping the charges," she said flatly.

"Maybe I should quit smoking," Dad said again as he tapped another cigarette from the pack.

I milled around in the kitchen, listening to them talk. It surprised me that Mother was taking such a stance about the charges. She usually let Dad make her decisions, but, supported by Edson Tucker, she held firm this time. I listened as she spoke, felt myself grow taller, and agreed. *She's right! We should be strong, testify in court and put these men in jail where they belong!* Then I listened to Dad, felt myself shrink like a cowering dog, and agreed. *We could move! Start over. Get out of here before the goons kill us all!* But if we ran away, we'd always be looking to see who was following us, suspecting everybody. Ordinary events would become nightmarish.

While Dad was still in the hospital and Mom was there with him, two young men had come to our house. We were so scared we didn't want to answer the door, thinking it might be Henry and Lester, but they knocked persistently. David hid with the rifle and Willie and I peeked through one of the little square windows on the front door. I knew Henry and Lester; Doris Ann and I had seen them many times at Uncle Jake's. They had even given us a ride home in the back of their truck once. The two men at the front door were much younger than Henry and Lester. They looked like teenagers.

"They could be hired thugs," Willie whispered.

"One of 'em has on a MOMA T-shirt," I whispered back. "I don't think thugs'd wear an art museum T-shirt."

"We're gonna open the door," Willie said, signaling for David to shoot if necessary. We opened the door just wide enough to hold the two of us—jittery, ready to jump straight to heaven if they pulled a gun.

"Is that LeMans in the front yard for sale?" one of the men asked. We stared at him, not comprehending what he was talking about. He turned and pointed at that broken-down LeMans that Stewart had purchased while he was home on leave; it was sitting on blocks and surrounded by weeds. "Is it for sale?" Willie and I leaned forward and looked at the car as if we had never seen it before. Just then David— enticed from his corner by the mention of automobiles—stepped out, the rifle forgotten but still cradled in his arms. The young man who had been asking about the car grabbed the other man and pulled him back down the steps.

"That's okay!" he cried. "We don't want anything; we don't want anything!" They ran back to their car and both of them piled in through the driver's-side door. David walked out on the porch.

"It's five hundred dollars!" he shouted. The young men cranked up their car and threw dirt in a wide arc getting out of the yard. David ran down the steps and into the yard, rifle still cradled in his arms, and shouted, "It's five hundred dollars, cash money, and the wheels are in the barn!"

That's how it would be if we tried to move away; we'd suspect the mailman, the paper boy and young men who tried to buy broken-down cars. Mother's way was better and, as she put it, "was right."

Blind Spot

*D*ad didn't stop smoking, but, except for getting himself to and from work, he did stop driving. Before the beating, he had had me or David drive for him occasionally, but now it was all the time, especially if he was going to the bar or the bootlegger. He was afraid to be alone, and being terrified myself, I understood and willingly drove him wherever he wanted to go.

I took my left hand from the steering wheel to point out a flock of egrets flying just outside the driver's-side window and the Cadillac veered off the road.

"Hey! Hey!" Dad shouted, grabbing the wheel and slowly easing the car back onto the road.

"You gotta pay attention, Southpaw," he said.

"Sorry." I tried to concentrate on the road in front of me. When Dad had brought me along as his driver that day, he'd explained, as I pulled slowly out of the yard, "I don't want to get picked up without a license." But he hadn't had a driver's license in twenty years. I had just turned sixteen and didn't have one either, but he didn't think they would put me in jail. "They might give us a warning," he said. We drove for hours through northern Alabama and then Mississippi. We didn't know where we were and Dad liked it that way. Once we were lost he quit looking over his shoulder, quit talking about the trial, and concentrated on teaching me to drive.

"There's a blind spot on your left," he said. "Always look behind you before moving into the left lane." He repeated this information every time I climbed behind the wheel, I guess because I was his only left-handed child: "Southpaw, Sinister, Gawky," he chided. "There's a blind spot on your left."

In small towns like Attalla, Tuscumbia and Iuka, we stopped at beer joints: ratty, shingled boxes with fluorescent beer signs in the windows. I liked to go because, as the driver, he treated me better than when I was just part of the horde of noisy kids around his house. And once we were sitting in a bar, he bought me peanuts and Cokes and gave me money: quarters for the jukebox.

Just before we reached the town of Corinth, Mississippi, he told me to pull over at a bar named Sarsaparilla's, a square, squat little building completely covered in bottle caps. Most of the caps were rusted and the brand couldn't be read anymore. Everything about Sarsaparilla's was rusty, including the "RC Cola" sign, the "Jazz" sign, two out-of-commission gas pumps that sat on a block of concrete in the middle of the parking area, the toothless bartender and the customers. We walked inside and sat at the bar, ignoring anyone brave enough to stare directly at Dad's battered face, or my butterfly-embellished crooked one. Since Dad had come home from the hospital, I had gotten somewhat used to how he looked. But strangers—especially women—sucked in their breath when they saw him for the first time. Dad ordered a Pabst Blue Ribbon for himself and an RC for me. I sipped my Coke, breathed the hypnotic mixture—stale smoke and alcohol—and watched the goings-on in the mirror behind the bar. I swiveled my stool back and forth, slowly, to glimpse a couple touching in the corner and a man passed out at a table. Right behind me two men argued over who had the fastest car and the straightest gun. Occasionally someone glanced curiously at Dad as he sipped his beer.

"Your braces are working out just fine," he said, lifting his beer in a salute to me. He turned and looked at a man at the end of the bar who was staring at us and the man turned away. Dad took a sip of his beer. "Since they pulled them molars, your teeth are straightening up pretty fast. Looking real good." He took another sip of the beer and made a sour face. "You'll look good as me before long." He placed the beer back on the bar. "That's without the bruises, of course." I flashed him a butterfly-metal smile, blushed and turned away.

My teeth *were* getting better, fast. My back teeth made contact when I chewed and my lips no longer bled at night. The progress of the braces caused a constant sense of excitement, like a buzzing, through my body. I had started looking at people when they spoke to me, not for very long, just a glance, but still—*looking* at them. I felt like the gladiolas that we planted, when they shot toward heaven: crackling, popping and full of promise.

One of the men who claimed to have the fastest car got up from the table behind us and sat next to Dad at the bar. He was a lot taller than Dad, but they were about the same age, and recognized each other as old military men.

"Iwo Jima and Saipan," the tall man said as he settled onto the barstool and stuck out his hand. Dad shook his hand.

"Saipan and Tinian," he said.

"Marine?" the tall man asked.

"Marine. You?"

"Same. Wounded?"

"Shot in the arm and bayoneted in the chest. Saipan," Dad answered, holding out his fist as if for proof.

"Well, I'll be damned. I was wounded on Saipan," the tall man said. He started to sock Dad on the shoulder but stopped short. "You look like you been in a recent war," he said, pointing to Dad's stitched, bruised and swollen face.

"Ah, just a little accident," Dad said, reaching into his pocket. He pulled out a fist of change and flipped a couple of quarters on the bar. I snatched them up, slid off the stool and moved toward the jukebox, leaving them to discuss the battle on the island of Saipan. They were comparing Purple Hearts as I pumped the quarters into the jukebox. I played Frank Sinatra, Loretta Lynn, Patsy Cline and Patsy Cline again, rocking back and forth and flipping through the selections as the music vibrated the floor. I was safe. We were far enough away from home, and lost enough, for me to stare dreamily at the album covers and fantasize about being a beautiful singer like Patsy Cline. I closed my eyes, swayed to the music and pretended I was the one singing the syrupy-sweet moans.

I drank two more RCs and Dad drank four more beers. He bought the first two himself, the third was bought by the tall man, and the last by the bartender, another WWII veteran. The bartender tried to buy him a shot of whiskey, but Dad refused it, asking instead for another beer. He had been avoiding whiskey ever since he got beaten up, swearing that it smelled like Uncle Jake's kitchen and prompted memories of the very moment he was hit on the head. When he first regained consciousness in the hospital and began to talk, he said he remembered Uncle Jake laughing just before he was hit. Later, when the police took his statement, he had no recollection of having said such a thing.

At dusk I convinced Dad it was time to head home. I didn't really want to leave, but I knew Mother would be waiting for us, keeping our dinner warm. We opened Sarsaparilla's bottle-cap-studded front door, waved and promised our new friends we would return soon.

I climbed behind the wheel, cranked the car and asked for directions. I didn't remember which way we had come and Dad didn't care. He was much happier lost in Mississippi, talking to a WWII veteran and sipping a beer, than back in Alabama with the constant fear of the goons and the knowledge that his brother was at least partially to blame.

"Drive east," he slurred. "Don't matter what road, just drive east. We'll drop south when we get into Alabama." I backed the car out of the parking area and pulled onto the road, heading east, mile after mile in the general direction of home. For a while Dad talked about the war, repeating part of the story I had heard him tell the tall man at the bar.

"Me and three of my buddies got separated from our platoon. We couldn't see a damned thing. Shells were exploding all over the island. We were scared; thought we were gonna die. We got shot. I got shot in the arm, Sully in the chest, and Nick got it twice in the thigh. Then they rushed us and used their bayonets. Later, back at the hospital, we found out we were some of the few who made it out alive. Most of our platoon had been killed. If we hadn't got separated, we'd've died with 'em." He fell silent and slumped in the seat.

It got darker. Trees faded into clumps of menacing shadows. Dad was falling asleep and—not wanting to be alone—I tapped his arm. He jumped, sat up straight and glared out the window as if someone were out there in the darkness. He looked over his shoulder, into the rearview mirror, and then settled back down. A few minutes later he began to talk, only his voice was strange—deeper, less intoxicated—and he told me a story I had never heard before.

"I was married before your mother," he said, turning his face toward the passenger-side window, "to a woman named Margie." I slowed down and glanced at him, catching his reflection in the dark window. His eyes were closed. "We had twins that died shortly after they were born. Somethin' wrong with 'em. I don't know what." He was quiet for a moment, then glanced at me. "She was hit by a car and killed while I was fightin' on the island of Saipan. Already buried by the time I got the news."

I drove in silence, too startled to think of anything to say. I knew he had been married before, but it was one of those things we knew better than to discuss out loud. After a few minutes he pointed ahead. "Here. Pull over at that service station just ahead; I'll show ya somethin'." He began rolling up his right sleeve as I pulled into the parking lot and stopped under a streetlight. I knew he was going to show me his tattoo and I felt uneasy. I liked to look at the thin black lines filled in with shades of reds and greens, but if I looked at his tattoo, I would also see the sickly bruises that covered his arm. The bruises made my stomach hurt.

Dad held his arm out for me to examine, turning it back and forth. He pointed to the large red tattoo in the middle of his lower arm. I looked at the tattoo and tried to ignore the purple bruise underneath. I had seen this tattoo many times before: my mother's name, encircled in a fully bloomed red rose. A pale blue ribbon under the faded blossom trailed "Rose of the Family."

"That's for your mother. The rose of the family," he said.

"Yeah," I said, nodding my head. I looked closer, examining the tiny veins in the pale green leaves, the thorns on the stem. Dad chuckled.

"When you were little-bittie, you used to put your nose against my arm and try to smell that rose."

"I remember that," I laughed. "And I thought I could really smell roses. Later, after I smelled real roses, I realized that was the smell of axle grease." He chuckled again and pushed the sleeve down.

"Yeah, that was back when I worked in the garage just down the street from our house in Eastaboga. Alice used to stand on a box and hand me tools as I worked. She was somethin'; she knew all the tools.

I'd ask for a crescent wrench and she'd ask me what size." He chuckled again as he buttoned his right cuff and unbuttoned his left. He pushed his sleeve as far as it would go and twisted his shoulder around to the light. There, high on his upper arm, circled by a deep green bruise, was the tattoo I had heard whispers about, the one he kept covered with an undershirt at all times. Thick navy-blue block letters spelled the name MARGIE. A black line drawn through the middle crossed it out. He tapped it gently with his swollen right index finger and said, "That was for her." He held it in the light and twisted it farther so he could see it, too. Then he rolled his sleeve back down and buttoned the cuff.

I didn't know what to say. I put the car in gear and drove into the darkness.

"I can tell you about *her*," he said, almost whispering, "because you'll understand, because you're left-handed." He paused, then added, "She—Margie—was left-handed. She would a' liked that."

I drove Dad to many bars after that night, hoping he would tell me the story of Margie again. There were so many questions I had thought to ask. *What did she look like? Were the twins girls or boys? What did my mother think about it?* But Dad never mentioned her again. I pondered the link he made between us: left-handed, southpaw, sinister, gawky. Most of all, I wondered if he had constantly told her about the blind spot on her left.

By the time Dad testified in court against Henry and Lester, the bruises and balloon-like swelling had faded. He looked older, thinner, and grayer at the temples. The cuts on his face had healed into scars that accentuated the lines around his eyes and tightened the corners of his mouth. Mother went to court with him, to make sure he got there and didn't slip away in fear to the bar.

"You can do this," she said. "I know you are strong enough to do this."

Lester Boswell received two sentences: life and ninety-nine years. He would be eligible for parole in twenty-five years. Henry Page received ninety-nine years and would be eligible for parole in fifteen years. Henry testified that Dad hadn't done anything to them, he had just made them mad and was in the wrong place at the wrong time. When I heard this, it made everything more confusing. *What about Uncle Jake? Why had he not stopped them?*

By the end of the trial, Dad had gone back to work at the Anniston Army Depot. We had gone back to our routine at school. But we were suspicious of strangers and scared of the dark. We no longer walked the roads along the bean fields or played kick-the-can in the yard at night. If an unfamiliar car turned into the driveway we ran for Mother's protection; and, though we tried not to, we paused and held our breath every time the cicadas stopped screaming.

Several days after Henry Page and Lester Boswell received their sentences, Dad went back to Uncle Jake's.

Russian Roulette

A few months after the trial, Aunt Nina died of a heart attack. Uncle Jake didn't seem to be very upset. In fact, she had fallen early in the day and he had left her lying on the floor until Dad arrived that evening. Uncle Jake didn't want the expense of an ambulance and couldn't lift her by himself, so he had waited until Dad could help him. Dad called the ambulance. Aunt Nina died the next morning.

Shortly after the funeral Uncle Jake gave us a freezer filled with pork and beef. Then he gave us a color television set. He made a trade with his son Kyle: his new stove and refrigerator for Kyle's old battered ones. He gave Mother a pitcher and bowl that had belonged to our grandmother, and he gave me a framed poster of Leutze's *Washington Crossing the Delaware*. It was unlike Uncle Jake to give anything away. He was what Dad called "tight." Usually, he even counted the Coke bottles when we visited, making sure we didn't take one with us when we left. When his newfound generosity began, we thought he was sorry for what had happened to Dad and was trying to make up for being too drunk to keep him from being hurt.

Then, once again, Roscoe Mansfield came to our house bringing bad news. He came in the back door, into the kitchen, without even knocking. He stuffed his hands into his pant pockets, stared at the aluminum tea bowl in Mother's hand and spoke directly to it, informing the bowl that Uncle Jake's house had burned during the night. Then he nodded his head and backed out the door. David and I rode over with Dad to see what could be done. Uncle Jake was sitting in his car with the driver's-side door open. He held his head with both hands as if it hurt terribly. The house was completely gone, burned to the ground. Smoke still drifted lazily from the charred rubble.

"Where's the police?" Dad asked as we climbed from our car.

Uncle Jake rubbed his head. "They've already come and gone."

Dad propped his arm on Uncle Jake's open car door and looked at the burned square patch. David and I squeezed into the space next to Dad and stared into the car at Uncle Jake. He pulled his glasses off, laid them on the dash and rubbed his eyes. He was tinted a sooty black except for the area around his eyes that had been protected by his glasses. He reached out and patted David on the shoulder, then smiled at me. He looked like a giant hoot owl.

"The fire engine, too?" David asked.

"The fire engine, too. There wasn't anything left for them to put out when they got here," Uncle Jake said. "By the time I walked all the way to Edson Tucker's to use the phone the whole damned thing was gone." He paused and held his chest as if he were having a heart attack. We had seen him do that countless times before. He held his chest when his oldest daughter moved her three younger sisters out of the house; he held his chest when the bait farm didn't make us rich and when the gladiolas didn't either; he held his chest when Dad got beaten up, when he was accused of being part of it and again, with relief, when he didn't go to jail.

"I stood and watched my whole life burn to ashes," he moaned, pulling himself up by the steering wheel and throwing his legs to the ground. He eased himself from the car, huffing and puffing, and waved one arm toward the charred remains. "All that's left of my life," he sighed.

Dad pushed a pack of cigarettes from his shirt pocket, tapped out a couple and offered one to Uncle Jake. Uncle Jake shook his head, leaned back into the car and pulled an almost full box of cigars from under the front seat. David elbowed me in the ribs to make sure I had noticed that Uncle Jake's prized Upmann cigars, which were usually locked in his rolltop desk, were now under the front seat of his car. I nudged him back. Uncle Jake lifted two cigars from the box, dropped one into his breast pocket and stuck one between his teeth. He chewed it and rolled it to the corner of his mouth. Dad held his

Zippo lighter out to light Uncle Jake's cigar, then lit his own cigarette. Uncle Jake blew smoke into the air. The sweet cigar smoke smelled stronger than the drifting smoke from the charred house and I backed away.

"I don't know how you can smoke them damned cigarettes," Uncle Jake said, waving his cigar in Dad's face. Dad looked at his feet, drew deeply on the cigarette, caught my eye and winked. He lifted his head, sent a row of smoke rings into the air and stared at what was left of the house.

David and I walked toward the large square of smoldering ashes. It was still hot, so we stopped a few feet away. David picked up a couple of rocks and threw one into the fire.

"Don't mess with it, Dave!" Uncle Jake shouted. He leaned against the door of the car and ran his hand through his thinning hair. "My insurance man is coming out this morning to inspect!" David nodded and dropped the other rock. We walked around the remains of the house to the backyard, where rows of metal septic-tank forms waited to be poured with cement and the tire swing still dangled from a tattered rope.

"He burned it," David whispered.

"Yep," I whispered back.

"Where do you think he's gonna live now?"

"With us," I whispered.

"Yep."

Uncle Jake moved in with us that afternoon. Mother made the living room into a bedroom: covered the couch with sheets, and folded his change of clothes onto the arm of the large Naughahyde chair that didn't quite match the couch. Uncle Jake had told us that the fire ran through the house quickly and that he had had time to grab only a couple of personal belongings: a change of clothes and the "kitty," a can filled with quarters, Kennedy halves, bills and checks from the septic-tank business. Luckily, he told Mother as he propped a rifle in the corner of the living room, his guns had been safely tucked in the trunk of his car. He lined up his pistols on the mantel: a pocket model Colt .25 automatic, a Guiseppe .32 automatic and a Smith & Wesson .38 Special. He pulled a Colt .38 Super from his belt just below his sagging belly and sat down in the Naugahyde chair. He popped the clip from the handle of the Colt .38 and put it on the floor, stood and lifted the Smith & Wesson .38 Special from the mantel. He sat there until dark, spinning the cylinder on the revolver, calling at intervals for Mother to bring him a "toddy."

Uncle Jake had been playing Russian roulette with his Smith & Wesson .38 revolver for years. Dad had told us about it—as a forewarning should he actually shoot himself. He described the game and the stupidity of it in detail, but we had never seen him actually play it until he moved in. He put one bullet in the chamber, spun the cylinder, then put the gun to his temple and pulled the trigger. Mother told us to stay out of the living room, to stay away from him when he was drinking—which was most of the time—and to stay away from his guns. She also told Dad to get him out of her house. They had the same conversation every day in the kitchen, immediately after Dad came home from work.

"Get him out of here, Stewart," Mother said as she emptied his lunch box and rinsed out his thermos, "before he manages to shoot himself in front of my children."

"I'm working on it, Dorris," Dad replied. "I'm working on it."

Doris Ann and I got off the school bus ahead of David and Willie, ran across the yard and slammed through the front door. We walked into the hall holding our schoolbooks in front of our chests like plated armor. In the four months Uncle Jake had been living with us, he had shot through the living room wall several times. He aimed toward the soybean fields—where the goons were supposed to be hiding—and fired through the wall. The holes were all relatively close to the window, as if he intended to fire through it, but missed. His firing time was around midnight, so Doris Ann and I had gotten into the habit of waiting until after midnight to attempt sleep. It was unnerving to think that a bullet might fly from the first floor through to the second while we were sleeping.

But we didn't necessarily have to be sleeping to be fired upon. The Saturday before, Dad and Uncle Jake had gotten into a gunfight. They had been sitting on the porch all afternoon, loading their guns, drinking Wild Turkey and arguing over something that their father was supposed to have done, when the argument got out of hand and they started shooting at each other. Well, sort of shooting at each other. Dad stood on the porch with the .22 rifle and Uncle Jake crouched behind a cedar tree in the front yard with his pocket model Colt .25. Uncle Jake yelled, "You rotten son of a bitch!" then fired over the soybean field. Dad yelled back, "You good-for-nothing lying bastard!" and fired over the soybean field in the other direction. Mom stood in front of Dad shouting, "Get down kids, get down!" and waving her arms frantically. We squatted but didn't make much effort to hide. With that particular technique they might have shot one of the cows in the pasture but not each other. They were more unnerving when they *weren't* trying to shoot each other. Just walking past the living room door could be more unnerving.

Doris Ann and I squeezed our schoolbooks to our chests, peeked into the living room, then sneaked by the doorway and walked into the TV room—the room we had been using as a living room since Uncle Jake had moved into our real living room. He usually stayed in the real living room, loading and unloading his guns, but as we entered the TV room we saw him, almost hidden, in Dad's large corduroy-covered chair. He had lined up a row of bullets, placing them upright like missiles, on the cold space heater against the wall. He held the .38 revolver in his lap. We stopped in the doorway and looked around, then cautiously walked past him to put our schoolbooks in their usual place on the ironing board. As we dropped our books there, Uncle Jake swiveled the chair to face us. "Babsy, Babsy, Babsy," he said. "And Darsy, Darsy, Darsy."

"Hi, Uncle Jake."

"Do you know that there's a spot right here," he said, tapping his temple with his index finger, "if you hit it just right, a bullet will go straight through your head without disturbing a single bone? One shot," he laughed and tapped the .38 against the spot.

"You'll be dead—but intact! One shot straight through the temple." He laughed again, straightened the .38, pushed it into his temple and pulled the trigger, shouting, "Blam!" with the click of the pin. Doris Ann and I screamed and covered our ears and Uncle Jake laughed, expelling the smell of whiskey into the air.

"I nearly bought it that time, by God!" He tilted the barrel of the pistol toward the ceiling. Doris Ann and I laughed nervously, then ran toward the doorway. Uncle Jake swiveled the chair to catch us, pointed the pistol at Doris Ann's head and pulled the trigger—just as Mother walked through the doorway. The pistol clicked, Doris Ann and I screamed again and Mother lunged across the room, knocking the pistol from Uncle Jake's hand.

"You don't have to kill yourself!" Mother screamed as she began pounding her fists on Uncle Jake's head. "*I'm* going to kill you!" Doris Ann and I jumped out of the way. Our jaws dropped. Uncle Jake covered his head with his arms and yelled, "Hey! Hey! Hey!" while Mother beat him on the head with her fists. He slumped farther in the chair and reached for the pistol on the floor. Mother—never missing a single whack to his skull—kicked it under the ironing board. It ricocheted off the wall and lodged behind the freezer full of pork and beef. Uncle Jake pushed himself from the chair, almost falling to the floor, and stumbled from the room. He staggered into the hall, bumped into David and Willie—who were on their way to the ironing board to drop off their schoolbooks—knocked the books from their hands and tripped on an opened speller. He slid to the floor. Mother kicked him in the rear and hit him on the back as hard as she could, screaming, "*I'm* going to kill you!"

David and Willie jumped out of the way and their jaws dropped, too. Uncle Jake pulled himself up from the floor and lurched toward the bathroom, hunched over like an old man. Doris Ann and I sneaked next to David and Willie and continued to gape. Uncle Jake clutched the top of his head with one hand and grabbed at the skirt of Mother's dress with the other. He caught her dress at the hip and pushed her back into the hall, ran into the bathroom, slammed the door and shoved the dead-bolt lock on the other side. The toilet lid slammed shut and there was a heavy thud of butt meeting seat. He heaved in oxygen and sputtered like an old bull.

Mother turned and marched toward the kitchen. We stood in a clump, speechless. We were used to Dad doing this kind of thing— *but not Mom!* While we waited for Mother's return, Doris Ann and I whispered to David and Willie what had happened. Uncle Jake sat on the toilet gasping for breath.

Mother had gone out to the red barn and retrieved a huge ten-penny nail and a hammer. She came back, marched up to the bathroom door, angled the nail so that it would go through and into the doorframe and hit it with the hammer, hard and straight. The door splintered slightly as she rapidly pounded the nail through the wood. At first, Uncle Jake thought she was pounding on the door with her fist.

"I'll come out! Don't you worry! I'll teach you a thing or two!" He gasped between sentences. By the time he recovered his wits and climbed from the toilet, it was too late. He slammed the dead-bolt back and tried the door, but it was already nailed securely shut.

"I'll show you a thing or two, by God!" he shouted, pounding his fist on the bathroom door. He pounded for only a minute before he began to heave for air again. He sat back down on the throne. The bathroom window was only a twelve-inch square. He couldn't get out there either. He was caught—with no whiskey and no gun—until Dad came home from work.

"I want him out of here!" Mother said as Dad climbed the steps. He handed over his lunch box and dropped his hard hat onto Janet's head.

"What's the trouble?" Dad asked, propping his hands on his hips and looking at all of us. We looked away, pretending disinterest and left the explanation to Mother.

"I want him out of here. I want him out of here tonight."

"Where is he?"

"He's in the bathroom." Mother took Janet's hand and walked toward the kitchen. Dad followed her and, since we had seen the whole thing and there was nothing to be kept from us, we followed.

Dad decided to move Uncle Jake into a mobile home that sat next to Metal Craft, a small machine shop that Uncle Jake had purchased with the life insurance on Aunt Nina. The trailer had been used as an office for the business, but Uncle Jake had let the secretary go and let the bills pile up on the beat-up wooden desk that sat in the living room area. The single bedroom was packed with boxes of old records, cartons of folded mailers for shipping the machine-shop bolts and screws, and two dozen oily gallon buckets of machine-shop rejects that Uncle Jake planned to find a use for. Dad was supposed to be a partner, so he had a key to the trailer. He left Uncle Jake nailed in the bathroom, collected cleaning supplies and kids, and set out to make the trailer livable.

He, David and Willie carried all the boxes and oily buckets out to the shop and stacked them in a corner while Doris Ann, John and I swept and scrubbed. I swept the floors, snapping orders to Doris Ann and John to pick up this, move that, scrub this, scrub that. As I swept, tufts of rotting carpet peeled from the floor. I pushed them back into place and stomped them flat. I was jumpy, worried that if we didn't do a good-enough job cleaning the trailer, Uncle Jake would continue to live with us. Uncle Jake was too scary to live with; and as long as Uncle Jake was at our house, Dad would be more irritable; he would drink more and he would continue to play with guns. I looked around the trailer at the rusted windows and the peeling wallpaper. *I wouldn't want to live here. This place doesn't even have a kitchen; it's got a sink and a half-size refrigerator, but no real kitchen. How's he gonna eat?*

After the trailer was as clean as possible, Dad brought over Willie's old army cot and set it up for Uncle Jake to sleep on. Then he sent David to the store for cereal and milk.

"He can eat that for breakfast," Dad said, pushing the carton of milk into the little refrigerator, "and your mother can make him a plate for dinner and I'll drive it over in the evening."

Dad took us back home, loaded up Uncle Jake's guns, clothes, whiskey and can of money, and took them to the trailer. When he came back, he released Uncle Jake from his powder-room prison.

After his fight with Mother, Uncle Jake had passed out in the bathroom. Dad pulled him from the throne and down the hall toward the front door, explaining that he was going to his new home. Uncle Jake couldn't remember fighting with Mother and couldn't remember firing the pistol at Doris Ann. At first he thought it was a joke. He acted surprised and laughed, but when he realized Dad was serious, he got angry.

"What the hell is this?!" He tried to pull away from Dad, who held him tight. "By God, I'm your brother! I'm your own flesh and blood! What kind of a man throws his own brother out in the cold! A god-damned worthless man, that's what!" Stone-faced, Dad walked on, pulling Uncle Jake firmly but gently. He opened the car door and sat Uncle Jake on the seat, but Uncle Jake wouldn't lift his legs inside. Dad bent to lift his legs and Uncle Jake tried to kick him in the face. Dad pushed the door shut, forcing Uncle Jake to pull his legs into the car. Uncle Jake was yelling, "You're no goddamned brother of mine," as they pulled from the yard.

The next evening, and for 365 more, Mother made Uncle Jake a dinner plate—meat, vegetables, bread—and Dad drove it over after he had eaten his own dinner. Sometimes, if he planned to stay and drink, he went alone. Otherwise, he took David or me along as an excuse to leave. I was afraid to go. Uncle Jake had been shooting holes in the walls of the trailer ever since he moved in. At first he tried to conceal them with Band-Aids. But as he drank more and more, he gave up trying to hide anything. All the windows were shot out and the wooden desk looked like a target. He left the front door ajar so he could see the goons should they happen to drive up. That way he could shoot them before they shot him. The grease-stained men who worked at Metal Craft were afraid to walk out into the gravel yard for fear of being shot. Twice since I had been going over with Dad to deliver dinner, Uncle Jake had shot at us before recognizing us.

Although I was afraid to go over there, I was more afraid Uncle Jake would move back in with us. I was in my junior year of high school and didn't think I could stand more frustration at home or school. I would sit the aluminum-foil-covered plate on my lap and ride over with Dad, gladly trading an hour of fear for the abnormal normalcy we had had before he'd ever moved in with us.

One evening Doris Ann and I were clearing the dishes from the table as Mother wrapped Uncle Jake's dinner with aluminum foil. She handed the plate to Dad.

"Jake said yesterday's orange Jell-O was too strong," Dad said. "You didn't put any leftovers on his plate today, did you?"

"How can orange Jell-O be too strong?" Mother snapped, placing her hands on her hips. "And no, there wasn't any left over. When have there ever been any leftovers?" Dad went out the back door without answering. Uncle Jake had been sending messages about Mother's cooking through Dad: the chicken's not crispy enough; the steamed carrots need some kind of sauce; the sliced tomatoes are too green; the orange Jell-O is too strong. Even from two miles away, Uncle Jake strained everybody's nerves. Mother scraped the few scraps left on our plates into the dog's dish. "I ought to poison the old fool," she said absently.

Doris Ann and I looked at each other, dropped the gathered silverware into the sink and walked out the back door. We sat on the back steps for a few moments, looked at each other again, then walked out into the yard, out of earshot. I started toward the red barn and Doris Ann said, "It's in the other barn," as if we had been discussing our thoughts aloud. We walked toward the other barn, the barn Edson Tucker had rented to a local farmer to house a few cows. We found the bright yellow box of rat poison in the hayloft against a clutter of buckets and old Mason jars. I picked it up and looked at the label.

"How much would it take, do you think?" I asked.

"How much to kill one rat?"

"A teaspoon. So we'd need . . . four tablespoons, maybe?"

"Five or six tablespoons," Doris Ann said, taking the box and reading the label.

"At least six tablespoons. It's a shot in the dark it'll work at all."

We hid the rat poison and waited for an evening when Mother made mashed potatoes for dinner. We couldn't think of another food that we could hide six tablespoons of rat poison in; even the mashed potatoes were thick and lumpy with the extra powder. Sweat ran down my arm as I stirred the lumpy mixture. I hadn't been sleeping well before, but since we hid the rat poison, I couldn't sleep at all. I had nightmares of being shot with Uncle Jake's .38. I was furious because Uncle Jake wouldn't die of the heart attack he'd been having for the past ten years.

Dad had taken him to the emergency room at least ten times in the past year for chest pains. But the doctors told him he needed to quit drinking and sent him home. Once Uncle Jake demanded that he be taken all the way to the University Hospital in Birmingham. David drove, Dad sat in the front passenger seat and I sat in the back with Uncle Jake. I spent the trip over, the time in the hospital waiting room and the trip back acting as his nurse: dishing out pills, ice packs and "nips" of Southern Comfort, working the entire time to shield my ears from his exploding speeches and avoiding his horrible breath.

When the emergency room doctor told him there was nothing wrong with his heart and that he needed to quit drinking, Uncle Jake knocked over the stand next to the gurney and pulled down the curtain that separated him from the next patient. "Worthless bastard!" he raged. "How did you get a goddamned license for practicing medicine in the first place?"

I held the plate of meat loaf, peas and mashed potatoes on my lap. Doris Ann had poured extra gravy on the mashed potatoes to hide the taste of the poison and, because my knees were shaking so badly, it was dripping from under the aluminum foil onto my legs. By the time we reached Uncle Jake's trailer, my thighs were splattered with gravy. I climbed slowly from the car, letting Dad go in ahead of me, and wiped the gravy from my legs onto my shorts. The fear in my stomach had climbed into my chest and I couldn't breathe. I walked shakily toward the concrete block steps, sweat running in a stream down my arm. I reached up for the doorknob and the sweat trickled back down my armpit, tickling my left side. I let go of the doorknob and tried to think. I had heard that if you killed someone, you had to carry their soul around for the rest of your life. *I don't want to carry Uncle Jake's soul!!—If he has one!*

I wanted to be free of Uncle Jake: his remarks to Mother, his hold on Dad, his guns, his goons, his whiskey and cigars, even the sickly-sweet smell of him that still haunted our living room. But I couldn't do this. I tore the aluminum foil from the plate and, using my fingers, raked the mashed potatoes into the gravel. I smeared them with my tennis shoe, kicked more gravel on top of them, climbed the steps and opened the door.

"Well, get the hell in here!" Dad yelled.

"I tripped," I lied, walking over and handing the plate to Uncle Jake without closing the door behind me. "Your mashed potatoes slid off the plate, Uncle Jake."

Dad shook his head. "Well, I'll be go to hell. Can't you be more careful than that?"

"It's all right, S.K.," Uncle Jake said. He sat in the swivel-desk chair and placed the plate on the wooden desk. "Dorris's gravy hurts my stomach anyway. It's got too much pepper in it for me."

I walked shakily out the door, down the steps and out to a row of cottonwoods that hid the trailer from the road. It was the only area around that wasn't covered with grease-soaked gravel and I needed to sit. Little swimmy things floated in a field of black before my eyes. I sat on the ground, pushed my legs toward the pink glow of the setting sun and wiped my hands in the warm grass, letting the blades scrape the poison from my fingers.

Six months later, Uncle Jake was dead. Shot through the head with his .38 revolver. Dad had taken his dinner to him and found the door wide open, the body just inside. He called Edson Tucker from the machine shop and drove home. He walked slowly in the front door, so pale we thought he might faint. Mother ran to help him into a chair.

"He's dead," Dad choked. "Shot."

"Are you sure he's dead?" Mother asked, smoothing Dad's hair with her palm.

"Yeah," Dad said. He paused a moment, then added, "The top of his skull's sitting on the step."

That evening Edson Tucker came by the house. Dad was at the funeral home, but Edson didn't ask for Dad, he asked for me. I thought Edson was one of the handsomest men I had ever seen. I slipped the butterfly brace from my mouth, stuck it in my pocket, and slapped both sides of my face to bring some color to my pale cheeks. I walked to the front porch, self-consciously crossing my arms over my chest, and expected him to ask if I could watch his children on Saturday night. Instead, he asked if we could ride down the road a piece. I climbed into his pickup still believing the visit had something to do with baby-sitting.

Edson drove out of the driveway, down the road a quarter of a mile, then cut onto a dirt road that ran through the soybean fields and eventually ended in his own backyard. We often took this route back to his house when he picked us up to baby-sit. The fields had been plowed in the fall and were covered with a thin layer of frost. When the soybeans were fully grown, the truck was completely hidden from view on this road; it could be detected only by the trail of dust as it rambled down the crusty path.

The road was extremely bumpy, used mostly by the tractors and combines, and I bounced in my seat, clutching the tattered seat cover to hold on. Edson slowed down so the bouncing wasn't so severe, glanced at me and said, "So tell me who did it. Was it S.K.? Did S.K. kill Jake?"

"What?" I asked, astonished.

"Was it S.K.?" he repeated. "You can tell me. God knows nobody would've blamed him. Down at the office—we're all so damned glad he's dead—we don't care who did it. He was an unbelievable pain in the ass."

I felt the blood drain from my head. I let go of the seat and turned to face Edson Tucker. "No! Dad wouldn't kill Uncle Jake. He idolized Uncle Jake," I said, repeating words I had heard Mother say. "He thought more of Uncle Jake than he did any of us. He would never do anything to hurt him."

"Well," Edson said. "I checked. He was at work all day. It wasn't your daddy."

"Then why did you ask me if it was?" I charged. The blood slowly crept back into my head and I shivered. I stared out the window trying to imagine Dad killing Uncle Jake, but couldn't. He absolutely would do anything for him. Then I tried to imagine Mother killing Uncle Jake, even though Edson had not mentioned her. When Uncle Jake had first moved in with us, Mother had waited on him just the way she waited on Dad. She didn't start resenting it until he proved to be so dangerous, and she continued waiting on him even then, until he pointed the gun at Doris Ann. No, Mother didn't kill him either. Besides, even if she could have found a way over there, who would have watched Janet, Darrell and Chris, and how could she have gotten Uncle Jake's gun away from him? How could anybody have gotten his gun away from him? He shot at everything that moved!

Edson flipped on the heat and it poured over my face. "Your Uncle Jake had lots of enemies," he said. "Anybody could've done it." I looked at Edson and looked away again. He sounded as if he were just *hoping* someone had finally gotten enough nerve to kill Uncle Jake.

"But it looks like he did shoot himself," Edson continued, "the way the bullet went through his head and all." I straightened in the seat and continued to stare out the window, thinking of how much better our lives would be now that Uncle Jake was finally dead.

"I don't care who killed him," I whispered.

"He had almost a thousand dollars in his billfold," Edson said. "You'd think if it was some lowlife, they'd've taken that money."

"So you suspect Dad because he wasn't robbed?" I asked curtly.

"You know he played Russian roulette all the time?" Edson said, ignoring my last remark.

"Yeah, I know."

"But it could've been suicide," Edson said. "It looks like suicide."

"What's the difference between Russian roulette and suicide?" I asked.

"Not much," Edson said, laughing. He reached over and snapped open the glove box and took out a pack of cigarettes. He pushed in the cigarette lighter, bumped the pack against the steering wheel and pulled one from the pack with his lips. He handed the pack to me and I put it back in the glove box. Edson pulled out the cigarette lighter, stuck it on the end of the cigarette and puffed. "No," he said, blowing smoke into the cab, "I believe he shot himself playing with that pistol." He reached over and cranked the window open an inch.

"Then why are we driving around in the soybean fields?" I asked.

3 A.M.

*D*ad had ordered Doris Ann and me to stand military-style, side by side, and count out loud the knots in the living room wall.

"One thousand one hundred one, one thousand one hundred two, one thousand one hundred three . . ." while Willie was ordered to open and close the living room door, gently, two thousand times.

Doris Ann and I had been caught skating in the house again. "We've got a chance to win a leather jacket, Dad!" I had said. "There's a skating-backward competition next Friday at the skating rink and it's just for ages fifteen through eighteen." Dad stared openmouthed as I tried to explain. "You win patches and sew them on the jacket, like race-car drivers." Dad wasn't grasping the importance of what I was telling him, so I changed tactics. "Besides, what else is there to do? We're twenty miles from town and two from the closest neighbor. There aren't any sidewalks and the road is bumpy, cracked blacktop. Anyway, how can we hurt hundred-year-old floors in a house that's falling down around our ears?"

"One thousand one hundred thirty-six, one thousand one hundred thirty-seven, one thousand one hundred thirty-eight."

"Hold your hands over your head!" Dad ordered. We obeyed. He sat in a kitchen chair several feet behind us, drinking a can of Pabst Blue Ribbon, half a six-pack at his feet. Mother, assessing his mood as being fairly harmless, had gone back to bed.

"One thousand one hundred forty-two, one thousand one hundred forty-three," with our hands over our heads. Doris Ann yawned.

"Do you want us to count the ones that are missing?" she asked, lowering her right hand to scratch her lower back. I smiled.

"Don't be smart," Dad said. "I'll keep you here all goddamned night." Doris Ann yawned again. I was glad we were facing the wall so Dad couldn't see us smiling. "One thousand one hundred thirty-five, one thousand one hundred thirty-six."

"Didn't we just do the thirties?" I asked.

"Yeah, maybe."

"One thousand one hundred forty-nine, one thousand one hundred fifty."

Earlier in the evening, right after Dad had caught Doris Ann and me skating in the hall, Willie had slammed through the living room door, an offense that always sent Dad into a lecture on social convention and etiquette.

"Jesus H. Christ!" he criticized. "Don't any of ya know how to enter a room? How do you get by in public flailing around like that? And the two of yas"—he pointed at me and Doris Ann—"ripping up the hardwood floors! You'd think the lot of yas was raised in a barn. Hell, I've seen more graceful pigs . . ." He glared at us in disgust, pondering what to do. We stood still, respectful, hoping our punishment would be mild, and watched the change come over him: His face kind of melted; he perked up and headed for the door. "Tell your mother I've gone to get a beer. The drunks at the Legion are at least capable of opening and closing a door." We waited until his car dropped over the horizon and pulled on our skates.

He had come home at 3 A.M., when the American Legion closed, hell-bent on teaching us a lesson before daybreak. Doris Ann and I were sentenced to the boring and much-hated punishment of counting the knots in the wall. Standing in our pajama shirts with jeans underneath, grumpy from being pulled from our warm bed, we counted in unison.

"One thousand one hundred fifty-one, one thousand one hundred fifty-two . . ."

Willie was sentenced to opening and closing the door like a gentleman, two thousand times. After half an hour of restrained door swings he mumbled something.

"What did you say?" Dad roared, lurching from his chair. "Did you just call your father—the man who brought you into this world—a son of a bitch!"

"No, sir," Willie said, instantly becoming more gentlemanly.

"Yes, by God, you did! I heard it with my own two ears!"

"No, sir."

"Yes, by God, you did! Now you say you're sorry you called me a son of a bitch every time you close that door!" He staggered back to his chair, opened another beer and settled down to watch the show.

"One thousand one hundred and seventy-five, one thousand one hundred and seventy-six."

"I'm sorry I called you a son of a bitch," Willie said, closing the door and opening it again. "I'm sorry I called you a son of a bitch."

"One thousand one hundred seventy-eight, one thousand one hundred seventy-nine, one thousand one hundred eighty." The numbers echoed in my brain and my eyes began to close. I dropped my arms and wobbled. Doris Ann laughed. I woke, elbowed her in the ribs—which made her drop her arms—and lifted my arms above my head again.

"Watch it!" Dad yelled. "Doris Ann, get your arms over your head!"

"It's her fault!" Doris Ann cried, lifting her arms in the air.

"Huh!" I said.

"All right, start over!"

"Ah, Dad," I said, "we're almost finished!" I knew from past sentences that there were exactly one thousand four hundred and twelve knots in the north wall, and that when we reached that number there was a possibility of getting to go to bed.

"Start over!" Dad slurred, trying to force his eyes to stay open. He reached down and pulled another beer from its plastic ring, popped the top and tipped it back. While he was busy chugging, I smacked Doris Ann. She smacked me back. Dad lowered his beer to the floor and glared at us, feigning alertness.

"One, two, three, four, five," we chimed. Dad began to sag in his chair.

"Ten, fifteen, twenty, twenty-five, thirty . . ." He didn't notice we were counting by fives and we started snickering as we counted, a rush of adrenaline waking us. "Thirty-five, forty, forty-five, fifty."

Willie smiled, also revived, and closed the door a little more force-fully. "I'm sorry I called you a son of a bitch." *Wham.* "I'm sorry I called you a son of a bitch." *Wham.* Dad sagged a little more, his eyes closed and his jaw dropped.

"Sixty, seventy, eighty, ninety." We giggled.

Wham. "I'm sorry I called you a son of a bitch." *Wham.* "I'm sorry I called you a son of a bitch." A gentle snore escaped Dad's lips. We laughed out loud.

"One hundred, two hundred, three hundred, four hundred . . ."

Wham! "I'm sorry you're a son of a bitch!" *Wham!* "I'm sorry you're a son of a bitch!" *Wham!* "I'm sorry you're a son of a bitch!"

3 A.M.

"Let's see how long you two boneheads can make it on your own!" Dad shoved David and me into the cool night and slammed the front door behind us. We sat on the front steps as Dad stomped back to the kitchen to charge Mother with our worthlessness.

"You want to climb up the trellis and go back to bed?" I asked, wrapping my flannel shirt a little tighter against the night.

"No," David said. He stared into the star-flecked sky. "Let's watch for a shooting star. If we don't see one in half an hour, we'll go back inside." The stars sparkled above the huge cedar trees in the front yard, and high in the sky arced a fingernail moon.

"Let's go down to the pond and watch from the Styrofoam boats," I suggested. The Styrofoam boats were actually two halves of a motorcycle shipping carton. David was working after school for Freeman Cycle in Bynum, a shop that sold several brands of motorcycles but specialized in Harley-Davidsons. He had talked his boss into giving him one of the motorcycle shipping cartons: a six-foot-long split carton of thick Styrofoam with a hollowed-out Harley shape in the center. It looked like a sliced peach with the pit removed, only more square. And since David had sold his beat-up car and bought a beat-up motorcycle, he had also talked his boss into delivering the Styrofoam to our house. He wanted to see if the halves would float like boats, so we had pulled them down to the pond and launched them. They floated like cupped lilies on the surface of the water, sinking only an inch or so when David crawled into the hollow to test the buoyancy with his weight.

*   *   *

We walked across the pasture to the boats, left upside down at the edge of the water the last time we dragged them from the pond. In the moonlight, they looked as if they were made of stone. We flipped them over and pushed them through the cattails that leaned liked lazy cane poles over the pool. We hopped aboard and stretched out on our backs as the boats rocked, then drifted smoothly in huge circles, bathed in moonlit shadows from a maple tree that hung over the water. David tucked his hands under his head.

"I've got sixty-two more days of school," he said. "Then I'm going in the Marines." He had been talking about joining the Marines for a year. He would use it, as Stewart had, to escape from Dad. I couldn't stand to think about what it would be like without David to fight with and confide in. He had visited Stewart in San Clemente for two weeks during the past summer, and it had felt as if he had been gone a year. The rest of us didn't know how to be as silly as David. We didn't play Rod Stewart's "Maggie May" twenty-seven times when we came in from school. And we would never have thought to tie a rope from the corner of the house to the oak tree and sail off the roof dangling from a pair of bicycle handlebars. It was David who put a pan of Alice's burned-to-charcoal biscuits on a nail in the kitchen and called it modern art; and David who made himself a home-rolled cigarette out of oregano and almost fried his lungs. He was silly. And without him, we weren't silly enough.

It suddenly occurred to me that *I* could join the military as soon as I graduated from high school, too. I only had my senior year to go. I put my hands under my head and considered this. I visualized myself in the Marine Corps uniform, then quickly changed to the Navy uniform: dark blue bell-bottoms.

A rustling around the pond interrupted my daydreaming and I sat up. David raised himself a little to look over the edge of his boat. The farmer's cows were inching curiously toward the pond. They circled it, sniffing the air, then stood with their heads extended over the water, lowing softly.

I mooed back, laughed at their startled expressions and said, "They wonder what we're doing floating in the pond at three in the morning." David propped himself on his elbows and laughed cynically. "*I* wonder what we're doing floating in the pond at three in the morning."

Quest for Beauty

I thought I could get away with renting a piano—rather than taking flying lessons, or any number of the other things I wanted to do—because Mother could play the piano and she played well. My siblings would be reluctant to tattle to Dad if I chose a side interest that delighted Mother. Everyone would be in favor of anything that gave her joy—everyone except Dad.

The idea of renting a piano came to me shortly after I moved back in with my parents. I had graduated from high school, married, had a baby and filed for a divorce—all in one short year. I could have waited and let my husband divorce me after I left, but I was afraid he'd drag it out, take forever, and I wanted to be free of him as quickly as possible. He had controlled every aspect of my life. I hadn't been allowed to work outside the home, or go anywhere, or have any friends. After a few months of marriage, I realized I was a captive house servant and all of my dreams were lost. In fact, living with my husband was worse than living with Dad. So I returned to the lesser of two evils.

My parents had moved again, into a shabby nine-room house on Coldwater Pump Road. The living room, dining room and kitchen were at the front of the house and two of the seven bedrooms split into an L-shape at the rear of the house. It was just days after I moved back in that Dad cleared a section of the yard for a garden—and introduced me to the idea of the rental store. He hammered stakes into the ground at each corner, then drove into Anniston and rented a rototiller.

*   *   *

Doris Ann maneuvered the rototiller up and down the length of the garden rows. John followed on her heels, anxious to take over, shouting over the noise of the machine that she was going too slow, digging too deep. I sat on the back steps to soothe my new baby and watched them. Doris Ann was just two years younger than I was. But at nineteen, I had already married, had a baby and gotten a divorce. I felt tired and desiccated, like an old leaf. My son, Jason, was the only thing that kept me firmly planted on the earth. He was perfect. When he opened his deep blue eyes and studied my face, his lips curled into a bow and his tiny hand wrapped around my finger and held it with complete assurance.

Dad walked through the back door, popped the top on a beer and sat beside me. After taking a sip, he put the can on the step between his feet and smiled.

"Doris Ann can run the hell out of that thing, can't she?"

"Yeah," I answered enviously. Doris Ann had always been stronger than me and, since I had just had a baby, she was now a lot stronger. She was also prettier, much prettier. She was, appropriately, Mother's namesake, having Mother's heart-shaped face and pale blue eyes. When we were younger, strangers would coo over her and touch her straight blond hair. One Easter Sunday when she was about six years old, the preacher from our church fell in love with her. We were hunting Easter eggs in the choir director's backyard. After following Doris Ann around for a while, chortling about how beautiful she looked in her new dress, the preacher took her hand and led her straight to the prize Easter egg we had all been searching for. We were singing in the choir at that time and Telle, our choir director, had bought Doris Ann and me new dresses for Easter. Mine was blue and Doris Ann's was pink. I thought my lace-trimmed blue dress was much prettier that her plain one, but I was painfully aware that I was an ugly kid in a pretty dress.

"Yeah," I said again to my father and rocked my knees back and forth, comforting myself as well as my son. "She does a real good job."

"You shoulda seen that rental place, Southpaw," Dad said, flashing his hazel eyes at me. "They had everything anybody could possibly want." I looked at him, interested, but more interested in having him talk to me for a little longer. He was in a good mood, excited about planting a garden, and I was tired and longed for company.

"Yeah?" I asked. He shook his head and reached out and ran his fingers along my baby's arm.

"I'm not kiddin' ya. Everything: lawn mowers, boat motors, stoves, typewriters, camping equipment, power tools, dishes, carpet cleaners, coffeepots, stereos, TVs, cameras. Everything! They even had candelabras like ol' Liberace sets on his piano. It was just amazing!" The mention of a piano raised the hair on my arms. I used to watch Mother play Aunt Janet's pump-organ and fantasize that I was playing instead. But Dad thought that playing any musical instrument was a waste of time and had long ago forbidden any of us to "waste our money" on such foolishness.

For a moment I daydreamed about renting a piano from the place my father was talking about. Afraid that he could read my thoughts, I looked out at the garden and said, "Wow!"

"And for next to nothing!" he continued, picking up his beer and holding it toward the rototiller. "It only cost me four bucks to rent that rototiller for a whole day and they rent stuff out cheaper than that by the week or the month."

I glanced at him again. "Wow."

"It was unbelievable," he said.

Dad's enthusiasm for the rental business was catching. He gave Willie the job of returning the rototiller. Willie returned with a rented movie projector and several library reels of Cape Canaveral. His passion had always been space exploration. When he was little, he told everyone he was going to be an astronaut, reciting NASA trivia and naming satellites and astronauts to prove it. He had a worn scrapbook filled with brown newspaper clippings following the space race from 1962 through the Apollo Program—which had just ended. He set up the projector in his bedroom. Too excited to wait until dark, he taped sheets over the windows to block out the light and showed us a blurry launching of *Mercury* and then *Apollo 11*, giving us details the narrator omitted.

The following Monday, I drove in my five-hundred-dollar clunker to the rental store on my lunch hour to find out if they rented pianos. I was working as a dental assistant, a job that my orthodontist had found for me after I graduated from high school. Paychecks at the dental office were handed out every Friday at 5 P.M., and just the feel of the check in my hand gave me an adrenaline rush. I wanted to dash out the door and buy all the things that I felt I had missed. In my eyes, everyone in the world was far ahead of me, had what I didn't have, held beauty in the palms of their hands. I thought my heart would burst if I couldn't be a part of it—get to touch beauty. I daydreamed of playing Beethoven's beautiful music, of painting great paintings like John Singer Sargent and dancing like Ginger Rogers—with a face that matched the grace with which I would waltz across the floor.

I didn't want just a little, I wanted everything! Every Friday I paid Mother for taking care of my son while I worked, paid ten dollars on my divorce, bought diapers and baby food, and put money aside—for my car payment, to put in a telephone and to rent a piano. Dad ranted when he came home from work to find the telephone, "a goddamned waste of money!" Even Alice made sarcastic remarks that I was trying to be better than I was. A month later the piano arrived, unbeknownst to Dad.

The rental store that had so impressed Dad didn't rent musical instruments, but they directed me to a store in the mall, Forest's Music, that did.

"Twenty dollars a month," the young salesman said, brushing his fingertips along the keys of a mahogany console Wurlitzer. "Free delivery and pickup." I felt my heartbeat quicken. I couldn't believe they would actually rent a piano to *me*—without even asking for a credit reference! I was so excited my knees quivered, but I forced myself to stay calm, inspecting the piano the way I had seen my father inspect cars, lifting the top and peering inside as if I knew what I was looking for. I closed it gently, then ran my palm along the smooth finish. It felt warm and vibrant, as if the music pulsed just under the lid, eager to be set free. *If I pay on my divorce every two weeks instead of every week—it'll take twice as long to pay it off but that doesn't matter. This is the most beautiful thing I've ever seen. Mom is going to love it!*

"Can I make the arrangements today?" I asked, anxious to get the contract signed and the piano delivered before someone with more sense took over and realized they were renting a Wurlitzer to common riffraff.

*   *   *

Forest's delivered the piano early in the morning while I was at work (and so was Dad). Mother had them bring the piano in the back door and put it in the very back room—farthest from the room with the TV set, the fan in the window and the dozen people who congregated there. But mostly farthest away from Dad—in a room that he hadn't entered since they moved in. We managed to keep it hidden for a year before he accidentally found it.

"If you don't have this goddamned piano out of here by six o'clock, I'll chop it up with the ax!" he shouted, slamming the phone down before I could try to reason with him. I looked at my watch. I didn't get off work until five o'clock and it was four already. I dropped the phone back on the cradle, lied to my boss, telling him the call had been a family emergency, and dashed out the door.

I ran from the parking lot at the mall into Forest's Music, grabbed the sleeve of the first salesman I found and panted, "You've got to pick up the piano from my house!" The salesman, a young man about my age, continued filling a circular rack with sheet music and stared at me as if I were a lunatic.

"Okay. Just let them know at the counter," he said nonchalantly, nodding his head toward the rear of the store. "They'll put you on the waiting list."

"No, I mean you have to pick it up *now!*" I grabbed his arm and urged him toward the rear of the store. "My dad's gonna chop it up if you don't get it out of there right now!"

"What?!" the salesman said, more perplexed than concerned.

"He's gonna chop it up!" I said frantically. He raised his eyebrows, laughed a little and shrugged his shoulders as if I were joking. Fear that I wasn't going to be taken seriously shot through my chest, and I pulled him toward the back of the store. He shuffled the sheet music and cleared his throat to get the attention of the elderly man sitting behind the counter. The man looked up, put his pen down and stood. It was cold in the store and my skin was damp with perspiration; I shivered as the salesman spoke.

"She thinks her father is going to chop up the piano she rented if we don't pick it up today," he said, nervously laughing and shrugging his shoulders again. I let go of the salesman's arm and turned my attention to the older gentleman.

"No, I'm telling you he's *going* to chop it up if we don't get it out of there today. Right now!" The elderly man also raised his eyebrows but he didn't laugh. He studied my white uniform and the plastic tag with my name and "Dental Assistant" written underneath. He opened a drawer, shuffled through it and pulled out a file with my name in the upper left-hand corner. I knew he was looking at the payment record, trying to determine if I was credible.

"Will he really do such a thing?" he asked, closing the file and dropping it onto the counter.

"Yes. He really will."

He picked up the phone and dialed. Pointing toward the front of the store, he said, "Jeffrey, help that woman," and turned his back to us. Jeffrey put the sheet music on the counter and walked toward the woman who had just entered the store. The elderly man dropped his chin and spoke sharply into the receiver. He listened a moment and said, "Tell him to forget that and come here. Right now. Yes, I'm positive. Have him call me immediately." He hung up the phone and turned back to me. He placed his hands on the counter, raised his eyebrows again and lowered them slowly.

"Well, young lady," he said. He paused, looked at his hands, looked up at me and asked, "Did you learn to play?"

Mother played seven bars of Beethoven's Minuet in G, then dropped her hands into her lap and gently sighed.

"This piano has a beautiful sound," she said, sliding from the bench. "Try it again." She turned back to her ironing. On the end of the ironing board sat a small glass bowl filled with chunks of Argo starch. She picked up a piece, bit the end off and held the rest of it out for me. I took the piece of starch with my teeth and let it drop into my mouth.

Mother had always loved the bland crunch of Argo starch. When she was pregnant she had had an insatiable appetite for it, but she'd had an even greater hunger for dirt. She craved the mineral salts and iron oxide impregnated in the soil. The same smooth earth that I sliced from damp banks to use as modeling clay, carving images of ducks, chicks and pigs. But as much as I loved the velvet clay that squished between my fingers and outlined my handprints, I couldn't understand her desire to eat it. *Eat dirt.* I had pushed my fingers into the warm, lurid mud, pulled them out and licked the tips, but the craving my mother felt for the acrid taste eluded me—until I became pregnant.

❧

I married as soon as I graduated from high school. I had tried to join the Navy but didn't pass the physical due to cardiac arrhythmia—my keepsake from the bout of rheumatic fever when I was thirteen. I didn't have a car and the city buses didn't come anywhere near the long expanse of soybean fields where we lived, making it impossible to get a job. So I married.

I met my husband when Doris Ann and I, out of boredom, walked to our closest neighbor's house. This young man was visiting there. He told me that he was recently divorced and looking for another wife.

"And I want a *pure* one this time," he said. "One that hasn't been ruined by another man." When he decided we should marry, I didn't even know how to say no—didn't even know I could say no. I won a husband with my virginity, something that was gone as soon as we married.

He and I moved farther south, where the soil was a mixture of pale dirt and dingy sand, useless for capturing the outline of my hand or for carving images. Instead of being surrounded by the boisterous company of my family, I was a lonely prisoner in a forbidding land. In less than a year, I returned to my mother from this faraway land with my belly swollen. I hurt all over. She packed my sore eyes with smooth, wet clay from the yard—to draw out the bruised blood— leaving me to rock in the old wooden rocker on the porch.

That evening, after a soft summer rain, we walked barefoot in the yard, leaving a trail of footprints behind us in the red Alabama mud. Nowhere else in the world had God been more generous with red: burgundy; mandarin; bronze; molten sun; arrogant, arrogant scarlet; staining white clapboard houses, hacked onto brickyard workers' handkerchiefs. The bright immutable copper saturated the ground straight through to China. We stopped in the middle of the large yard. I walked into a soggy patch of ground and squished the mud between my toes.

"I'm afraid, Mom," I said. "I can't think anymore, can't feel anything. Except what's eating me away inside."

"Describe it to me," she whispered.

"It's like I'm dying inside; I need something. I don't know what . . . Yes, I do. It's what I've always needed. It's everything. I need everything! I feel like I'm never going to have anybody; nobody's going to love me—not for very long, anyway. There's always going to be prettier women . . . And it's more than just that. I feel like I'll just dry up and blow away if I don't get something; get to *be* something; *somebody!* I want to paint beautiful paintings and play beautiful music and dance beautiful dances! And I want to look in the mirror and see a beautiful face instead of this . . ." I choked on the last word and turned my face away from hers. The braces I had been wearing for four years had straightened my teeth, but the upper portion of my face remained too long, exposing teeth and gums above a receding lower jaw. I was thankful for straight teeth and gums that no longer bled, but had hoped, somehow, for a more complete transformation of my face. I had hoped for beauty. I turned toward her again but stared at my feet.

"I'm not anything; I've got nothing; and I'm pregnant and broke." I shook my head and took a deep breath, struggling to hold back tears, knowing I was asking too much of my mother to hear this. As we stood there, her feet began to move in the pattern of a broken box-step. I had seen her do this shuffle-step many times before, whenever any of us displayed our emotions. Since the first time I saw this unconscious dance, it had reminded me of my head-rocking: a response to emotional overload. My sisters and I called the box-step "the disaster dance."

I took another deep breath and tried to concentrate on the soft, red earth beneath my feet, ashamed that I was adding the weight of my unhappiness to her troubles. We walked on in silence to the edge of the front yard. Mother snapped a small limb from a tree and stooped to the ground. She pried a clay-encrusted stone from the earth, stood up and held it to my lips. I turned my head away. She moved directly in front of me, touched the red stone to my lips and said, "Take it; it's good." I sucked the stone from between her fingers and let it settle on my tongue. I felt a sudden flush and the child in my womb moved, stirred by the earth, the blood-red clay, Southern dirt laden with maltha, gilsonite and iron, feeding the unspeakable hunger. The flush climbed up my cheeks and a lively warmth radiated through me. My baby—*my baby*—would soon be born. I rolled the stone against my teeth, making a pool on my tongue, and swallowed the bittersweet muddy water.

The starch dissolved on my tongue as I slid onto the piano bench. I ran my fingers along the black-and-white keys, icy to the touch even through the thin white dress gloves I wore. I moved my fingers to the keys and played, attempting to imitate the grace and rhythm with which my mother had played the Beethoven minuet, but it sounded choppy and slow. I dropped my hands into my lap, frustrated. Mother parked the iron on its end while she adjusted the shirt she was ironing; steam hissed into the air. "Patience," she said.

Patience. *I don't have any patience.* I tugged the gloves from my hands, dropped them onto the bench beside me and tried again. The music flowed more easily, smooth and light. Without the gloves, my hands felt weightless and my fingers seemed capable of reaching far beyond the length of a chord. I played the minuet and believed that not only was I searching for the music, but the music was searching for me. The melody resonated in light, airy rhythms. But very quickly my fingers grew numb with cold and the music grew choppy and slow again. I slid from the bench, disappointed at being forced to leave the piano, and walked back to the living room to warm up.

The back room was quiet except for the sound of the piano, the hissing of the iron and an occasional word of instruction or encouragement from Mother. The lighting was dim and furnishings scant: a single bed, a small dresser displaying a model of *Apollo 11*, a broken rocker that Mother used to hold the ironing, an ironing board and the piano. Walking from the back room to the living room was like traveling through a wormhole in space and ending up on another planet. I walked through door after door in the cold darkness, quietly shutting them behind me, then opened the one to the living room. Heat, blinding light, the babbling TV and the smell of popcorn assaulted me. I waded through the shabby furniture, thick with people—Dad, Willie, Doris Ann, John, Janet, Alice and her kids, Darrell and Chris, who were lifting kernels of popcorn from the plastic bowls as I picked my way through them to the heater. Mom had stretched a clothesline from one end of the living room to the other and hung several pairs of jeans out to dry; dirty water dripped from the cuffs and sizzled as it splashed onto the hot space heater. Janet's black cats, Houdini and Pete, licked the water puddled on the floor. I pushed Houdini out of the way with my foot, held my hands close to the heat and rubbed life back into my fingers. Lady, Janet's dog, slept in the middle of the floor and Janet was using her belly as a pillow. She looked up at me from the floor and covered her mouth as if smiling would reveal our secret, and turned back to the TV.

A few minutes later Mother also came to warm up, bringing a cup of hot tea for herself and another for me. She asked the others if they would like a cup and returned to the kitchen for two more. We stood in front of the heater and drank our tea. When we were warm again we went back to the piano, through the darkness, one at a time so our departure wouldn't be noticed.

We kept the piano hidden in the back room for a year, covered with a sheet to ward off kids and roaches, and asked everyone to keep our secret. And they did, even the little ones: Janet was seven years old, Darrell was just five and Chris was three, but none of them ever mentioned, in Dad's presence, the piano in the back room. Out of his presence, they told everyone.

"We've got a piano," Janet told the cashier as Mother and I lifted groceries from the cart and put them on the checkout counter. The cashier smiled and said, "Sure you do." Darrell told the mailman almost every day, and John brought his doubting buddies in, two and three at a time, and pulled the sheet from the piano as if he were a museum docent and the piano rare dinosaur bones. They stared, mouths gaping, in disbelief. It had that same effect on me and sometimes I sneaked back during the night and slipped the sheet off just to make sure it was still there. It made us feel wealthy. We actually looked forward to getting home from work and school. We argued less and looked at each other with admiration when someone played "Mary Had a Little Lamb" or "Yankee Doodle" without any mistakes. When Dad was gone, we gathered in the back room to listen to Mom play, then took turns attempting to play ourselves.

Through the summer piano sessions, we kept a fan blowing on our backs to keep us cool. But when winter came, we froze. The back bedrooms were closed off to hold the heat at the front of the house. We played the piano wearing thin white hand-me-down gloves Aunt Lola had sent. They were restricting, but we could practice twice as long before retreating to the space heater in the living room. Until our bodies began to shake, we warmed our gloved hands on Mother's iron, sliding one hand over the hot surface, then the other, and clutching them together as if in prayer. Once our teeth began to chatter, we withdrew to the living room. Dad didn't pay any attention to our coming and going. Mother ironed clothes every evening in the back room, so she had a reason to be out of sight; and I had my son, Jason. Every night I rocked him to sleep in the rocker next to Dad's chair, then carried him to bed. After tucking him into his crib, I sneaked to the piano until it was time for Dad to go to bed. If he wasn't going to the bar, he never got up from his chair; he simply called "Dorris!" until she came to see what he wanted. The only real threat was when he got up to go to the bathroom. So Janet, Darrell and Chris served as sentinels, running to warn us whenever he got up. They were so charmed with the music that occasionally we discovered all three of them standing right behind the piano bench, watching and listening.

Willie, Doris Ann and John weren't interested in learning to play, but they did learn "Chopsticks." They pecked at the keyboard, one on the base keys, another on treble, until Mother ran them off. Even Alice, who thought I was "putting on airs," wanted to play. She chose Marchetti's "Fascination" as a piece to commit to memory and practiced with the same diligence with which she had memorized poetry as a child. While she practiced, I paced back and forth behind the bench, anxious for her to get out of my way. Mother ironed, listening intently, providing instruction and encouragement. When I got on her nerves with my pacing, she sat the iron on its end, dropped her brow into a frown and looked at me—all that was needed to stop any of us in our tracks.

"Study your charts," she said. She had made music charts on sheets of notebook paper.

"The treble clef has five lines and four spaces," she explained. "Each line and space represents a note. Start with the bottom line and memorize: Every Good Boy Does Fine. The first letter of each word represents the name of the line. For the spaces it's F-A-C-E, face. For the bass clef," she said, drawing a small dot and looping a long tail through the lines, then drawing the notes on the lines and spaces, "it's Grizzly Bears Don't Fly Airplanes for the lines and All Cars Eat Gas for the spaces." She also made a chart for the order of flats: Bears Eat All Day Go Catch Fish, and a chart of the order of sharps: Fat Cats Go Down Alleys Eating Bologna.

"And you've got to count," Mother said. "Each note has to get the appropriate time or it sounds awful. You can't play without counting."

At work, my employer drilled decay from teeth and I held the suction, silently reciting, *A whole note gets four counts; a dotted half note gets three counts; a half note gets two counts; a dotted quarter note gets one and a half counts. Grizzly Bears Don't Fly Airplanes. Grizzly Bears Don't Fly Airplanes.*

Mother tried to remember what she had learned in her childhood piano lessons, but most of it was too advanced for me. She spoke of major chords and augmented chords and inversions while I searched for middle C. Eventually I sought a piano teacher and began lessons.

Sally Allen was tall, thin, very old and very stately. She lived alone and had a strong sense of command. She had chosen, instead of marriage, to spend her life singing in New York. Her house was spotless and her furnishings sparse. The living room furnishings included a boxy chair, a square natural-wood table and five Japanese paper Noguchi lamps in various sizes that looked like visitors from outer space. In the middle of the room sat a black grand piano that flaunted a black-and-white photograph of Ms. Allen and violinist Isaac Stern standing in front of Carnegie Hall. The walls exhibited more photos, each one in a black-lacquered frame and labeled in neat, tight handwriting: Sally Allen and Richard Rodgers (*South Pacific*); Sally Allen, Jerome Kern and Oscar Hammerstein II, 1949. Above the mantel in the living room was a large group photo of a black-tie event where she sat at a long table with a group of celebrities, including the dancer Fred Astaire. When I asked about the photograph, Ms. Allen stared into it and sighed, as if she had finally let go of something, the same way Mother sighed when she looked at her old photos.

Ms. Allen was everything my mother could have been had she chosen not to marry, yet there was that same sadness when she looked around the room, as if she too had made a bad choice. I admired her greatly, wanted to know what she knew, wanted to be like her and was scared to death of her. She thought I could learn so much more than I could possibly learn. At the end of our first lesson she said, "Here's your assignment for next week," and handed me a photocopy of Beethoven's Minuet in G and Giordani's "Caro mio ben," on which she had written the phonetic pronunciation above the Italian.

"Memorize the Italian," she said. "And study the melody. I think after you learn to play it, you should learn to sing it." I could barely speak the English language and she wanted me to speak Italian! To sing Italian! I took the music home, still shaking from my lesson, and showed it to Mother.

She smiled. "Oh, I *like* this woman." She flipped through the pages, propped Giordani's music against the piano stand, straightened her shoulders, cupped her hands in front of her abdomen and burst into song: "Ca-ro mio ben, cre-di-mial-men, sen-za di te lan-gui-sce il cor, Ca-ro mio ben, sen-za di te- lan-gui-sec il cor."

He Made the Stars Also

I had remarried, gotten a job at a natural-history museum and moved into Anniston. Mother continued to take care of my son, Jason, while I worked. One evening I drove into her yard and she was sitting on the porch swing sobbing. I thought someone had died and fear ran through me. I climbed the steps and stood in front of her, holding my breath and expecting the worst.

"I've wasted my life," she cried, wiping her nose with the back of her hand. "I could have done so many things, but I wasted my life on him." I closed my eyes, waited for my heart to begin beating again and slid onto the swing beside her. I knew she was talking about my father. When I was seventeen, I had tried to talk her into divorcing him. I was tired of his drinking, tired of being thrown out of the house and angry with him because he wouldn't help me fix Stewart's old car so I could get a job. He was angry with me, too. Stewart, who was overseas in the military, had given me the broken-down LeMans that he had left sitting in the front yard. Dad, believing Stewart owed the car to him, wouldn't repair it for me. When I pointed out my need to get a job and asked him to put a new starter in it, he refused.

"It's your car; you fix it. You'll rot in hell before I'll lift a finger to it!"

I was furious. For days afterward I made subtle pleas for Mother to leave him. Finally I raged.

"We can get jobs and take care of everybody!" I said. "And we can do a better job than he's doing!" Mother slapped me hard.

"That's my husband you're talking about!" she cried. She stepped back, startled, and her jaw dropped slightly. I caught my breath and held my stinging cheek. She had slapped me only once before, when I was five years old. She had gone outside to chop wood for the fireplace and had instructed us not to go outside until she returned. We didn't have an inside bathroom and David needed to go pee. Stewart refused to go with him to the outhouse and suggested that he pee through a knot-hole in the floor. David was afraid he might miss and pee on the floor, so he lay down over the knot. We were gathered around watching him when Mother came in the door. She didn't say it, but I knew that—as she slapped each one of us—her version of what was happening was different from ours. Somehow perverse.

When she slapped me at age seventeen, I felt the same way about her passionate defense of Dad; it was somehow misguided. That was the first time I realized how completely her identity lay with him. He wasn't just married to her, he *was* her, and she couldn't even consider the possibility of leaving him. I thought about my own history with marriage. At twenty-five, I'd never been in what could be called a *good marriage*. Both of mine had been one-sided; I did the giving and they did the taking. But I'd never been willing to completely surrender myself the way Mother had with Dad.

I pushed the swing with my foot and looked over at my son. Jason and Chris, Alice's son, had stripped out of their shirts and were digging in the dirt with plastic shovels. Mother got out of the swing, picked up Jason's shirt, slid back onto the swing and wiped her eyes on the sleeve.

"You haven't wasted your life, Mom," I comforted. "Look at all you've done. None of us would have made it through high school if you hadn't been here for us. And we couldn't go to school and work now if you didn't take care of our kids." Even as the words came out of my mouth I knew they were hollow. She was talking about *her* life, what *she* could have accomplished, and I was just adding to the list of what she had given up and was still giving up.

"He's given my car to Nancy," Mother said, blowing her nose on the T-shirt. An angry flush climbed my cheeks. Dad had promised to teach Mother to drive for her fifty-fourth birthday. Months earlier, he had bought her a car, a used 1970 baby-blue Cadillac, but had lent it to a friend, presumably until Mom's birthday. Her birthday had come and gone. The driving lessons had been postponed and the car had yet to make it into the yard. Dad was supposed to have brought the car home the night before. I knew he had lent the car, but I didn't know it was to a woman, especially *that* woman.

We had often gone to the American Legion to drop off Dad or pick him up, but we didn't start going in and sitting at the bar with him until John came home on Army leave and grew tired of waiting for Dad to come home. John had followed Stewart and David into military service, but for different reasons. His relationship with Dad was amicable. John joined the Army for the college money they offered. When he came home on leave, he'd go to the Legion to find Dad. He eventually talked me into coming along. After a while, whenever we wanted to see Dad, we went to the American Legion.

Doris Ann and I would sit at the bar and drink a Coke while Dad had a beer. On several occasions we had watched Nancy slither among the men, run her hands across their shoulders, tease them into buying her a drink or dancing with her. She was around forty-five years old and very pretty, but the bottle-blond bouffant hairdo, red lipstick and low-cut blouses cheapened her beauty. Also, she talked too much and laughed too loud. I wasn't surprised that Dad had hooked up with Nancy. I only wondered how long it had been going on.

"He just *loaned* her your car, Mom," I said. "He's going to get it back."

"No, he's not. He gave it to her. He came home last night without the car. And later—after I sat up half the night listening to his drunken nonsense—when we went to bed, he undressed and didn't have on his underwear. When I asked him where he had been, where he had left his underwear, he accused me of stealing." She burst into tears again. "Accused *me* of stealing his underwear! And didn't even have enough sense not to tell me where he'd been, where he'd left my car. With his underwear—that's where he left it!"

I felt sick. She had him this time and he wasn't going to be able to turn it around so that it was her fault. It made sense. He had been so mean lately, meaner than usual. He seethed every time he came home—*when* he came home. And, as usual, most of it was directed at

Mother. He complained about her cooking, her housekeeping, her clothes and her hair. In other words, if he went to the bar every night, it was her fault. Thinking back on it, I realized he had been seeing Nancy for some time. He had been meaner than usual to everyone. The previous winter, he'd woken me up and thrown me out of the house so many times that I'd finally moved into an apartment.

I knew the money I was contributing each week was much needed, and for that reason I felt guilty about moving out. I felt most guilty about taking Jason away from his grandfather. Though Jason would still see his much-adored grandmother during the day, he wouldn't see his equally adored grandfather. Dad had never liked babies. He didn't help care for them. He didn't hold them. Yet my baby had eyes for my father from the day he was born. Sometimes I couldn't believe that he was mine. He had cotton-blond hair, bright blue eyes and a gleeful, contagious laugh—but it was his fearlessness that I thought most unlike me.

From the time he could crawl, Jason went straight for his grandfather's chair. I pulled him away, tried to warn him, but Jason was not to be stopped. He tenaciously crawled into his grandfather's lap, slapped the newspaper aside and pulled himself up, getting face-to-face with the devil. Dad grumbled and called me to come and get him, but Jason crawled back as soon as he was free, chortling fearlessly at his grandfather's protests. Even my mother couldn't convince Jason of the danger. After countless attacks, Dad surrendered. Jason met him at the door every evening when he came home from work and smothered him with affection. In return, Dad picked him up, gave him Halls cough drops and called him "Buddy."

By his first birthday, he sat in his grandfather's lap every evening sucking the mentholated balls he had become addicted to. It was a startling relationship, and I was hesitant to jeopardize it, but I needed sleep in order to work.

And recently Dad had become even more intolerant of all of us. A few days earlier when I'd come to pick up Jason, I heard him snap at Janet, something he had never done before. At the sight of him, the dog slinked behind the house, the cats slithered under parked cars and the "baby-sat kids" turned to stone.

*   *   *

Mother wadded the T-shirt into a ball and dropped it into her lap. "What should I do?" she asked. I was astonished. She had never asked anyone for advice before. And she was asking *me*. My second husband was off somewhere—our divorce inevitable—and she was asking *me* for relationship advice. *You can pour what I know about relationships into a thimble.* I held my breath for a moment, then released it in a long sigh. "What do you *want* to do?"

"I want to *kill* him."

"Yeah, well, besides killing him, what do you want to do?"

"Well," she said, straightening her shoulders and clenching her jaw, "if he doesn't want to be with me, then I don't want to be with him. I don't need him; I can get a job." She scooted from the swing and went inside. I told Jason and Chris to stay in the yard and followed her. She pulled a cardboard box from the closet, emptied the collection of shoes and hats it contained onto the floor, dropped it by the bookcase and began pulling the encyclopedias from the shelf.

The encyclopedias! Every time Dad ran away from home, which happened about fifteen times a year, he took the encyclopedias. For us kids, it was like watching the same play over and over again.

"Get a box, David," Dad said, "and get my *World Book* encyclopedias packed up." He sat on the couch—calmly, having decided, once again, to leave—and smoked his cigarette. I had been told to take down the light-up picture of *The Last Supper*, and stood awkwardly with it in my arms, not sure if he wanted it taken out to the car or if he planned to make a huge pile in the middle of the floor this time. "Put my light-up picture right there, Barbara"—he pointed—"and get my *Man o' War* poster off that wall." I put the picture facedown on the floor and walked into the kitchen. Mother sat at the table drinking a cup of hot tea.

"Is he loading it in the car?" she asked.

"No. He's making a pile on the floor." I pulled a table knife from the dish rack and slipped it into my back pocket. Mother nodded and took a sip of tea.

"Let me know when he's ready for his junk from the trunk," she said.

"Yes, ma'am." I picked up a kitchen chair and walked back to the living room. David had gotten a box and dropped it in front of the bookcase. I sat the chair next to the box.

"Doris Ann, help your sister," Dad said, pointing toward the poster. Doris Ann walked over and held the chair so it wouldn't fall over.

"Now there's a pointless venture," David sneered as I climbed onto the seat to take down the poster.

"You want to trade jobs?" I asked, tapping his back with my bare toes.

"Nope. One redundancy is just as redundant as another." He started to pull the encyclopedias from the shelf. "You know we're just gonna have to put it all back again at three in the morning." I nodded my head and pulled the kitchen knife from my back pocket. I stood for a moment and admired the furiously competitive racehorse that had won the Preakness and the Belmont stakes in the same year. Man o' War stood like a champion: tall and proud, with a ring of flowers around his long neck. The poster was almost all horse; a patch of green grass anchored him to the earth and he was surrounded by clear blue sky. I tapped David with my toes again.

"I'd like to be reincarnated as this racehorse," I whispered.

"You already *look* like a horse," he said, squatting with an armload of books to avoid being kicked. Doris Ann giggled. I ignored them and pried a thumbtack from the poster. Dad had left Mother so often—taking the poster each time—that the corners had disappeared into a tattered, pin-pricked curve, and each time it was returned to its place of honor it had to be pinned farther into the sky. I pried another thumbtack loose, dreading the lecture we would receive just before Dad walked out the front door. Holding a hand in the center of the poster, I forced the last thumbtack from the wall and the poster rolled. It no longer bounced into a tight coil as it used to, so I rolled it tighter and put a rubber band around it. Willie and John came into the living room carrying Dad's fishing poles and tackle box. They laid them on the floor next to the light-up picture and waited for orders. I dropped the poster by the fishing poles and studied the pile to see what still had to be gathered: his clothes, beer stein, pistol and his war medals—items that Mother would have to gather.

"Barbara, tell your mother to get my belongings from her trunk,"

Dad said, exhaling a lazy ripple of smoke. I walked into the kitchen, told Mother he wanted his stuff from the trunk, and quickly walked back to the living room. If I had to listen to this story again, I wanted to sit in the rocking chair so I could at least rock. Willie saw me coming and made a beeline for the black-lacquered rocker, but I beat him by half a second. He groaned and flopped down on the couch between Doris Ann and John. Mother walked into the living room and put Dad's things from her trunk on the floor. She left the room, returned with two grocery bags of clothes and dropped them to the floor. She brushed her hands as if they were dusty, leaned against the wall and shoved her hands into her dress pockets.

"Now," Dad began. He drew his cigarettes from his shirt pocket and tapped them against his wrist. David, who had been standing by the empty bookcase, walked over and sat on the box with the encyclopedias just out of Dad's vision. He crossed his legs, pretended to hold a cigarette, and mouthed, *I'm leaving your mother,* as Dad said it out loud. We stifled laughter; even Mother had to look away to hide a smile. John laughed out loud. Dad was about to poke a cigarette between his lips, but he dropped his hand back to his knee.

"Boy, do you want me to take a belt to you?" he asked.

"No, sir," John said, wiggling around on the couch. "These broken springs are tickling my back." Mother lowered her eyebrows and David stopped imitating Dad.

"Your mother saw to it that we could never remain married," Dad continued, nipping the cigarette with his lips and digging in his pocket for matches. He lit the cigarette, blew out the match and dropped it into the empty beer can at his feet. "In fact, she *destroyed* our marriage by being unfaithful. That's right," he said, shaking his head and looking at each of us as if we should be shocked. "Your mother, this woman right here," he said, nabbing the cigarette between his fingers and pointing at Mother, "had an affair with a pot salesman."

He blew smoke into the air, stood, paced across the floor and then turned to look at each of us. "A goddamned pot salesman!" He paced again, stopping in the middle of the room. "She left me in Philadelphia by myself and run off with him! She run off with a goddamned pot salesman! Hell, she didn't even pick a real man; she picked a pot salesman—a man that walks around selling pots and pans and brushes to *women* all day. A goddamned pantywaist." He walked to the open front door, stared into the darkness, and spoke as if addressing someone on the front porch.

"I was barely healed from being wounded in the war and your mother's out sneaking around with a pot salesman. We hadn't been married more than two or three years. I give her everything. She didn't have to work. She didn't have to do a damned thing but clean the house and cook, and she didn't do that very well!" He kicked the screen door, caught it so that it stopped wide open, and turned to face us. "Now load my stuff in the Cadillac and let me get the hell out of here before I have to hurt somebody!" he shouted.

We jumped from our chairs and loaded the car. Dad picked up the box containing the pistol and tucked it under his arm. When he finally drove away we were exhausted and went to bed. He returned several hours later, drunker than when he left.

"David! Barbara! Willie!" he called. We climbed from our beds and staggered toward the front door. "Get my *World Book* encyclopedias out of the car and put them back in the bookcase!"

Mother dropped the last encyclopedia into the box and I helped her carry it outside, pushing it to the edge of the porch so it blocked the path to the front door. She walked through the house, came back, tossed two fishing poles and his tackle box onto the pile and walked through the house again.

Even though Mother had never broken anything, I was afraid the news of Dad's affair might push her in that direction. I stood in the doorway and stared at the light-up picture of *The Last Supper* hanging next to Dad's chair. If she was going to smash something, that would be it. I had admired its beauty all my life, had even thought the Jesus sitting at the table possessed the power to keep us safe. While Mother was out of the room, I lifted it from the wall and placed it, facedown, on the far side of the books. She came back and dropped a paper bag of clothes next to the box. She glanced at the picture and spit out a short "Hmph." I hoped she thought I was being helpful rather than disloyal. I followed her back to the bedroom, where she stuffed more clothes into paper bags.

I leaned in the doorway and watched, wondering if she would really make him leave; and if he left, how she would pay the rent and buy groceries; what would she do? And if he left, what would *he* do? Where would he live? Who would cook his meals? Who would shave him every morning? Mother had been shaving him and combing his hair every morning since they got married—except for the year that I shaved him.

I had always watched my mother as she glided the double-edged razor over my father's face, and when I was fourteen, I wanted to give it a try. After ignoring my pleas for several days, Dad looked up at Mother and said, "Let her shave me." He looked at me and said, "Don't cut me now." And for a year, I didn't cut him. Then, overnight, I did. Three nicks in three days, closer each time to the thick blue vein that bulged from his neck. On the fourth day, as I walked toward the living room with the pan of hot water and the razor, I told Mother I didn't want to shave him anymore. She took the pan and razor. Without looking at me or questioning me, she walked on toward the living room where Dad waited.

I shoved my hands into the pockets of my jeans and turned my attention back to Mother. Maybe she could get a job. She'd been home for so long, though. Alice and I would have to put our kids in day care. Then a revelation struck like lightning: *Wait a minute! She's going to leave him now? Now that we're all grown and out of the house! Now that Janet's the only one left at home!* Anger engulfed me. I walked back to the front porch, dropped onto the porch swing and gave it a quick shove. *You mean he could do anything to us—anything to her!—as long as he didn't sleep with another woman?* Anger surged through me; I felt strong and fierce—able to snap like toothpicks the wooden poles that held up the porch. I wanted to stomp and kick and smash everything in my path. But instead I lay down in the swing, put the back of my hand over my eyes and concentrated on the kaleidoscope of trees and sky flashing between my fingers.

Mother dropped two bags of clothes onto the front porch. "Will you teach me to drive?" I sat up in the swing and moved over so she could sit.

"Sure," I said.

"Can we start this evening? Willie will be home shortly. He can watch the kids while we're gone."

Mother shifted the Maverick from first to second, grinding the gears, pumped the brakes and turned the corner, barely missing a car that was waiting to pull onto Highway 78. I paled but didn't speak. She already knew she'd been going too fast to turn the corner and, besides, she was my mother.

"I just can't seem to get the gist of shifting," she said. We continued down the road, passing Edson Tucker's place, the overgrown shambles where Uncle Jake used to live and the field of soybeans that once had been gladiolas. The July soybeans were at their peak and still, after all these years, a scattering of bright gladiolas shot from the sea of green like painted arrows. I pointed them out, reciting their names: "Ballerina, White Cloud, Dynasty and Rapid Red. Rapid Red was the prettiest of them all, Mom." She smiled but didn't take her eyes from the road.

"What a fiasco," she said, lurching forward as she shifted into third. "Only your father and his brother could have thought up such a scheme." I laughed and turned my attention back to the driving lesson.

The Maverick was a particularly difficult car to drive; the seat didn't move forward enough, so, unless you were man-sized, it was hard to reach the pedals. Also, the clutch was stiff, and with an inexperienced driver the car lurched with every shift of the gears.

When my five-hundred-dollar car died, Dad and I had gone to the Sunny King Ford used-car lot to see what was available. He picked out the Maverick: a 1968 candy-apple red five-speed.

"This is a beaut," he said, poking his head under the hood. "Really nice engine. Clean as a whistle."

"I can't drive a stick, Dad. Can we look at an automatic?"

"This is the best car for the money, right here," he said, tapping the front fender with his index finger. He had worked as a mechanic most of his life. In fact, he had held on to his job repairing tanks and small military weaponry at the Anniston Army Depot for many years. He knew engines. That's why I had asked him to come.

I climbed inside the Maverick and played with the clutch. It was stiff. I stuck my head out of the window and requested, again, that we look at an automatic.

An hour later we walked from Sunny King's long blue building into the car lot, where my just-purchased five-speed Maverick sat next to Dad's automatic Cadillac. I expected him to drive the stick-shift home and I would drive the automatic, but he climbed into the Cadillac and leaned out the window.

"Just push in the clutch, shift into gear, give it some gas and let out the clutch. It's that simple." He put his car in gear. "Any idiot can do it," he said as he threw up his hand in farewell and drove away.

I didn't dare give the same advice to my mother. Besides, my anger had subsided, and it felt so good to be taken into her confidence, to be needed by her, that I didn't care if she destroyed the car.

Dad came and got his belongings with no complaint, thinking he would move right in with Nancy. She let him stay with her for six days, then tossed him out. He moved into a small roach-infested apartment in Bynum, two blocks from the American Legion, and tried to rekindle his relationship with Mother. But the world had been created in six days, and while he was off in adulterous bliss, it had been re-created. In six days Mother had learned to drive and gotten a job. She had applied for a cashier's position at Wakefield's, the swankiest clothing store in Anniston, made the highest score ever achieved on their aptitude test, and was given the job of assistant credit manager.

The next evening she asked me to take her to the Ford dealership to see if she could purchase a car. I thought the idea was ridiculous. She had not worked in years, she had no credit history and no down payment. But I took her anyway and sat next to her chewing on my fingernails as she spoke with Sunny King. She was wearing pale pink lipstick and had on a pale rose pantsuit—charged on her new Wake-field's charge account. Her soft gray-streaked hair fell in short curls around her face; she looked like an older version of Joanne Woodward. She delivered her story as straightforwardly as possible: "I'm recently divorced. I'm not asking for charity or sympathy but simply an oppor-tunity to rebuild my life. I haven't been part of the work force for a while," she apologized, "but I'm presently working at Wakefield's Department Store. I can make the payments and they'll never be late."

Sunny King, a handsome man in his forties and one of the wealthiest men in the area, was married to a beautiful blonde and associated with the city's elite. Our worlds were as different as night and day, but he listened as if she were his own mother, then, much to my astonishment, pulled out papers and financed the loan himself. It was late by the time he escorted Mother to her newly purchased Honda. A full moon hung overhead.

"Look at that moon," Mother said, pointing upward as Sunny opened the car door for her. We looked into the night sky. "So unassuming," she said as she climbed into the car, "you'd never know it had the power to move oceans."

"That moon's got nothing on you," Sunny King said as he gently closed her door.

Des Moines, Iowa

1987

Move the Stone Aside

One evening John called me. He was stationed at Fort Sill, Oklahoma, and was about to be sent overseas again. I had just moved to Des Moines, Iowa—the final destination after getting the inevitable divorce from my second husband and running away to art school in Florida. John was calling me because he had lost his birth certificate and was having trouble getting a new one. He had applied for it using military forms that required the listing of his next older sibling and the next younger one. He listed Doris Ann as the older sibling and Mary Louise as the younger. Two weeks later the form was returned. They could not find a Mary Louise Moss. As much a coward as the rest of us when it came to questioning Mother about her past, he called me instead.

"Why wouldn't they be able to find her birth certificate?" he asked.

"Maybe because she died," I said. "Tell them to look for a death certificate." Talking about Mary in such a factual way filled me with sorrow. I couldn't explain it, but I had always missed her, imagining that *she* was the one sibling who would have been like me. I imagined that she would have thrown her arms around me and walked arm in arm with me as we talked. There was a distance between me and my other siblings, a protective barrier that kept us just short of loving each other enough—created, I supposed, because Mom and Dad were never comfortable with hugs and kisses, or, for that matter, tears. So we weren't either. That same distance, I also supposed, would have been there for Mary had she lived.

John sent the form back, suggesting that they look for a death certificate for Mary Louise, but, once again, it was returned. No record of Mary's birth or death could be found by the state of Alabama.

"My commanding officer is starting to give me funny looks," John complained. "He thinks it's weird that I don't know who my brothers and sisters are. Why wouldn't there be a birth or death certificate for that baby? Are you sure Mom had her in the same clinic as the rest of us?"

"As far as I know," I said. "She always said that was where she was born."

"Call her," John ordered. "Call her and ask her."

"Why can't you call her?"

"I'm not calling her. Besides, she'll tell you stuff she won't tell anybody else. She's used to you hounding her."

"Thanks," I said sarcastically.

"You know what I mean," he said. "*Please* call her. I've gotta get this damned birth certificate. They're starting to think I'm nuts."

I called Mother that evening and asked if Mary had been born at the same clinic where most of us had been born. She didn't speak for a long time, and when she did, she sounded tired, drained of energy.

"Oh, honey," she said, "that was a long time ago."

"But she *was* born at Norell Clinic in Pell City, wasn't she?"

"Yes."

"Then why wouldn't there be a birth certificate?"

"Oh, I probably forgot to report it."

"Mom, you weren't responsible for reporting the birth, the clinic was. There isn't a death certificate either." There was silence again at the other end of the phone line.

"I'm sure I just forgot to report it. That was a long time ago. I don't really remember."

"Well, maybe they could find something if John gave them the exact date of her birth."

"Honey, I don't remember what day she was born. I blocked all of that out long ago."

I felt guilty about pressing her, but tried once more. "Well, what *month* was she born in? Maybe that would help. I told John she was born in 1961, but I'm not even sure of *that*. All I can remember is that Dad left for Pennsylvania not long after she died." When Mother spoke again, the tone of her voice had changed; the tiredness had been replaced with a sharp edge similar to the one she used when she scolded us as children, a sharpness that made you fearful and at the same time ashamed that you had upset her.

"I really don't remember," she said. "I blocked it out—let go of it—a long time ago."

The state of Alabama did a statewide search for records of Mary Louise Moss, but didn't find anything. In the meantime, John started over, filling out the military birth certificate request form with Doris Ann as his next older sibling and Janet as the younger. He received a new birth certificate within two weeks and was satisfied to forget about the missing records.

But the incident haunted me. What I had been told as a child about Mary's birth and death had always bothered me. I reexamined what little I knew: She was born at Norell Clinic; she was a blue baby and stayed on a monitor for three days. She died. Dad—blind-drunk at the time—buried her at Blue-Eye Creek Cemetery, but couldn't remember exactly where. Once, when—as Dad's driver—I had insisted on stopping at the graveyard, he claimed that the reason he couldn't remember was because it had been dark. Did he really bury her at *night,* or was that an excuse, given to a child who wouldn't know better, to cover drunkenness?

When I was pregnant with Jason, I searched for Mary's grave, trudging through the overgrown graveyard beside Blue-Eye Creek Baptist Church and scraping dirt and debris away from the names on every stone. But then, she didn't have a stone; and Dad had never been able to pinpoint exactly *where* in the cemetery she had been buried. I questioned the pastor of the church, but he said they hadn't buried anyone in that graveyard in fifty years. Rather than question Mother, I gave up the search.

Now I thought of other things that bothered me about Mary's death. Where was Mother while this burial was taking place? Was the body sent to a mortuary? Did the hospital or the mortuary actually relinquish the body to Dad? Those were the most prominent questions. But there were others. Exactly *what* was Mother blocking out? Why was it forbidden to speak of Mary Louise? And why would Dad go to the trouble of writing—in elaborate script—each of our names, dates of birth and places of birth in the family Bible, only to stop abruptly after John?

I brooded over the mystery of it all, and mused over the impact this dead sister had had on my life. While in art school, I developed an iconography that reflected upon Southern folklore, traditions and family. Dad was often depicted as a tornado or a bolt of lightning, Mother by a fragile house on stilts—like the Kimberly house—with indigo skies filled with stars: nine stars, one for each child, the small faded one symbolic of Mary. She appeared in my artwork as shadowy, thin, obscure, barely visible—but always present. She emerged as a single sunflower growing beside the steps, a red-winged blackbird on the roof, or as a blue, elaborately decorated cup steaming with hot, sweet tea.

A few days after John received his new birth certificate, I called the woman who had done the statewide search for Mary.

"I couldn't find a thing," she said in a familiar down-home accent. "If I had to guess—having been in this job for twenty years—I'd say your parents had that baby adopted."

"That doesn't make any sense," I said hoarsely. "Why would they keep all of us and have her adopted?"

The woman sighed. "The fact is, they were probably broke and somebody offered 'em some money. It happens more often than I care to think about."

"But there would still be records," I insisted.

"I know this is hard to hear, but the only logical explanation is that they made the birth certificate out in the last name of the adoptive parents. That's why we can't find it. You could still track her down if you wanted. It'd take some time; that clinic's been closed down for years. But, honey, I'd guess you've got yourself a sister out there some-where."

"Truth," Said the Traveler, "Is a Breath, a Wind, a Shadow, a Phantom."

When it was time for me to leave Sarasota, Florida, where I had attended art school, and move to Des Moines, Iowa, where I would attend graduate school, I didn't have enough money to make the move, but deep in my heart, I had always believed there was at least one person who could help me financially if I got desperate—Dad. He had often helped my brothers buy cars and motorcycles, and he had given Alice money on several occasions before she went back to school and got a civil service job.

As it turned out, I didn't have to call him to help me move. In late July, a couple of weeks before fall semester was to begin, the First Baptist Church in Sarasota, where I was a member, collected money and gave me a wonderful send-off party, complete with cake, ice cream and tears. They thought of everything: money, wool sweaters for the northern winters and a book on how to act like a Yankee. By that time the Maverick had died and I owned a well-worn Honda Civic without a trailer hitch. One of the men in my Bible-study class hooked my packed U-Haul trailer to his utility vehicle and transported it from Sarasota to Anniston, Alabama, almost halfway to my final destination. Jason, now twelve, and I spent a few days with Mother, and then Stewart hooked the U-Haul to his truck and took us on to Des

Moines. We arrived in East Des Moines around midnight, checked into a motel, unhooked the trailer and went to bed.

The next morning Stewart took a look around. There was a strip mall across the street that had a tattoo parlor and a cycle shop, obviously the local hangout for a gang of motorcycle riders. In the corner of the parking lot was a display of velvet paintings and wall hangings, American flags, baseball caps and cheaply made cowboy hats.

"You're moving to the land of tattooed girls," Stewart said.

"There's got to be more to Des Moines than this," I said. "Let's go look at the university." We found Drake University on the other side of town, and looked at some apartments in nice neighborhoods. But I couldn't afford the rent.

"I'm taking you back home," Stewart said. "You don't have enough money to rent anything decent, and I don't think Mom would want me to just leave you where you are now. That place doesn't look safe. And it's too far away from the university. And what's Jason gonna do? How much money do you have left? You better come back home with me."

I calmed him down and promised to call if I couldn't find a place to live by the end of the week. Stewart reluctantly drove away, leaving us standing in the motel parking lot.

After two days of hopeless searching for safe, affordable housing, I called a friend in Sarasota who had grown up in Des Moines and begged for help. He called a real estate friend in Des Moines and she rescued us from the motel. She had teenage children of her own, so she understood what I meant by "safe," and knew just the place for us, a duplex on Hillcrest Drive, a quarter of a mile from the local high school and a mile from Drake University. She even hooked the U-Haul to her car and helped us unload. I couldn't afford the rent on the duplex, but decided not to worry about that until later.

When *later* came, I realized what an incredible find the apartment was, and how indebted I was to the woman who found it for us. I borrowed as much as possible on my Guaranteed Student Loan so we could stay there, and made a financial plan to cover rent, groceries and gasoline. But the financial plan didn't allow for emergencies. Several months after we moved to Des Moines, Jason, who had just turned thirteen, came down with mononucleosis. The doctor said Jason would have to come in every two weeks until his blood count returned to normal, usually about three months. We didn't have medical insurance, or any other kind of insurance, for that matter. The doctor's fee alone would be sixty dollars a month.

I called Mother and asked what she thought about calling Dad for money.

"I wish I had it to give you, so you wouldn't have to ask him," she said. "If I had it, I'd send it to you. I don't know about your father. Do you have any other options?"

"I could apply for government help, Mom," I said, blushing with embarrassment, even though we were talking on the phone.

In our family, government help had always been considered unacceptable. I had thought about applying before, but couldn't get past my pride. Instead, I had worked two jobs. But I had looked over my graduate school class load and knew that wouldn't be possible this time. Mother was silent for a moment, then said, "Call your father. He helps the boys occasionally. He makes enough. Doris C. keeps him pretty close to home, so I don't think he's drinking it all away. Call him, honey. He might give it to you."

I had talked to Dad several times in the eleven months since moving to Des Moines. As soon as I found a place to live I had called to let him know I was okay; I called him on his birthday and on Thanksgiving Day. Recently I had called him more often than that because I wanted to find out more about Mary Louise. The subject of Mary had been hard to bring up. Hints didn't work. Finally, I mentioned John's difficulty getting a copy of his birth certificate, but Dad made no comment. I even told him the woman who did the statewide search for Mary suggested that the baby might have been put up for adoption. But Dad only said, "Hmph," and moved the conversation back to me.

"When are you coming home, Southpaw? How much education does one little girl need?"

Before I called to ask Dad for money, I planned the telephone conversation in my head. I'd make small talk for a few minutes, ask about Doris C., the woman he had married four years earlier, and then I'd tell him the situation with Jason. I had decided to ask for three hundred dollars. One hundred dollars a month for the next three months, just enough to pay the doctor and buy medicine. I was confident he would send it to me. But when I finally made the call, he said, "Hell,

I can't lend you a hundred dollars. I got eight kids; what if they all wanted a hundred dollars? Besides, Doris has already put the nix on loanin' any more money to kids."

I was stunned. Through the years of struggling, living as a full-time student and single parent, I had convinced myself that he would come through for me if I really needed him. I was wrong. He was as he had always been: unavailable in every way. I hung up the phone and stared at the wall, chilled. Then I got angry.

"Last month Mom told me that he helped David buy another motorcycle!" I yelled, flinging the phone to the floor. I stomped around the apartment, while Jason sat on the stairs watching and listening.

Jason was a good listener. Through the years he and I had clung together, determined to create a different destiny for ourselves. He had walked the streets of Sarasota with me, collecting Coke cans to buy food. He had been my assistant, handing me brushes and buckets of paints, when I took an under-the-table job painting designs on surfboards. And he had taken a baby-sitting job—five nights a week—that lasted for three years. Going to art school had been my dream, but without Jason it would have been impossible. Alone, I would have been too scared to keep going.

Jason had seen me have a fit before, but nothing like this one. I kicked a wooden folding chair and it collapsed to the floor.

"And Dad can't tell me he doesn't have any money!" I yelled. "He sits in that leather rocker holdin' that damned two-hundred-dollar poodle. Hell, he pays twenty dollars a month just to get that dog's toenails polished." I slapped a cigar box of drawing pencils off the table and kicked them around the room. "Doris C. didn't stop him from buying a half dozen cars and a half dozen motorcycles last year, but she puts the *nix* on . . . I don't believe she told him that! He made that up 'cause I'm a *girl!* Everybody knows *girls* don't count! I might as well be a turnip!" A portfolio of nudes leaned against the wall in the living room. I pulled out the portfolio and started ripping them up one at a time. Jason came over, moved the portfolio out of my way and put his arms around me. I burst into tears and cried, "He could just give me some of the money he got for selling Mary Louise."

Anniston, Alabama

1990

And All We Need of Hell

*D*ad was so reckless that it seemed he could have stepped quickly in any direction, at any time, and freed himself of his body. I've been afraid he would die since I was old enough to be afraid of anything. Now that fear has come true. My brothers and sisters and I gather around his casket at the funeral parlor, inching closer to each other as if for warmth.

"He didn't say good-bye," Alice whispers. The rest of us shake our heads. Mother comes into the viewing room to gather us under her wing like ducklings. She tugs on Alice's arm, knowing we will follow.

"Come on," she says. "Let them close the casket."

Several family members, including me, sent gladiolas to the funeral home, thinking Dad would have gotten a kick out of it. Baskets of Irish Lass, Night Owl, Heart's Desire and Pearl. The parlor attendant moves the gladiola arrangements out of his way. I lag behind as the others leave the room. Everything is happening too fast. *Dad died yesterday morning, and today we are burying him. I want a church service. I want hymns and a sermon. I want more time.* Doris C. scheduled the funeral for the very next day. "Because what he did is an unpardonable sin," she said.

I look around wanting to curse her, but there's no one left in the viewing room but me. *I need more time. I need something that's his, something to keep.* I walk quickly back to the casket, see the VFW hat folded on his chest, and take it.

"What are you doing?" David asks. I jump.

"I need it with me," I say, clutching the hat. My brothers walk up in a group just as David takes the hat away from me.

"He needs it with him," he says, laying it back on Dad's chest and wrapping his arm around my shoulders.

"It's time to close the casket," says the parlor attendant.

I suck in a sharp breath. "Let me look at him one more time." David lets go of me and stands with the others in shared sorrow, watching me. I don't care. I want that hat. I stare at Dad and try to think of how to get it without their seeing me. I bend down and kiss his cold cheek.

My lips are close to the Band-Aid that conceals the thin round hole tunneled through his temple, proving Uncle Jake's one-shot theory.

Dad had been diagnosed with lung cancer the month before. He had received one painful chemotherapy treatment, then shot himself when he got home. It is so like him to bail out when pain moves in his direction. He had never been sick before. He'd suffered from occasional bar-fight injuries and he had that horrible beating years ago, but those wounds were considered badges of honor, something to be proud of. He preferred to inflict pain. And, once again, he has, just when I thought he couldn't hurt me anymore.

Of all the accidents and injuries I had worried about, I never thought to worry about suicide. How was I to know? Mother told me only last night that he had often threatened suicide. No wonder she never left him. No wonder she never thought of anyone else. She must have been immobilized with that fear for thirty-five years. I put my hands on the edge of the casket and stare at my father.

"Thank you," I whisper. "Thank you for not killing yourself while you were with Mother." I examine his face, the face she was so in love with. It has visible power, even in death. I want to keep his deep-set eyes and high cheekbones and wish I had thought to make a plaster mold of him—a death mask. I wish I had thought to press his hands in clay, or ink them with cadmium red and press his fingerprints onto rag paper, to keep—or maybe to tear up, or to burn, to rid myself of the anger that sits like a stone in my heart. Tears fall from my chin into the casket. I touch Dad's hand and turn to walk away. The boys are gone. I turn back to take the hat, but the parlor attendant has already closed the casket.

He was a thief, my father.

Epilogue
Anniston, Alabama
1984

from "I Have Had to Learn to Live With My Face"

I wonder how we learn to live
with our faces?
They must hide so much pain,
so many deep trenches of blood,
so much that it would terrorize and drive others away, if they
could see it. The struggle to control it
articulates the face.
And what about those people
with elegant noses and rich lips?

What do they spend their lives struggling for?

Am I wrong I constantly ask myself
to value the struggle
more than the results?
Or only to accept a beautiful face
if it has been toiled for?

Tonight I move alone in my face;
want to forgive all the men whom I've loved
who've betrayed me.
After all, the great betrayer is that one I carry around each day,
which I sleep with at night. My own face,
angry building I fought to restore
imbued with arrogance, anger, pride and scorn.
To love this face
would be to love a desert mountain,
a killer, rocky, water hard to find, no trees anywhere
perhaps I do not expect anyone
to be strange enough to love it;
but you.

DIANE WAKOSKI

Changing Faces

When I was thirteen and recovering from rheumatic fever, I began to exercise. I was stiff and sore and afraid that if I didn't move and stretch as soon as I could sit up, my joints would freeze, my thin muscles would deteriorate even more and I wouldn't be able to move at all. At first I just attempted to walk, then touch my knees. Eventually the daily routine progressed to toe-touches and jumping jacks. Although I got stronger, over the years I continued to have attacks of strep throat that produced a multitude of symptoms: erratic heartbeat, sore joints, mouth ulcers, spiral-shaped skin nodules, sun sensitivity and blanched fingers and toes. I had strep throat so often—twenty-three times before I was hospitalized—I could tell by a sluggish feeling in my limbs when my fever was about to shoot sky-high.

By the time I was twenty-six, daily exercise had become a form of prayer; I stretched, laid my hands upon my knees, ran them down the rough nodules on my legs and prayed to be healed. I had blamed God for letting me get sick and blamed Him for giving me such a twisted, mummy face. Mummy face. That was it. As a child, I had found my face staring back at me from a mummy who'd fallen from a cliff and smashed her face. I had been angry about that mummy all my life. But I was tired of being angry. I wanted change. I had heard my mother say, "You can catch more flies with honey than vinegar," so I sidled up to God. Prayed to be reborn. Prayed to be *physically* reborn. *God, this body is a lemon, an Edsel. You must have bodies around that I could use; healthy bodies—one with Venus's face attached to it. You could change my*

face and let my body grow stronger, gradually, over a year, so no one notices.
I envisioned all the vexations of my body melting away and my
mummy face simultaneously transforming itself to look like Audrey
Hepburn's. Even the scars of anger and pain evaporated. And since the
Bible said, *Ask and it shall be given,* I anxiously awaited the mutation.

Eager to help God in every possible way with the expected modifi-
cations, I painted landscapes and traded them for a membership to
a spa that had a track, a weight room, sauna and whirlpool. My body
became less gangly. I was proud of the small muscles in my arms, and
had been told how lucky I was to be tall and thin by several women at
the spa who were working to lose weight.

A particularly handsome man in his thirties also worked out at the
spa. He talked to the women, only the pretty women, as he helped
them lift weights, standing with his pelvis close to their faces while
they lay on the bench and struggled with barbells. One day we passed,
going through the door to the track; he and another man were going
out and I was going in. I stopped on the other side of the door to tie
my shoe and heard a remark he made about me to his friend.

"She's got some nice legs," he said. "A nice body, really. I wouldn't
mind nailing her. But I'd have to put a bag over her head." They
laughed.

It felt like being hit with a stick. I sat down on the floor and covered my face with my hands, sick and angry, remembering where I
had heard that remark before.

I was sixteen years old, a tenth grader in high school. I went through
the lunchroom line and picked my way through crowded tables looking for a place to sit. The lunchroom was packed with students and I
considered not eating. But I had already suffered the embarrassment
of picking up a free lunch token—a bright-red plastic hexagon dis-
tributed in the hallway in front of God and everybody by the assistant
principal—and the embarrassment of handing it to the lunchroom
attendant, so I searched for a safe place to sit, away from the athletes
and cheerleaders. I finally spotted a group of unpopular kids, two
girls and a boy, sitting in the far corner. I slid my tray onto their table,
asking if they minded if I joined them. The girls stopped eating and

stared at me. The boy dropped his grilled cheese sandwich onto his plate. "Only if you put a bag over your head," he said as he pushed his chair back and collected his books. Only slightly less rude than the boy, the girls claimed they were finished anyway and walked away giggling. I sat facing the wall with my chin in my hands, letting the silent tears soak my sandwich.

After the incident at the spa, my fever soared and I was admitted to the hospital again.

Dr. Wallace glanced at the chart that hung from the foot of my bed, jotted something down and looked at his watch. "You can get out of here in the morning," he said. "I want you to come into the office in a few days. I'm going to give you weekly injections of strep, like an allergy shot, and see if we can build up immunity to it. And at some point we need to remove those tonsils."

"Just remove my head," I said. Dr. Wallace had heard my wish to "fix" my face.

"They're doing some new experimental facial surgery over at the University Hospital in Birmingham," he said. "Moving bones around, something. I don't know." I propped myself up on my elbows and looked out the window, my mind racing: *Who owns a car that can make it to Birmingham? How much time will I have to take off from work? How much does it cost?*

"I'll see if I can find out something and let you know," he said. "But I don't think you're well enough for a tonsillectomy, much less some new radical—*experiment.*"

During an appointment at the University Hospital in Birmingham I was told that I was not only a perfect candidate for the surgery (called an upper and lower advancement), but that I could get it for almost nothing by serving as a *teaching tool;* several med students and a film crew would accompany Dr. Matthias, the attending surgeon. I booked the surgery and drove home to tell my parents. Mother said that if it was what I wanted, then she thought it was a good idea. But Dad said, "You won't look like us anymore!"

"I already don't look like us, Dad," I cried. "I don't look like anybody in this family, or anybody's family, for that matter! Look! My teeth and gums hang down like I've got dentures that dropped from the roof of my mouth! And I have *no* lower jaw! I'm a troll!"

"I just don't want you getting too far ahead of yourself," he said. "You *had* to have braces, and you *had* to play the piano, and you *had* to paint pictures and take all them dance classes. What good did it do you? You're not making a dime more money working at the museum than you were at the dentist office. It was a waste of time. And now you're gonna have surgery. Where's that gonna get you? By the time you're through, you won't even recognize yourself!"

I'll recognize myself. I've always been right here, underneath, like an underground spring. Several months later, as I was wheeled into surgery, I told the doctor, "Just cut away everything that's not me."

An incredible number of people—doctors, nurses, med students—wearing scrubs and masks stood around in the operating room. I was buck-naked except for a flimsy sheet, and they were all male—even the anesthesiologist and the nurses. But I wasn't shy of the young men's seeing my face—which usually brought ridicule—because they were doctors, or at least *almost* doctors, and they were there to saw it off, like a nasty growth. So, for the first time, I was looking right into people's faces—which was something I normally didn't do. But this time I could look, stare, even—because I was like a canvas and they were artists about to re-create me. It was the most exciting thing in the world to think there was a possibility I'd no longer be sneered at, after a lifetime of being called "Bucktooth," and "Dogface" and "Ugly."

For someone to say "You need a bag over your head"—that's all it takes. You'll cut your head in half and you won't even care. But I *was* scared. *What if they mess up and I look worse afterward?* Dr. Matthias had told me important nerves had to be severed and that there was a danger of my face collapsing. I knew a woman who had a stroke that affected the left side of her face. When she smiled, the right side, eyes and mouth, curled up, but the left side sagged as if it were made of Silly Putty. I envisioned waking up with a lumpy, sagging chin like the one I had made out of Silly Putty as a girl. *Please, God, don't let them make it worse; don't let my face sag.*

I hoped God would understand and not be angry with me for

being so vain. *If you'll let me have a nice face, I'll be good from now on. And I won't do anything else to myself—no fake boobs or tattooed eyeliner.* I didn't mind promising not to get breast enlargements—I was okay in that department—but I had intended, someday, to get tattooed lips and eyeliner; and since God knew it too, I thought He would realize that I was willing to compromise. Still, I was so scared, the gurney I lay on rattled until the anesthesiologist told me to count from one hundred backward.

I woke from the surgery that had promised a new face just as the sun began to drop below the window of my room. I struggled to sit up in the hospital bed and began to vomit bright-red blood into my cupped hands. It spilled over my fingers onto a towel my mother hurriedly thrust under my hands and splashed in large round blotches onto her wrists. The nurse came and said it was to be expected. "After all, they cut through your palate and sinuses." She took away the soiled towels and blankets, shook out clean ones and tucked them into the sides of the bed. She checked the IV in my right arm and went away, coming back seconds later with a pair of surgical scissors on a shoestring that she pulled over my head so the scissors dangled like a necklace.

"The doctor left orders for you to wear these scissors around your neck for the next six weeks, until they cut the wires free," she explained. "Now if you get choked, clip all the surgical wires so you can breathe."

I looked at Mother. My mouth was wired together, so I couldn't talk, but she knew I thought that was an absurd plan. *If I'm choking, how am I supposed to cut thirty tight little wires from my braces?* She smiled and sat on the edge of the bed as the nurse left the room.

"I brought you a present," she said, waiting for me to lift my head from the pillow before she placed the gift on my lap. It was a beautiful leather-bound copy of *The Ugly Duckling.* I opened the book and read silently: "The ugly duckling walked to the water's edge and peered at his reflection. Instead of a cute, cheerful face, he saw a huge bill and big, buggy eyes. The sight shocked him so much that he ran and hid behind a tree trunk." Two large tears rolled down my swollen cheeks and settled in the corners of my mouth.

"No crying," Mother said, closing the book and handing me a tissue. "You don't want to use those scissors, do you?"

In the past few years—as I had worked out with weights, gone to college, and made plans to "fix" my face—Mother had given me several copies of *The Ugly Duckling*. She claimed my outside had not had time to catch up with my inside.

Before years of braces forced my horribly protruding upper teeth into shape, I could put Janet's baby fist into my mouth without opening it, a trick that made her laugh and me cry, secretly. I accosted God, *I cannot be me with this face!* He didn't answer. I sought Him through chants, left notes for Him in the collection basket at the Methodist Church and the First Baptist Church, and at Mary's feet at Saint Patrick's. Talked to Him at the plaster-and-plastic grottoes along Mudd Street. Cursed Him and called Him dead. Begged for His forgiveness—only to ask, in the next breath, if He'd given my request any thought.

About a year before my face surgery, Mother and I were working in the garden, harvesting new potatoes, when a monarch butterfly landed on the handle of my hoe. Seconds later the sky was eerily dark, pulsating with countless orange butterflies. They fluttered around our faces, lighting on our arms and shoulders. Mother thought they must have flown off-course because they didn't usually migrate past our house.

"Goodness," she said, "*one* monarch butterfly lighting on you is supposed to bring change. Just look at all of *these*." She lifted her orange-and-black-spotted arm into the air. "I'm not sure I can stand that much change."

"I can," I said, blowing on a butterfly that was trying to land on my mouth. "I want my face to change."

"Be careful what you ask for," Mother said, "you just might get it."

I knew the surgery had altered my appearance when I came home from the hospital and my son, Jason, who was six years old, didn't recognize me. He got off the school bus and ran inside calling me, glancing my way as he raced right by. Mother had to go get him and point me out. His eyes widened as if he'd seen a ghost. He hesitated briefly, but then smiled and hugged me. I was swollen and bruised, my mouth was wired together and my nose had been accidentally broken during surgery and had not yet been repaired. Even with all of that, I looked better than before surgery.

"Wow," he said. "That's really you?" I assured him it was. He studied my face, hair and shoulders, and then picked up my left hand and examined each finger as if he were checking my fingerprints.

Finally! A nice face! Move it, shape it, wire it back together. One hundred and forty-four sutures inside my mouth, like a quilt stitched from underneath; cut away here, add there, stitch, stitch, stitch. Hurt like hell. But never did the pain—even the endless aching sleepless nights of ice packs, painkillers and tears—outweigh the pain of living ugly. Never did the pumpkin-sized swelling seem worse than any one sneer from any one man I'd ever seen looking at my face. And the physical pain—the cutting, biting, throbbing—was like the old familiar toothaches, sore throats and fevers, in that an end was always in sight.

The swelling subsided and the severed nerves began to repair, tingling my cheeks, nose, teeth and lips as if they were waking from Novocaine. For six months I ate baby food, clear soups and vitamin-fortified milk shakes. Jason made a game of the milk shakes, mixing combinations for me to guess the ingredients: peanut butter and banana; peaches, pineapple and pears; and chocolate and marshmallow cream. At night I dreamed of hamburgers. I craved regular food so fiercely that once I attempted to liquefy pot roast, popping it into the blender with carrots, potatoes and milk.

My palate had been moved forward in the surgery and when my jaws were finally freed, I had to learn to make words again. Even simple words like *I* or *me* took concentration. *Fish, funny* and *forbidden* were almost impossible. I sounded like a babe just learning to talk. Still, I thought, I've got a face!

But a lifetime of fantasizing about being a model, an artist and a folksinger did not prepare me for the drastic change in my appearance. I avoided mirrors until the bruises and the swelling subsided. When I finally looked, I didn't recognize the attractive, heart-shaped face that looked back: straight nose, full cheeks, small, well-defined jaw, an upper lip that settled right in the middle of my two front teeth—teeth that fit together like puzzle pieces. My whole face was smaller, fit my neck and shoulders. I ran my tongue over smooth lips, ran my fingers over my nose and jaw. Even the parts that I knew had not been changed looked different. *Has my forehead always been that high? Were my eyes always that deep-set, that color?* When I exhausted myself staring, I started to cry. Cried for days. Cried with relief for the nice face, cried for the loss of the old, familiar one, and cried for the end of such a long struggle.

Within a few months of the surgery, men began to approach me: at work, at church, at the grocery store. I cried even more. I thought of all the days and nights I had spent lonely, desperate for a smile from someone. Now they pursued me for my face. I hated them for it and yet seldom refused their attention. The art of refusal is gradually learned by young women through repetition and it was not a tactic I had ever needed. It was all new to me; the struts and accidental touches. This was a game where everyone knew the rules except me. Until surgery, I had no idea just how easy it was for the average woman to attract men. Just walk across a room and they watch.

Three months after surgery I went back to the spa where I had worked out before surgery. I had just finished running laps and slowed to a walk when the man who wanted to put a bag over my head jogged up beside me.

"Hey," he said, breathlessly. "Since you're new here, how about I show you around." My new jaw dropped and the hair stood up on the back of my neck. I ran from the building to my car, drove home and called Dr. Matthias.

"I want my old face back!" I cried. "It's not me anymore; it's someone else!"

He had me see a counselor. I saw her for a year, all the way through the healing and settling of this new face—a complete metamorphosis, everything I had begged of God. I loved the new face. It really was like being reborn. But now I had the peculiar problem of not recognizing myself. Once, while walking down the sidewalk in Atlanta, I saw my reflection in a glass-front skyscraper and didn't realize it was me until the attractive woman walking my way vanished when the glass panels met. I didn't recognize myself—how could I expect others to recognize me?

One day John, who had joined the Army right after high school, called me to pick him up at a gymnasium at Fort McClellan. He had been overseas for months and had forgotten that I had written him about my surgery. I waited by the designated doorway for over an hour scanning the crowd of young men in olive-drab uniforms, trying to find John. When I spotted him, I marched over and began to bawl him out. He stared at me with his jaw on the floor.

"How was I suppose to know it was you? I recognize the voice—but I've never seen that *face* before in my life!"

The reaction to my new face from family members ranged from the extreme—like John's—to the benign. After picking John up at Fort McClellan and dropping his duffel at Mom's, we went to visit David, who worked for the Harley-Davidson Company building and test-driving motorcycles. Spanking-new Harleys—too valuable to leave outside—crowded his living room. He sat on a sheet on the living room floor working intently on an engine. Shiny new parts lined the white sheet like surgical instruments.

"Hey," John said.

"Hey," David said, glancing up. "Give me a second." He fiddled with the engine. "Who's your friend?" he asked, glancing at me and back to the engine.

"It's Barbara!" John said. David looked at me.

"Oh, it is Barbara." He turned back to the engine. "Here, Barbara, put your finger right there and hold that wire steady while I tighten this up."

I had a brand-new life. New friends: male and female. Men asked me out. I got asked to join book groups and to go to parties. But inside my heart there was the knowledge that I would not have been asked if I were still ugly.

For a while after running into the man *who needed a bag,* I declined all invitations, certain that I would never have been asked had I not changed my face. Changing faces brought a new world to my fingertips and I felt resentful and shamefully happy at the same time. I was delighted to get the attention I had so desperately lacked all my life; at the same time I resented the way I was treated before, and resented no longer feeling capable of telling good guys from bad guys. Before the surgery, it was easy.

When I was twelve and living in Kimberly, I went to Sandlin's store for my mother. Before I arrived, the store owner had called the police about a girl who was stealing. I was standing at the counter, digging into my pocket for change, when a police officer came in and grabbed me by the collar. "You little thief," he said as he twisted my arm behind my back. The grocer got his attention and told him it was the girl by the cosmetic rack, a pretty blonde. He let go of me and looked at the girl. I could see the wheels turn in his head. *She can't be the one.* He took her elbow and escorted her to the police car without apologizing to me. That was how it worked. The bad guys were mean to me because of my looks . . . and the good guys (and there were few good guys) weren't.

After the surgery, the signals for distinguishing good guys from bad guys were missing. I was lost in a field of rabbits and rats and couldn't tell one from the other. Looking like the average woman, I found myself doing things for men that I didn't want to do just because I was flattered that they had asked me. I dated men I didn't want to date, picked up their cleaning and went along with their politics. (I even dated a Republican!) I worked diligently to fit into their lifestyle. I lost my focus, lost myself. Anything for this man who was now interested, anything, before he found out that I was a fraud, that he had been making love to an ugly woman.

I wouldn't change back now that I've gotten somewhat used to having so much. But I constantly question the sincerity of those around me. My counselor listens to my anger, acknowledges my tears and understands my resentment toward these people that are in my life, even the ones I love.

"How do I know they love *me?*"

"You'll get the hang of it in time," she says. "It's in their eyes. Look in their eyes."

This is hard to do. I'm not used to looking into other people's eyes. And even if I look, how will I discern which person would have treated me differently had I never gotten this new face? How will I ever be sure?

In my heart, I know that *most* of them would treat me differently; I know, because I've lived on the other side of this face.

These days I often stand in front of the mirror and draw my face, not because I'm satisfied with it, but because it's cheaper than paying a model. Occasionally I can make out the family resemblance: Dad's forehead and Mother's chin, can even feel their presence in my bones—feel the charcoal as it defines my jawline on the paper—feel it on my face like a touch. It's not a beautiful face, but it's not bad, I tell myself. Yet still, as I work, my hands burn to reshape it: smooth out the jaw, heighten the cheekbones; and I can't help but have a jealous heart for those who were born with beauty. Oh, how I've wished and prayed for it. *Change me! Change me into Zeus's daughter, the goddess of beauty!* And this face has changed—and changed—and changed, and strangely enough has looked more like my family with each revival.

Barbara Robinette Moss was the 1996 winner of the Gold Medal for Personal Essay in the William Faulkner Creative Writing Contest. That winning essay grew into this book and still serves as its first chapter. Barbara is a full-time writer and artist and lives with her husband in Iowa City, Iowa.

CHANGE ME INTO ZEUS'S DAUGHTER
DISCUSSION POINTS

1.   What is the meaning of the title *Change Me into Zeus's Daughter?* To what extent do you think a person's identity is wrapped up in her/his physical appearance? Do you think the connection between physical appearance and identity is different in women than it is in men? How?

2.   In its stunning opening pages, Barbara Robinette Moss's memoir details the pain of growing up in a family so poor that a pesticide-treated bag of seed looks good enough to eat, and of being controlled by a tyrannical, alcoholic father. What emotions does the book evoke? How does Moss keep her childhood account of grinding poverty, neglect, and abuse from becoming overly depressing or self-pitying?

3.   Critics have compared Barbara Robinette Moss's memoir to Frank McCourt's best-selling memoir *Angela's Ashes*. What other books does *Change Me into Zeus's Daughter* call to mind? Why do you think this kind of intimate memoir of family life has become such a popular form of literary expression?

4.   "He inflicted pain recreationally, both physical and emotional. It was his hobby, his pastime," Barbara Robinette Moss recalls at her father's funeral. How well-rounded is the author's portrait of her father? Did you find it believable? To what extent do you think her picture of him is distorted by memory and the passage of time?

5.   One reviewer of *Change Me into Zeus's Daughter* has remarked that the child's perspective of this memoir does not penetrate the mysteries of the parents' relationship, leaving the reader to wonder at the "tangle of emotions that drove her father to be so brutal and her mother so sheepishly deferential." Do you agree or disagree with this judgment? Do you think the more sophisticated perspective of adulthood is truer than that of childhood—or is it merely different? Why?

6.   Despite the severe deprivation they must endure, the author and her seven siblings share an extraordinary emotional bond. Discuss the ways in which they support one another, united in their adoration of their mother and in their conflicted feelings of love and hate for their father.

7.   Describing her mother's devotion to their father, Moss writes: "She seemed to crave him as much as he craved alcohol." Why do you think that Dorris, who would offer herself up time and again to absorb her husband's brutality to shield her children, was unable or unwilling to take the one step that would truly protect them—leaving him? Do you think that this kind of abusive relationship is best understood as an addiction? Do you think she felt she had any other choices?

8.   When the author has grown up and become a mother herself, her mother at last finds the motivation to leave the marriage. She has discovered that her husband is cheating on her. Barbara, who has always idolized her mother, rages silently in anger and resentment: *"She's going to leave him now? Now that we're all grown and out of the house? You mean he could do anything to us—anything to her—as long as he didn't sleep with another woman?"* Did this loving mother effectively place a higher premium on sexual fidelity than she did on the welfare of her children? Why do you think some women are willing to endure terrible indignities in a marriage but will leave as soon as they are confronted with evidence of their husband's unfaithfulness?

9.   "In our family, government help had always been considered unacceptable," Moss says. Do you think the pride demonstrated by this attitude is well founded? How do you think the author's childhood could have been different had her mother sought help? What values do you impart to your children by either accepting or foregoing government help?

10.   Toward the book's close, as Moss struggles to be a full-time student and single mom, she asks her father for a small loan to help her pay some unexpected medical bills. Devastated when he turns her down, she is sure he doesn't take her need seriously because she is a girl. How did Moss's mother, in her own words and deeds, express her views on a woman's worth?

Browse our complete list of guides and download them for free at:
www.simonsays.com/reading_guides.html